Modern Classroom Assessment

Modern Classroom Assessment

Bruce B. Frey
The University of Kansas

Los Angeles | London | New Delhi
Singapore | Washington DC

Los Angeles | London | New Delhi
Singapore | Washington DC

FOR INFORMATION:

SAGE Publications, Inc.

2455 Teller Road

Thousand Oaks, California 91320

E-mail: order@sagepub.com

SAGE Publications Ltd.

1 Oliver's Yard

55 City Road

London EC1Y 1SP

United Kingdom

SAGE Publications India Pvt. Ltd.

B 1/I 1 Mohan Cooperative Industrial Area

Mathura Road, New Delhi 110 044

India

SAGE Publications Asia-Pacific Pte. Ltd.

3 Church Street

#10-04 Samsung Hub

Singapore 049483

Photo Credits:
iStock: 27, 100, 245, 271, 310
Thinkstock: 51, 67, 79, 103, 114, 240, 266, 297, 309

Printed in the United States of America

Library of Congress Cataloging-in-Publication Data

A catalog record of this book is available from the Library of Congress.

9781452203492

Acquisitions Editor: Reid Hester

Associate Editor: Theresa Accomazzo

Editorial Assistant: Sarita Sarak

Production Editor: Brittany Bauhaus

Copy Editor: Deanna Noga

Typesetter: C&M Digitals (P) Ltd.

Proofreader: Scott Oney

Indexer: Kathy Paperchontis

Cover Designer: Candice Harman

Marketing Manager: Terra Schultz

This book is printed on acid-free paper.

13 14 15 16 17 10 9 8 7 6 5 4 3 2 1

Brief Contents

DETAILED CONTENTS

PREFACE

As a college professor and researcher in education, I've used and reviewed dozens of classroom assessment textbooks. Some books cover the basic types and strategies of classroom assessment with a little theory and research thrown in, but don't provide enough concrete examples of what this looks like in today's schools. Other texts are essentially example after example of multiple-choice formats and performance-based assessments, without much guidance about why those examples work or are consistent with theories or research about how students think and learn. I wanted a book that does both. It's always seemed to me that there was a critical need for a book that covers all the major, research-based approaches to student-centered teacher-designed assessment in today's modern world, while also sharing tons of detailed models of what teachers actually do. The goal for *Modern Classroom Assessment* is to go beyond simply listing the basic assessment formats by exploring five broad up-to-date approaches or philosophies to assessment with the supporting scholarship and theory to guide their appropriate use. Most important, though, my mission in writing this book was to make these sometimes abstract concepts and guidelines clear and practical by including as many real-world illustrations and examples as I could fit between these covers.

The five modern ways of approaching classroom assessment that form the heart of this book include almost everything a teacher needs to know about classroom assessment. These approaches are the following:

1. Formative Assessment

   Providing frequent feedback directly to students so they can monitor and control their own learning is the *only* assessment approach that has been found to affect learning and increase test scores. And formative assessment opens up the definition of what classroom assessment *is* and what its purpose should be. This is not your father's end-of-the-year high stakes exam. This process for collecting and sharing information is a collaboration between students and their teacher and is covered in Chapter 4: Formative Assessment.

2. Traditional Paper-and-Pencil Assessment

   The tried-and-true, efficient, objectively scored approaches to quickly and reliably assessing achievement include multiple-choice questions, matching, true-false, short answer, and combinations of those approaches. In many contexts and for many purposes in the modern classroom, these approaches fall short of teachers' needs. Sometimes forgotten, however, is that even today these methods often are the best and fairest choice. Chapter 5: Summative Assessment: Traditional Paper-and-Pencil Tests focuses on this still most common of approaches.

3. Performance-Based Assessment
   Twenty-five years ago, this approach was new and quickly gained popularity. The idea was to go beyond the measurement of low-level knowledge by asking students to perform a skill or create a product and assess student ability. This approach led by necessity to new scoring options, such as the creation of subjective scoring rubrics that increased validity, but it can lead to unique reliability difficulties. Chapter 7: Performance-Based Assessment examines this important approach to classroom assessment.

4. Authentic Assessment
   A current and very modern *best practice* in the field of classroom assessment is to use assessment tasks that match real-world expectations. This approach increases the usefulness of classroom assessment across all ages—preschool through graduate school to on the job. Assessment that is authentic is intrinsically interesting and focuses on the "important stuff" like critical thinking and transferable skills. Chapter 8: Authentic Assessment is dedicated to realistic assessment.

5. Universal Design of Assessment
   Modern methods of test design emphasize accessibility and fairness for all children, regardless of gender, first language, ethnicity, or disability. Basic standards exist that can and should be applied to classroom assessment in all contexts and at all levels. This book is unique in the focus it provides on universal design of assessment and what it means for the classroom teacher. Chapter 9: Universal Test Design provides that focus.

Supporting the discussion of these five key assessment approaches are several other crucial topics:

- Chapter 3: Basic Assessment Strategy: Categories of Learning, Objectives, and Backward Design provides a smart way for creating effective tests and assignments that work well for any of the broad assessment approaches.
- Chapter 6: Constructed-Response Items and Scoring Rubrics focuses on the design and scoring of complex assessments, assignments, and tasks.
- Chapter 10: Test Accommodations explores what classroom teachers can and should do to make any assessment fairer and its scores more meaningful for individual students.

- Chapter 11: Understanding Scores From Classroom Assessments and Chapter 13: Standardized Tests handle the heavy lifting by covering the statistical and analytical methods for interpreting student performance. The tricks of the trade for talking about standardized test scores with parents are discussed.
- Chapter 12: Making the Grade presents a variety of philosophies for designing grading systems and assigning that all-important letter grade. How to discuss grades with parents is explored.

A BOOK FOR TEACHERS

Modern Classroom Assessment was planned from the start for the future school teacher. The target audience is the undergraduate college student in a teacher education program. If that's you, I wrote this book with you in mind. If you're an experienced teacher or a graduate student, you'll still find *Modern Classroom Assessment* to be valuable, though. By design, the book is mostly full of hundreds of applied examples, applications, and authentic illustrations of what modern teachers do and the assessment choices they make, but the examples are always discussed in the context of theory and educational research. So the hope is primarily that you will get clear guidance and ideas about today's best practices in the classroom. It may be that that is all you need. "Just tell me what good teachers do!" It might be, though, that you'd like to know more about the theory or scholarship that supports the claim that a practice is "best." That's here, too. Perhaps most important, I've tried to provide a richness of detail in our discussions of different formats, purposes, and grand strategies of assessment so you can solve assessment problems and apply the broad assessment approaches emphasized here to the unique specifics of your own classroom and your own students.

SPECIAL FEATURES

To help foster a depth of understanding about both application and theory in the world of classroom assessment, we have included a variety of unique features in each chapter. These include the following:

Stories From the Classroom

Many chapters begin with a story about a teacher with a problem. Part 1 ends with a cliff-hanger, with Part 2 appearing at the end of the chapter. I hope that by seeing real-world dilemmas with real-world classroom assessment solutions, the meaningful application of that chapter's ideas and suggestions will make a lot more sense.

Good Question!

These are questions that students may wish to ask their instructor, but for some reason often don't. You can think of these as Frequently Unasked Questions. I've taken the liberty of asking and answering these questions for you!

Real-World Choices Teachers Make

As professionals, classroom teachers routinely make choices among assessment options. They have been trained, know best practice, and often are aware of the theory and research behind some strategy or approach. In the real world, though, even knowing all that sometimes doesn't make the right choice clear. Wherever this section appears, we take a look at the issues and information that help real-world teachers make quality choices.

Technology

This feature spotlights computerized, electronic, or web-based resources, which in today's world make assessment easier and more useful.

A Closer Look

Sometimes a theory, study, or idea deserves closer inspection. Rather than slowing down the conversation, I've placed these discussions in their own spaces. They are there for those interested, but can be skipped by you or your instructor. Think of this feature as an HD or high-definition option for a higher resolution picture.

There's a Stat for That!

Scores, item responses, student performance, validity analyses, and reliability estimates all produce numbers. These focused presentations on useful statistical and mathematical procedures are designed to be readable, meaningful, and useful in the real world without expecting students to be statisticians.

Organizational Tools in Each Chapter

Every chapter includes these guideposts and outlines to make it clear what the purpose of each chapter is, what will be covered, and how to think about what you just read:

- Chapter Objectives
  Think of these as the instructional objectives for each chapter.

- Looking Ahead

  Here are the major points in what you're about to read. This section comes at the start of each chapter.

- Looking Back

  These are reminders of the critical points that we just covered. This section comes at the end of each chapter.

- Things to Think About

  These are questions for discussion or self-reflection to clarify your own thoughts about the key points in each chapter.

- On the Web

  A brief list of websites that provides further support, examples, and insights is found at the end of each chapter.

ANCILLARIES

Two websites created especially for *Modern Classroom Assessment* provide all sorts of free resources to help both teachers and students:

Instructor Teaching Site

A password-protected site, available at www.sagepub.com/frey, features resources that have been designed to help instructors plan and teach their courses. These resources include an extensive test bank, chapter-specific PowerPoint presentations, lecture notes, class activities, sample syllabi for semester and quarter courses, and links to SAGE journal articles with accompanying review questions.

Student Study Site

An open-access study site is available at www.sagepub.com/frey. This site includes eFlashcards, web quizzes, web resources, additional rubrics, and links to SAGE journal articles.

ACKNOWLEDGMENTS

A critical contribution to *Modern Classroom Assessment* was made by almost two dozen reviewers. To these college professors, experts in classroom assessment, and top teachers, I give my heartfelt thanks for their careful thought, evaluation, and suggestions. Without their input, this book would, quite honestly, not be very good.

I'd especially like to single out among this group my colleague and friend Professor Robert Harrington, whose close consideration of a few key chapters was especially instructive. Thank you, Bob, for your yeoman's work!

A team of SAGE editors provided strong guidance and support during the development of *Modern Classroom Assessment*. It began with acquisitions editor Diane McDaniel, who thought this book sounded like a good idea. Then Megan Krattli took the ball and ran with it. Theresa Accomazzo finished up, under the guidance of Reid Hester. These four folks are very good at their jobs and have been a pleasure to work with. Thanks, SAGE gang!

Neil Salkind, prolific author and well-respected goofball, helped make this book happen and continues as my friend and guide. Two research assistants helped with some important components of this text. Stephani Howarter and Zach Conrad did all I asked and did it on time. They are both very smart. Thank you.

I'd like to acknowledge the support of my wife, Dr. Bonnie Johnson. As always, I'd have accomplished little in life without her.

Finally, the author and SAGE would like to acknowledge the contributions of the following reviewers:

William Boone, *Miami University*

Betsy Botts, *University of West Florida*

Maureen Davin, *Bethune Cookman College*

Cheryl Van De Mark, *University of Central Florida*

Debra Dirksen, *Western New Mexico University*

Carolyn Doolittle, *Baker University*

Karen Eifler, *University of Portland*

Robert Ferrera, *Notre Dame de Namur University*

James Gasparino, *Florida Gulf Coast University*

Marva Gavins, *University of Houston–Clear Lake*

Ramona Hall, *Cameron University*

Martha Jane Harris, *Texas A & M University–Texarkana*

Susan Hibbard, *Florida Gulf Coast University*

Adria Karle, *Florida International University*

Patricia Lutz, *Kutztown University*

Kathleen Makuch, *Wilkes University*

Elda E. Martinez, *University of The Incarnate Word*

Saramma Mathew, *Troy University*

Nelson Maylone, *Eastern Michigan University*

David McMullen, *Bradley University*

Gayle Mindes, *DePaul University*

Cindi Nixon, *Francis Marion University*

Judith Presley, *Tennessee State University*

Germaine Taggart, *Fort Hays State University*

Jahnette Wilson, *University of Houston*

Eunmi Yang, *Stonehill College*

About the Author

Bruce B. Frey, PhD, is an award-winning teacher and scholar at The University of Kansas. His areas of research include classroom assessment and instrument development. Dr. Frey is the author of the popular introductory statistics book, *Statistics Hacks*, and the co-editor of the *Encyclopedia of Research Design*. In his spare time, he collects comic books, and is especially fond of 1960's DC stories wherein super-pets turn against their superhero masters.

CHAPTER 1

MODERN CLASSROOM ASSESSMENT

Looking Ahead in This Chapter

The world of classroom assessment is different now than in the old days. Modern classrooms use a wide variety of assessment approaches depending on the purpose of the assessment and the teacher's philosophy.

---------- ৵৵৵ ----------

Objectives

After studying this chapter, you should be able to define the five approaches to modern classroom assessment:

- Traditional paper-and-pencil assessment
- Performance-based assessment
- Formative assessment
- Authentic assessment
- Universal test design

---------- ৵৵৵ ----------

"Then Miss Wilder closed her speller and said sadly that she was disappointed and grieved. . . . 'Carrie, you may go to the blackboard. I want to see you write, "cataract," "separate," and "exasperate," on the board, correctly, fifty times each.' She said it with a kind of triumph in her voice. Laura tried to control her temper, but she could not. She was furious. It was meant as a punishment for poor little Carrie, to make her stand ashamed before the whole school. It was not fair . . . ! Carrie went miserably but bravely to the blackboard. She was trembling and she had to wink back tears but she would not cry."

Laura Ingalls Wilder describing an 1880s South Dakota classroom
Little Town on the Prairie (1941)

In the last 20 years (which is only last week in terms of how slowly things have progressed in the centuries-long history of public education), big changes have occurred in classrooms across the United States. As the *Little House* excerpt that opened this chapter illustrates, assessment has always been a part of school life (and not always used in positive ways), but the amount of assessment and, more important, the variety of different forms and purposes of assessment have increased dramatically. As research from the last two decades describes, there has been a virtual explosion of assessment in modern classrooms for a while now. Here are some typical findings from across the last 25 years or so:

- 54 teacher-made tests are used in a typical classroom per year (Marso & Pigge, 1988).
- Many millions of unique assessments are created yearly nationwide (Worthen, Borg, & White, 1993).
- Assessment in one form or another can take up more than 25% of a teacher's day (Stiggins, 2007).
- Assessment has become an integral part of teachers' identities, and there is a worldwide call also to make assessment training integral to teacher training, as well (Pope, Green, Johnson, & Mitchell, 2009).

Consequently, researchers beginning in the late 1980s and early 1990s have called for more explicit training of classroom teachers in the areas of classroom assessment.

Like many aspects of teaching, quality classroom assessment plays a critical role in affecting student learning and has a research-based set of best practices.

- Comm. w/ parents

This skill, like one or two other important teaching skills, is sometimes treated as one of those important things that teachers are all magically able to do as soon as they are hired (Bennett & Gitomer, 2009; Stiggins & Chappuis, 2005; Wang, Wang, & Huang, 2008). Of course, as is true with other practices central to any professional and intellectual work, there are theories and empirical scholarship that inform modern classroom assessment. However, even into this decade, the typical teacher education program has no assessment course requirement, and many states do not mandate that teachers receive training in assessment. Teachers have historically received little or no training or support after certification. The formal assessment training teachers do receive tends to focus on large-scale test administration and standardized test score interpretation rather than on philosophies of assessment, the large variety of assessment formats available, assessment design strategies, or item-writing guidelines.

Ed TPA

Little has changed even in the last few years in the assessment-heavy nature of the classroom environment (Callahan, Griffo, & Pearson, 2009; Müller & Burdette, 2007) or the level of classroom teachers' assessment knowledge (Stiggins & Chappuis, 2005). Unfortunately, there still is a lack of agreement on the importance of classroom assessment training for teachers, and teacher educators tend to focus too much on standardized tests regarding training teachers, and neglect the teacher-made test (Stiggins, 2007). Teachers report that they need more training in assessment (Stiggins & Duke, 2008), but the majority of teacher educators do not believe it is essential to train teachers in modern assessment methods such as authentic assessment and portfolio assessment (Farkas & Duffett, 2008). Finally, and perhaps most ironically, considering the impact of the federal No Child Left Behind legislation on the increase in testing, the recently enacted U.S. definition of a "highly qualified teacher" does not require any training in assessment (Müller & Burdette, 2007).

The classroom assessment of today is not the common image of the anxiety-causing multiple-choice tests as popularized by media of today and yesterday and the center of nightmarish memories for some of your parents and grandparents and maybe for you, too, though, to be honest, that occasionally frightening format is still a *part* of classroom assessment and, if we are still being honest, a big part. Fortunately there are ways to make multiple-choice tests, and similar formats, more useful and less frightening. We know so much more now about the tried-and-true paper-and-pencil test that even that old-timey tool can be used more fairly and powerfully. Also, there are many other ways of assessing knowledge and skills, and many modern uses of assessment for purposes beyond simply assigning a class grade. To paraphrase an Oldsmobile car commercial from a while back, this is not your father's classroom assessment.

In today's classrooms, teachers still wish to assess knowledge and skill. That has not changed much in the last couple hundred years. Some of the methods for doing that well are new, but they do not represent dramatic paradigm shifts or important new ways of thinking about classroom assessment. There *are* some changes afoot, however; there *are* new goals, new purposes, new roles, and new perspectives for classroom assessment.

The perspectives of what a test was and why it should be used were fairly limited for most of our history. Within a stack of real, but old, textbooks, these examples of the past's narrow range of classroom assessment perspectives can be found:

1904   A book for elementary teachers with arithmetic exercises comforts the reader in the preface with the assurance that the "extreme 'spiral method'" is not applied in the assessment strategies therein because it is "scrappy, uninteresting and lacking in continuity" and pledges that "there is offered an abundance of the oral and written drill which is necessary for fixing number facts in the mind."(Smith, 1904, pp. iii–iv)

1918   "To the work of the teacher in the classroom (standardized tests) give a definiteness heretofore unknown. To use a military term, they set the 'limited objectives' for each subject of the course of study, which the teacher is expected to reach, but beyond which she is not expected to go. They prevent a waste of teaching energy by preventing over-emphasis, and set standards in instruction which are indisputable because they are based on the school practice of the best schools in the United States." (Cubberly, 1918, p. vi)

1924   "Recently . . . a still better method for the evaluation of work which teachers . . . are doing has been evolved. This new method consists in the setting up . . . a series of carefully devised 'standardized tests' . . . which will do for education what has been done for agriculture." (Monroe, DeVoss, & Kelly, 1924, pp. xii–xiii)

1930   A survey of physical education teachers lists seven factors that determine students' grades, ranked in order of use. First on the list is attendance. Last on the list is performance or achievement. (Bovard & Cozens, 1930)

1941   "A fairly large number of tests have been constructed to measure either general or special vocabularies. [One particularly effective test] lists 45 words which seemed adequate to appraise general vocabulary from the mental ages of 6 to 22 years. . . . Usually only two words are needed to indicate one year's growth." (Greene, 1941)

Fortunately, the modern teacher can choose from an array of broad theoretical approaches to classroom assessment, a variety of frameworks depending on the purpose of the assessment. The most exciting part of the modern classroom regarding assessment is that the different purposes for assessment that teachers of today consider before choosing an assessment approach include purposes of assessment that might not even have entered the mind of most of the teachers of just a few years ago! Not to give away too much of what is inside the chapters ahead, but:

- Assessment can be used *for* learning, to actually *increase* learning,
- Assessment can be used to improve instruction and allow *students* to control their own learning,
- Assessments can be designed to mirror the real world with the real world's accompanying realistic expectations and evaluations, and
- Assessments can finally be designed to meaningfully include everyone in today's diverse classrooms.

Defining Classroom Assessment

Q: This is already a few pages into the first chapter of this classroom assessment textbook. Could we have a definition of *classroom assessment*?

A: Sure, let's start with a dictionary-like definition and then let's go with a more informal definition. The latter one is the working definition used for this book.

Formal Definition

Classroom Assessment: Systematic collection of information about students' abilities, characteristics, skills, understanding, and knowledge developed, administered, and scored by a teacher for the purposes of evaluation.

Working Definition

Classroom Assessment: Assessment in the classroom includes a broad set of activities where information is gathered and evaluations are made. Mostly, it refers to information and evaluations about students and their learning, but there are other measurement goals, as well. This book uses the term to refer to tests and other formal or informal data-gathering strategies used by teachers to assess their students and themselves. The assessments can be used before, during, or after instruction, at any time during the learning process. The information can be used by teachers to improve instruction, by students to control their own learning, or both. Performance on assessments might or might not be graded or contribute to a course grade.

FIVE MODERN CLASSROOM ASSESSMENT PERSPECTIVES

"The future is not a result of choices among alternative paths offered by the present, but a place that is created—created first in the mind and will, created next in activity. The future is not some place we are going to, but one we are creating. The paths are not to be found, but made, and the activity of making them, changes both the maker and the destination."

John Schaar, Political Theorist

The heart of this book, Chapters 4 through 9, presents five approaches to modern classroom assessment. These approaches are different ways of thinking about assessment. They are choices that teachers make based on their philosophies, their goals, and their beliefs about the value and purpose of classroom assessment. As the quotation that opens this section suggests, teachers can build a classroom assessment culture driven by the thoughts and knowledge they have about assessment specifically and teaching in general.

These five approaches are described here. Though there are separate chapters devoted to each perspective and they are discussed as independent ways of treating assessment, there is some overlap among the five approaches. They do differ in important ways, however. They differ in their purpose, in the nature of the data they produce, in their intended audience, and in some cases in the assumptions they make about children and about learning.

1. **Traditional Paper-and-Pencil Assessment.** These popular, efficient, objectively scored approaches to quickly and reliably assessing achievement include multiple-choice questions, matching, true-false, fill-in-the-blank, short answer, and combinations of those approaches. Traditional assessment (earning this label for lack of a better name) is typically used for assessing *knowledge*. In many contexts and for many purposes in the modern classroom, this approach is still the best and is still a valuable tool for classroom assessment. More and more frequently, however, these approaches, when used by themselves, fall short of modern teachers' needs.

2. **Performance-Based Assessment.** Thirty-five years ago, this approach was seen as newfangled, but it quickly gained popularity and now is so common that many consider it as traditional as a multiple-choice test. The idea is to go beyond the measurement of low-level knowledge and understanding by asking students to perform a skill or create a product and assess student ability. This framework led by necessity to new scoring options, such as the creation of subjective scoring rubrics or guides that can do a good job of getting at exactly what teachers wish to measure, but can lead to unique scoring difficulties because of the judgments required. Performance assessment is typically used for assessing *skill* or *ability*.

3. **Formative Assessment.** Data collection that occurs during instruction not only can guide the teacher on instructional effectiveness, but also can let students know where they are and how they are doing. Formative assessment is typically used to give *feedback* to students and teachers about how things are going and does not affect grades. More important, providing frequent feedback directly to students so they can monitor and control their own learning is just about the only assessment approach that has been found to directly affect learning (and, of particular importance to administrators, increase standardized test scores).

4. **Authentic Assessment.** A "best practice" in the modern classroom is to utilize assessment tasks that match real-world expectations. Authentic assessment typically requires students to perform in ways that are valued *outside the classroom*. This approach may increase the meaningfulness of classroom assessment across all ages, preschool through graduate school. Understanding this approach to assessment has difficulties, though, because, as we will see, it turns out that the field of education can't decide what it means to say that an assessment is *authentic*. The idea that assessment tasks should be intrinsically meaningful and motivating and require skills or knowledge that is valued in the world is a powerful one, though, and can produce some powerful assessments.

Authentic Assessment and Performance-Based Assessment

Q: Is authentic assessment the same thing as performance-based assessment?

A: Sometimes when authentic assessment is discussed among teachers, educational researchers, textbook authors, and those who train teachers, it is confused with performance-based assessment. This is likely because one advantage of performance-based assessment over traditional paper-and-pencil approaches is that it is probably more authentic. After all, nothing is more artificial and nonauthentic than a multiple-choice test. However, just because an assessment is performance-based doesn't guarantee, of course, that it is authentic. As is discussed in great detail in Chapter 8, an assessment (regardless of whether it is a traditional format or performance-based) is authentic when the assessment task is intrinsically meaningful and represents a skill and activity that is valued outside the classroom.

5. **Universal Test Design.** Modern methods of test design emphasize accessibility and fairness for all children, regardless of gender, first language, ethnicity, or disability. Basic standards exist that can and should be applied to classroom assessment in all contexts and at all levels. Application of these standards can ensure that testing, whether teacher-developed or state-mandated, is inclusive and measures what it is supposed to. Assessments following universal design principles are typically used when the classroom teacher is concerned that irrelevant student characteristics might affect performance. And when you think about it, is a teacher ever *not* concerned about that?

In the past, the classroom assessment environment was almost entirely traditional paper-and-pencil assessment with, especially in the last few decades, some performance-based assessment activity. Times are changing, and the field has begun to recognize the value of modern approaches such as formative assessment, authentic assessment, and universal design of assessment. This is clear from a quick look at the frequency of the use of terms representing these five approaches to classroom assessment as they appear in books published over the last 100 years. Figure 1.1 shows the relative use of these terms over time in English-language books. While the traditional multiple-choice test and performance assessment still predominate in the modern classroom, our three other approaches have arisen almost out of nowhere of late and are now part of the conversation, part of modern classroom assessment.

The five approaches emphasized in this book, are derived from different theoretical frameworks, emphasizing different purposes of assessment, but they are not mutually exclusive. The modern teacher does not have to pick one philosophy at the expense of another, one approach over another, but can focus on the purpose for a particular assessment and choose different approaches that are consistent with that goal. A teacher can design a traditional paper-and-pencil

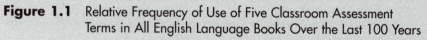

Figure 1.1 Relative Frequency of Use of Five Classroom Assessment Terms in All English Language Books Over the Last 100 Years

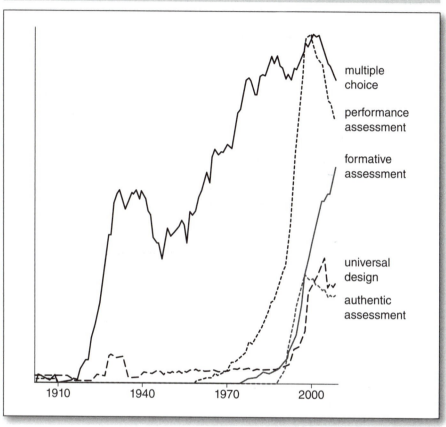

Source: Produced on Google nGram software, Michel et al., 2010.

test that follows universal accessibility guidelines. A single classroom assessment might be performance-based and authentic and formative. Most authentic assessments are probably performance-based, but many performance-based assessments are not authentic. A formative assessment might inform both the teacher and the student and parents. Modern classroom assessment is multifaceted.

"We are not arguing that one assessment approach is good and another bad: the key issue is around fitness for purpose."
(Gipps & Cumming, 2005, p. 3)

Choosing an Assessment Approach

In today's classrooms, assessment is used for a variety of purposes. The longtime reason for assessment was, essentially, to assign a grade. In the real world, teachers can choose to use assessment for several different, but important, reasons. Sometimes a combination of reasons is in play:

- Assessment *for* learning. Teachers gather information about where students are "at" (what they know and can do) and how they are reacting to instruction. The purpose is to design and revise instruction so that it is the most effective.
- Assessment *as* learning. Data is gathered either *by* or *for* students to help them understand how they learn. This is the formative assessment approach. The purpose is so students develop learning skills and control their own learning.
- Assessment *of* learning. Data is gathered to reach a conclusion about how much students have learned after instruction is done. Until fairly recently, this was the only use of classroom assessment. The purpose is to share with the students and others how much they have achieved.

In a modern classroom environment, all three purposes drive teachers' assessment choices.

The five approaches to classroom assessment consist of a set of three different formats or types of assessment designs (traditional, performance-based, and authentic), a new way of thinking about the purpose of assessment (formative), and an overall philosophy about the usefulness of a given assessment (universal test design) for all students. Figure 1.2 provides a visual summary of the key characteristics of these five ways of thinking about classroom assessment. Triangles, which diminish in size as one travels across the figure, are used to represent the five types of classroom assessment. Triangles are used because, though there are some defining qualities that make the approaches different, they are not complete absolutes. For instance, clever and creative teachers could find ways to measure ability using a bunch of matching items (a traditional format)

Figure 1.2 Key Characteristics of the Five Approaches to Modern Classroom Assessment

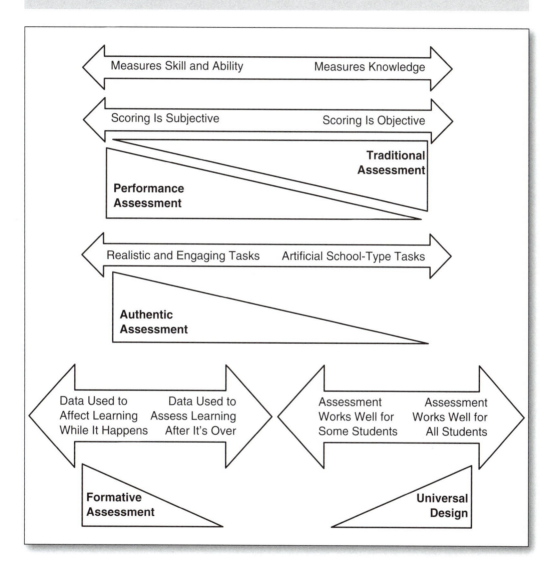

instead of a performance assessment; it is just less common and more difficult. Likewise, it is the goal of universal design to include all students with the same assessment, but that is not always possible or fair. Further, the approaches are not necessarily distinct; they certainly can and do overlap conceptually. For example, useful formative assessment could be performance-based or tradition-ally designed, but the most effective formative assessment has objective, not subjective, scoring. Some performance-based assessment is authentic; some is not. A single test could include traditionally formatted multiple-choice items and also have a performance-based component. Classroom assessments using any of these approaches could be developed using the principles of universal design. And so on.

THINGS TO THINK ABOUT

1. You've taken many multiple-choice tests in your life. How well do you think your scores on these *traditional* paper-and-pencil tests have reflected your true level of understanding?

2. Why are *performance-based* assessments usually more interesting for students?

3. What *formative* assessments have you been part of lately?

4. What is it about traditional paper-and-pencil assessment that might be considered not *authentic*?

5. What might an assessment that follows the principles of *universal design* look like?

Looking Back in This Chapter

- Traditional paper-and-pencil assessment is used to measure knowledge and basic understanding. It is usually scored objectively.
- Performance-based assessment is used to measure skill and ability. It is usually scored subjectively.
- Formative assessment is used to provide feedback to students and teachers. It allows students and teachers to monitor their own learning and teaching and change their behavior.
- Authentic assessment is used when teachers want their assessment tasks to mirror methods, skills, and behaviors that are valued outside the classroom in the real world.
- Universal test design is used when teachers want the assessment to be under-standable and fair to all their students.

ON THE WEB

National Teaching and Learning Forum Library provides overviews of classroom assessment
http://www.ntlf.com/html/lib/lib.htm

Assessment methods summarized
http://www.pbs.org/teacherline/courses/inst325/docs/inst325_stiggins.pdf

Linking classroom assessment with learning
http://www.ets.org/Media/Tests/TOEFL_Institutional_Testing_Program/ELLM2002.pdf

What teachers need to know about assessment
http://echo.edres.org:8080/nea/teachers.pdf

STUDENT STUDY SITE

Visit **www.sagepub.com/frey** to access additional study tools including eFlashcards, web quizzes, web resources, additional rubrics, and links to SAGE journal articles.

REFERENCES

Bennett, R. E., & Gitomer, D. H. (2009). Transforming K–12 assessment: Integrating accountability testing, formative assessment, and professional support. *Educational Assessment in the 21st Century*, 43–61.

Bovard, J. F., & Cozens, F. W. (1930). *Tests and measurement in physical education*. Philadelphia, PA: W. B. Saunders.

Callahan, M., Griffo, V., & Pearson, P. D. (2009). Teacher knowledge and teaching reading. In F. Falk-Ross, S. Szabo, M. B. Sampson, & M. M. Foote (Eds.), *Literacy issues during changing times: A call to action*. Arlington, TX: College Reading Association.

Cubberly, E. P. (1918). In W. S. Monroe (Ed.), *Measuring the results of teaching*. Boston, MA: Houghton Mifflin.

Farkas, S., & Duffett, A. (2008). Results from a national teacher survey. In *High achieving students in the era of NCLB* (pp. 49–82). Washington, DC: Thomas B. Fordham Institute.

Gipps, C., & Cumming, J. J. (2005). Assessing literacy. In A. Cumming (Ed.), *Handbook of educational policy: Literacy*. Dordrecht, The Netherlands: Springer.

Greene, E. B. (1941). *Measurements of human behavior*. New York, NY: Odyssey Press.

Marso, R. N., & Pigge, F. L. (1988). *An analysis of teacher-made tests: Testing practices, cognitive demands, and item construction errors*. Paper presented at the annual meeting of the National Council on Measurement in Education, New Orleans, LA. ERIC Document Reproduction Service No. 298 174.

Michel, J.-B., Shen, Y. K., Aiden, A. P., Veres, A., Gray, M. K., Brockman, W., . . . Aiden, E. L. (2011). Quantitative analysis of culture using millions of digitized books. *Science, 331*(6014), 176–182.

Monroe, W. S., DeVoss, J. C., & Kelly, F. J. (1924). *Educational tests and measurements*. Cambridge, MA: Riverside Press.

Müller, E., & Burdette, P. (2007, May). Highly qualified teachers and special education: Several state approaches. *In Forum*, 1–14.

Pope, N., Green, S. K., Johnson, R. L., & Mitchell, M. (2009). *Examining teacher ethical dilemmas in classroom assessment*. Orlando, FL: Elsevier.

Smith, D. E. (1904). *Primary arithmetic*. Boston, MA: Ginn & Company.

Stiggins, R. (2007, October 17). Five assessment myths and their consequences. *Education Week*, 1–5.

Stiggins, R., & Chappuis, J. (2005). Using student-involved classroom assessment to close achievement gaps. *Theory Into Practice*, 44(1), 11–18.

Stiggins, R., & Duke, D. (2008). Effective instructional leadership requires authentic leadership. *The Phi Delta Kappan*, 90(4), 285–291.

Wang, T. H., Wang, K. H., & Huang, S. C. (2008). Designing a web-based assessment environment for improving pre-service teacher assessment literacy. *Computers & Education*, 51(1), 448–462.

Worthen, B. R., Borg, W. R., & White, K. R. (1993). *Measurement and evaluation in the schools*. White Plains, NY: Longman.

CHAPTER 2

THE LANGUAGE OF CLASSROOM ASSESSMENT

***Looking Ahead* in This Chapter**

By getting comfortable with seven key terms and concepts in classroom assessment, we can begin to understand almost all there is to know in the world of teacher-made tests.

—————— ৵৵৵ ——————

Objectives

After studying this chapter, you should be able to

- Define:
    - **validity**
    - **reliability**
    - **construct**
    - **objective scoring**
    - **subjective scoring**
    - **norm-referenced**
    - **criterion-referenced**
- Explain the different categories of validity evidence
- Explain the different categories of reliability evidence
- List common statistical methods for estimating validity and reliability
- Explain key professional standards and ethics for classroom assessment

—————— ৵৵৵ ——————

"Oh, Stewardess . . . I can speak jive."

Mrs. Schiff (Barbara Billingsley), the movie *Airplane!*

There are seven basic terms, some technical jargon, which are thrown around time and time again in this book. These seven words are representative of the language of measurement and, more specifically, the language of classroom assessment. Two of the words, validity and reliability, are foundational concepts; get comfortable with these two concepts and you essentially know everything you need to know about classroom assessment. The remaining five terms—construct, objective, subjective, norm-referenced, and criterion-referenced—provide a shared terminology that will allow for a meaningful conversation between you and me and the world of education.

CONSTRUCT

A construct (pronounced CON-struct; it's a noun, not a verb) is the invisible trait you wish to assess. In the classroom, constructs are typically knowledge, understanding, skills, attitudes, traits, and so on. In the broader world of educational and psychological measurement, constructs include things like intelligence, depression, learning disabilities, aptitude, and personality. Because abstract characteristics cannot be seen and measured or reported directly (like weight or height or age), they must be defined theoretically by whoever wishes to assess them. So the first step in developing, for example, an intelligence test is to decide what intelligence is. Then, one develops an instrument or method for measuring intelligence as defined however it has been built up in the mind of the developer. This invisible trait is called a construct for that reason—it must be imagined, defined, or *built* by a researcher or assessor. For teachers who wish to assess knowledge, for example, the nature of the knowledge and its "shape," the domains or content areas to be assessed, and the depth of knowledge expected are defined first (sometimes intuitively, sometimes informally, sometimes formally), and an assessment approach is developed that is consistent with that definition. The goal of classroom assessment is to measure constructs with high *validity* and *reliability*. Those key words are defined next.

VALIDITY

Validity is the characteristic of an assessment which measures what it is *supposed* to measure. "Supposed" means a couple of things; it means that the assessment measures what you assume it does, and it means that the assessment measures what it is intended to measure. The official "handbook" for educational and psychological testing, prepared by the professional organizations in these areas, the American Educational Research Association (AERA), the American Psychological Association (APA), and the National Council on Measurement in Education (NCME), describes validity as the "most fundamental consideration in developing and evaluating tests" and defines it as "the degree to which evidence and theory support the interpretations of test scores entailed by proposed uses of tests" (AERA, APA, & NCME, 1999, p. 9).

There are a variety of ways to classify the various arguments or types of evidence that might justify a belief that an assessment score is valid. A traditional approach is to identify three types of validity evidence, three strategies one could use to make a decision as to the degree of validity associated with any particular assessment. These classical categories are *content-based validity*, *criterion-based validity*, and *construct-based validity*.

Content validity means that the items on a test are a fair and representative sample of the items that should be on the test. For example, most teachers have a well-defined set of objectives or content areas that an assessment should cover. If that framework guides the item selection and development for a classroom assessment, then one could reasonably conclude that the assessment produces scores with some content validity. Though intellectually interested, perhaps, in all three types of validity, it is content validity on which teachers typically focus. Assessing whether objectives are met, and making sure that a test covers what was taught—these are the common purposes of assessment for classroom teachers.

your content is valid

There's a Stat for That!

Content Validity

There is a quantitative way that teachers and others who use and develop assessments can estimate content validity. The *content validity ratio* provides a single tidy number that estimates how well a single item fairly represents all the items that should or could be on the test (because it represents the topic, it was taught, it asks about a key concept, etc.). The index was developed for job aptitude tests and some types of achievement tests, but it works equally well for classroom assessments designed to measure knowledge. A group of judges or experts (like, say, teachers) examine a group of items on a test meant to assess knowledge in some identified domain. For each item, each expert indicates whether the question is essential (covers a central or major fact,

(Continued)

(Continued)

point, or aspect of the domain), of some importance (somewhat relevant, but not essential to the intended domain), or unrelated to the topic. The total number of judges (N) and the number of judges who categorize an item as essential ($N_{essential}$) are determined, and a quick calculation produces the content validity ratio:

$$\text{Content Validity Ratio} = \frac{N_{essential} - N/2}{N/2}$$

Of course, it is hard to get a group of expert teachers together to do these sorts of analyses; so fortunately, there is an easy way for a lone, curious classroom teacher to use this analytic method. A single teacher can rate each item and then run this formula on the whole group of items. A number greater than 0 is hoped for and the closer to 1.0, the better. By the way, we divide by 2 in this equation to make sure that chance doesn't play a role.

your score is valid

Criterion-based validity means that performance on an assessment is related to scores on another assessment that measures the same thing or something similar. This sort of evidence is particularly important for standardized tests (like school readiness screening tests or the ACT and SAT tests) that are used to predict or estimate performance on some other important outcome or measure (such as performance in kindergarten or college). For example, I might argue that the Frey Intelligence Test (which I just whipped up in my basement laboratory) does in fact measure intelligence because students score about the same on it (relatively speaking) as they do on the Wechsler Intelligence Scale for Children (a commonly used intelligence test). My test is cheaper and shorter, I might claim in my brochures, so use it instead of the Wechsler. I demonstrate that it measures intelligence (or, at least, whatever the Wechsler measures) by showing a relationship between scores on my test and scores on the Wechsler.

Teachers are not especially interested in this evidence for their classroom-based assessments because their assessments are usually not meant to be a predictor of future performance or an estimate of current performance on some other measure. Classroom assessments might, in fact, be very good indicators of performance on other assessments, of course, but that is rarely their intended purpose (and remember, validity speaks to the intended purpose of an assessment).

There's a Stat for That!

Correlation Coefficient

Some validity arguments, especially criterion validity arguments, are based on demonstrating a relationship between two sets of scores. To produce a single persuasive number to demonstrate criterion validity, one can compute a correlation coefficient. Correlation coefficients are used to estimate the strength of a relationship between two variables (such as two sets of scores). Variables are correlated if, when compared in two columns side-by-side, a change in the value of one variable is associated with a change in the value of the other variable. The formula for the most commonly used correlation (technically referred to as the Pearson product-moment correlation) is

$$\frac{\Sigma(Z_x Z_y)}{N-1}$$

Some of the terms used in this formula are described in great detail in Chapters 12 and 13, so for now, just know that Z_x and Z_y are standardized values representing two columns of scores (the distance between each raw score and the mean of that column of scores, divided by the standard deviation for that column of scores), N is the number of pairs of scores (or scores in either column), and Σ means to sum up. This formula always produces a value between -1.00 and $+1.00$. Positive signs indicate the relationship is in the same direction. As one value increases, the other value increases. Negative signs indicate the relationship is in the opposite direction. As one value increases, the other value decreases. Assessments tend to be scored such that that a high score means more of the construct, so reported criterion validity coefficients tend to be positive. In measurement, correlations are interpreted so that an absolute value of .70 to 1.00 is considered strong or large, .30 to .70 is moderate or medium, and 0.00 to .30 is weak or small. The higher the correlation between two tests, the stronger the argument that the tests measure the same construct.

Construct validity is the broadest category of validity, and this category includes the bulk of validity arguments that can be made. The construct validity argument is that performance on the assessment really does reflect the underlying knowledge, skill, or trait that is intended to be measured. If the scores on a test are higher for students who have more of whatever invisible "thing" you think you are assessing than for students who have less of that thing, then that suggests that your scores have some construct validity. Remember that measurement people call that invisible thing the *construct*, and most validity evidence is construct validity evidence.

Construct Validity

Q: The definition of *construct* validity sounds suspiciously like the basic definition of validity *itself*. So what's the difference?

A: Construct validity arguments tend to reference some operational theory or conceptual definition of the trait, skill, or knowledge base being assessed, while content and criterion validity arguments do not. It's a smart question, though, because some measurement theorists have maintained that there are not really different types of validity. A respected measurement philosopher, Samuel Messick (1989), for example, argued for decades for a unitary definition of validity, suggesting that every validity argument is, essentially, a construct validity argument; all validity is construct validity. Others, though, point out that for practitioners, like teachers and other test developers, categories and types are useful for planning and strategizing and making decisions about the quality of an assessment (e.g., Crocker, 2003; Kane, 2008; Lissitz & Samuelsen, 2007), so most textbook authors and teacher educators have stuck with the traditional categories.

Construct Validity

For construct validity of individual items, an index that real-life teachers might calculate can be used to judge whether each test question measures what it is supposed to measure. The **item discrimination index** gives an indication as to the relationship between the level of knowledge students have and how high they scored on a test. The best way to see this relationship is to *correlate* (see *There's a Stat for That* in Chapter 2) the "score" on a single item (often a 0 for wrong and a 1 for right) with the total score on the test and hope for a positive correlation. The idea is that if that item is measuring the same thing as the rest of the test, it has some construct validity.

Even today, with computers in our pockets, calculating a correlation coefficient is difficult sometimes. A method designed just for classroom teachers has easier math and produces estimates very close to what a correlation coefficient would find. This technique requires you to take all your scored tests and put them into two piles—a high scoring pile and a low scoring pile. As to what counts as a high or low score depends on the distribution of scores your students produced. Just pick a **cut score** (a point at which to split a distribution of scores into two halves) that gives you two roughly equal-sized groups. Now in each group, calculate the **difficulty index** (see the *There's a Stat for That* earlier in this chapter). Once you have two difficulty indices for each item (one for the high group and one for the low group), subtract one from the other:

**Item Discrimination Index = Difficulty Index (High Group)
− Difficulty Index (Low Group)**

You would expect, at the minimum, for all your items' discrimination indices to be greater than 0. If they are negative, that means, for some reason, people who knew less (at least as measured by the total test score) were more likely to get that question right! This can happen when an item is tricky in some unintended way. For example, students who know more might be drawn more to a good distractor (one that uses a correct term, but in the wrong context, perhaps) than students who know less and do not even find that distractor plausible.

RELIABILITY

Applying good learning strategies, let's immediately create a sentence that uses both key terms we have covered so far: *Validity is the characteristic of an assessment that measures the intended construct.* Assessments that are valid, then, are probably of high quality. A second characteristic, reliability, is required, though, before we can be confident that our assessments work as intended. Teachers typically give an assessment only one time to any given group of students, and that assessment is only made up of a small sample of potential tasks or items. So it is important that a test or assessment be representative of a student's true level of performance. An individual score on a test should represent the typical score that student would receive. Imagine that a student took the same assessment hundreds of times in a row, all in a brief period of time. She would not get exactly the same score each time, of course, because there would be some randomness in her performance. On some occasion she might guess correctly on a multiple-choice question that she usually would miss, or in a different context, she might stumble while performing a complicated dance move that she nails in practice. Sometimes the poor kid might be exhausted (maybe from taking the same test hundreds of times as required by our experiment) and miss things she knows. Or she might have had a particularly potent vitamin water right before the quiz and do better than normal. The point is there will be variability in her scores. The average of those scores is her typical score. A reliable assessment *produces* students' typical scores.

Classical Test Theory

There is a theory of measurement that has been used for more than a century to understand the nature of the scores produced by classroom assessments and all educational and psychological tests (Thorndike, 1904). All these years later, Classical Test Theory is still the foundation of our definition of reliability. The entire theory can be summarized by this conceptual equation:

Observed Score = True Score + Error Score

Or as many educational psychology grad students have gleefully shouted during their doctoral comprehensive exams, "O = T + E!" It is elegant in its simplicity. The theory points out that the score a person gets on an assessment is made up of two components—the score he or she would typically get and some amount of random fluctuation away from that typical level of performance. *True Score* is that theoretical average score across many hundreds of times of taking the same test that we discussed in our definition of reliability. Implications and consequences of this intuitive equation have allowed educational researchers and theorists to, among other things, produce statistical estimates of reliability, make probability statements about what a student's true score is compared with the score he actually got on a test, predict the likelihood that he would do better if he retook the SAT, and produce very precise and reliable standardized tests.

If the scores produced by an assessment are close to the typical scores, they are precise (close to typical) and consistent (scores for the same student will, theoretically, be about the same across multiple administrations). Reliable assessments produce precise and consistent scores. Evidence for reliability of assessments, then, generally takes the form of showing consistency in some way. Three different ways to think about reliability are *inter-rater reliability*, consistency in the actual scoring of an assessment; *test-retest reliability*, consistency across time; and *internal reliability*, consistency within an assessment itself.

Inter-rater reliability is probably the type of reliability that classroom teachers focus on most. *Rater* refers to whoever scores the assessment, and inter-rater reliability refers to consistency in scores regardless of who scores an assessment. Imagine a traditional paper-and-pencil test, such as a multiple-choice test, with an accurate answer key (the cheat sheet a teacher has that lists all the items and the correct answers). For any example of a completed test, it doesn't matter who scores it. The student will get the same score. Any small inconsistency in scores for that individual on that one test administration would be due to random human error on the part of the scorer. Multiple-choice tests have very high inter-rater reliability. Now, imagine an assessment that requires students to paint a self-portrait. Even if a teacher has put together a good scoring rubric (a detailed set of scoring rules) that breaks the assignment down into different components that must be present, the quality of performance will likely be a matter of judgment. Two different teachers, or the same teacher in two different moods, might disagree on what the score should be. Consequently, performance assessments tend to have lower inter-rater reliability than multiple-choice tests.

Test-retest reliability refers to stability across time. The basic definition of reliability suggests that performance on a reliable measure means that the student gets the same score every time. A simple experiment, sometimes actually run by standardized test developers, would be to give the exact same test twice to the same group of people with only a short time between administrations (one does not want the actual level of the intended construct to change). By correlating the two sets of scores (see *There's a Stat for That: Correlation Coefficient* in this chapter), one could get a good sense of test-retest reliability.

Internal reliability looks at consistency in scoring on the individual items within a single test (or part of a test). If you get some of the items correct, does that predict that you will get most of the others correct? Though it is useful to combine many scores into a total score, it only makes sense if the many scores measure the same thing (or *construct*). Internal reliability determines whether it makes sense to combine those observations. Analyses for this type of reliability are somewhat easier than for other reliability approaches because the assessment is only given once and is only scored by one person. It does require more sophisticated statistical analysis, however, using correlations among scores from all the items with each other, and it is most favored by commercial test developers and educational researchers.

Reliability Analysis in the Classroom

Good Question!

Q: I can see that, in theory maybe, it's good to know about different types of reliability and ways of investigating them, but in the real world, classroom teachers don't actually ever do reliability analyses, do they?

A: No. Not usually. As professionals, well-trained teachers in the real world do, however, think about how the choices they make regarding structuring assessments and developing scoring rules might affect the reliability of those scores from the perspective of test-retest or internal reliability, and, especially, inter-rater reliability. Of course, some real-world teachers actually do reliability analyses, especially if they are into *action research* and want to be superconfident that the assessments they use regularly are fair and useful.

Estimating Reliability

There's a Stat for That!

There are a variety of quantitative tools for estimating reliability. The **correlation coefficient** (see *There's a Stat for That: Correlation Coefficient*) is useful for exploring test-retest reliability, as described elsewhere in this chapter. It can also be used to look at agreement among two scorers for the total test score or for looking at the inter-rater reliability of individual items. Another use of the correlation coefficient for reliability estimation is for internal reliability. To see if performance is consistent across the items within one assessment, one can split the test in half (e.g., create a subscore for the first half of the items and another subscore for the second half of the items) and correlate the two halves. Sometimes, internal reliability is called *split-half reliability* for this reason.

There are other useful statistics that are used by researchers or measurement-savvy teachers. For inter-rater reliability, a *percentage of agreement* can be computed. Two teachers, for example, might independently score the same stack of tests. When their scores are compared, they will have agreed some percentage of the time. For instance, if out of 30 tests, they assigned the same scores as each other on 26 of them, their percentage of agreement is 26/30 or 86.7%. Researchers generally interpret percentages of agreement greater than 85% as good.

For internal reliability, a modern statistic, **coefficient alpha** or α, has replaced the split-half correlation coefficient as the preferred estimate. Though it uses a slightly different statistical approach than the correlation coefficient, it takes into account the correlations among all the items with each other. Coefficient alpha is better than a split-half correlation because there are many ways to create two halves of a test, and any two halves one chooses are essentially arbitrary. It turns out, conveniently, that coefficient alpha is the average split-half correlation one would get if they divided the test into every conceivable pair of halves. So, in a sense, it is the fairest internal reliability estimate. The complicated mathematical formula for this approach has been around forever (Cronbach, 1951), but computers have made it a breeze to calculate, so nowadays it is found in almost every test manual or educational research paper. Alpha is almost always between 0.00 and 1.0, and the closer to 1, the better. A common rule of thumb for coefficient alpha is that values greater than .70 suggest good reliability.

COMPARING AND CONTRASTING VALIDITY AND RELIABILITY

As the chapters ahead present the different perspectives on modern classroom assessment, the distinctive roles that validity and reliability concerns play in each approach are explored. As you may have noticed, there are important differences between the two concepts, but they also seem related.

One similarity between validity and reliability is that they both indicate the amount of error in the measurement. The error that validity is concerned with is *systematic* error. There is something about the structure of the assessment that either measures the construct of interest or does not. A test with no validity simply does not measure the contrast of interest—ever, for anyone. The error that reliability is concerned with is random error. A test with no reliability produces random scores; it is not consistent. It might by chance occasionally hit the nail on the head, but it cannot do so consistently.

A way in which validity and reliability differ is that a test can be reliable, but still not be valid. This makes sense because validity refers to whether an assessment is working for its intended purpose and reliability just means the scores are consistent. A math quiz that is made up of word problems may be partly assessing verbal skills, but the teacher may intend for it to be a pure assessment of mathematical ability. Data from the assessment could

Figure 2.1 Reliability and Three Types of Validity Evidence

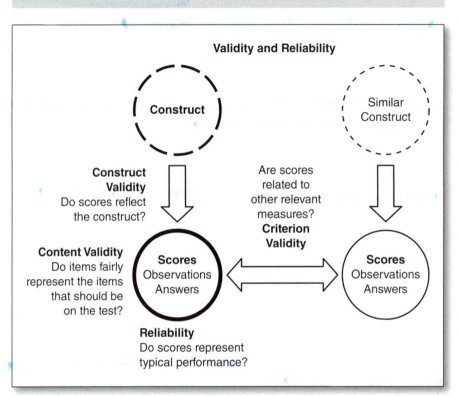

Validity and Reliability

Construct

Similar Construct

Construct Validity
Do scores reflect the construct?

Are scores related to other relevant measures?
Criterion Validity

Content Validity
Do items fairly represent the items that should be on the test?

Scores
Observations
Answers

Scores
Observations
Answers

Reliability
Do scores represent typical performance?

indicate high reliability, but if it is not working for its intended purpose (a math measure), it is not valid. On the other hand, if a test is *not* reliable it cannot be valid. A test with no reliability is producing random numbers as scores; it is producing zero information. A test cannot both measure nothing and measure something. So for a test to be valid it must first be reliable. Once reliability is established, then all the requirements for validity come into play.

Figure 2.1 provides a visualization of the three types of validity and includes reliability, as well. Reliability is placed near the scores themselves as an indication that the level of reliability is purely a mathematical function of how the assessment scores behave and is independent of any theoretical discussion about invisible constructs and whether the scores represent them.

Real-World Choices Teachers Make

Choosing the Type of Validity and Reliability That Matters

Though there are official definitions of types of validity and reliability evidence, choosing which evidence is appropriate, which evidence is more or less persuasive, producing quality instruments, and identifying what data is trustworthy is not so clear-cut. Part of the art of assessment is figuring out which data and arguments are relevant in any given assessment situation. To demonstrate how these choices might be made, let's use an interesting outside-the-classroom example.

This comes from the spooky real-life adventures of ghost hunting. Benjamin Radford (2010) describes in his book, *Scientific Paranormal Investigations*, some common ghost-busting mistakes as they relate to validity and reliability issues with astral assessment. Regarding validity, Radford believes that ghost hunters often misinterpret evidence, such as floating orbs of light visible on video or haunting images of mysterious shadows in dark rooms, as evidence of the supernatural. It turns out, though, that light reflected off of the dust or insects commonly found in old spooky structures can create images of floating lights on video and a random shadowy shape can look like "the old man who died here 100 years ago today," if one has preconceptions about what one will find. The methods ghost hunters often use may have low reliability, as well. Better or more observations (e.g., items on an assessment) tend to increase reliability, for example, but many *X-files* types insist on assessing a haunted house on only one occasion, overnight, with the lights *off!* As a measurement strategy, this is unlikely to produce typical "scores." Further, the fancy electronic equipment, such as Geiger counters, infrared cameras, and electromagnetic frequency (EMF) detectors paranormal investigators like to use measure phenomena that, at best, appear inconsistently and have not yet been shown to produce data related to the construct of interest: ghosties. Radford concludes that if ghost hunters wish to produce convincing evidence, then they need to perform their assessments with greater validity and reliability.

Of our seven important words, we have handled the biggies—**construct**, **validity**, and **reliability**. The remaining terms describe characteristics of scores that influence the validity and reliability of classroom assessment.

OBJECTIVE AND SUBJECTIVE SCORING

Having just presented reliability and its different types, it is a good time to emphasize that it is the scores of an assessment (not the assessment itself) that are reliable or not. Consequently, the nature of the scoring rules used for an assessment has a direct effect on reliability. This is especially true for inter-rater reliability.

Objective scoring means that there is no judgment involved in assigning a score to an item or a test. If a bubble-sheet-reading computer or trained chimpanzee or carnival sideshow tic-tac-toe-playing chicken or anyone picking up the answer key can score an assessment, and they would do it all the same way, then the scoring is objective. Many traditional paper-and-pencil test formats, such as multiple-choice, matching, fill-in-the-blank, and true/false, are scored objectively. There is one single correct answer (usually), and if the response given by the student matches the response called for in the scoring rules, then the student gets credit for a correct response. Subjective scoring means that there is judgment involved. Two different smart people, following the exact same guidelines, might reasonably disagree on what score is deserved. Many performance-based assessments and authentic assessments are subjective because they often use scoring systems that leave room for evaluative judgment. In fact, it is the evaluative judgments involved in these assessments that help increase their perceived value and validity.

In a *Good Question* in this chapter, it was admitted that real-world teachers, even great teachers, probably don't spend a lot of time worrying about test-retest or internal reliability, but they *are* concerned about inter-rater reliability. Fortunately, teachers have a lot of control over this aspect of reliability. They can increase inter-rater reliability for their classroom assessments by devising scoring rules that are as objective as possible.

NORM-REFERENCED AND CRITERION-REFERENCED SCORING

For spring break, Tim and Melissa decided to vacation in the deepest, darkest jungles of a faraway land. As they walked along a narrow path, a tiger leaped out! "We better try to outrun it!" Melissa yelled. "OK," Tim agreed, running along beside her as the tiger gave chase, "but good luck, because you don't run fast!" "I don't have to run fast," Melissa pointed out, "I just have to run faster than you!"

In the story above, while Melissa speaks a bit harshly, she is technically correct. If the goal is to avoid being eaten, being faster than the other meal option is all it takes. Melissa is evaluating the situation as a **norm-referenced** assessment. Norm-referenced scoring means that performance is interpreted by comparing scores to each other; the information in a score comes from referencing what is normal. Tim's philosophy is that you are either fast or you are not. There is a criterion for what it means to be fast, and whether one is fast or not is independent of how fast other people are. His assessment approach is criterion-referenced.

Classroom teachers use both criterion-referenced score interpretation and norm-referenced interpretations all the time. If everyone can get an A on a test or on a report card by meeting some set of standards, objectives, or criteria, then a criterion-referenced philosophy is at work. If the grading is "on a curve" or individual scores have meaning only in comparison with how others performed, then a norm-referenced philosophy is being used. Norm-referenced evaluations are so common in education that you may not even realize that someone (a teacher, policymaker, administrator, test developer) has chosen that approach over a criterion-referenced interpretation. Of course, criterion-referenced assessments are also common and just as much a part of the classroom culture as norm-referenced, but it may not be clear that there is a real difference in the meaning of assessments depending on which philosophy is applied. Table 2.1 provides common examples of criterion- and norm-referenced assessment phrases and snippets of thinking to illustrate the differences.

Table 2.1   Criterion-Referenced and Norm-Referenced Assessment Phrases

Criterion-Referenced	Norm-Referenced
She has mastered the material.	She is the best in the class.
He has met six objectives.	He is at the 83rd percentile.
He turned in a well-written essay.	He scored a standardized score of 600 on the SAT.
Anyone scoring 70% to 79% correct on this test gets a C.	Anyone scoring close to average on this test gets a C.
She is great at math.	Her IQ is 115.
He might qualify for special education services because he acts out in class.	He might qualify for special education services because he scores in the lowest 2% on the Behavior Rating Scale.

PROFESSIONAL STANDARDS AND ETHICS

Three professional organizations made up of educators, psychologists, and other developers and users of tests—the American Educational Research Association (AERA), the American Psychological Association (APA), and the national Council on Measurement in Education (NCME)—have worked together to establish standards of professional and ethical behavior related to measurement and published a manual for those who develop, use, or interpret assessments (AERA, APA, & NCME, 1999). Most of the ethical standards are centered on two of our seven key terms, *validity* and *reliability*.

Ethics are agreed-on standards or codes of behavior for professionals, such as teachers or test developers, to support quality and socially responsible outcomes. As a professional, a teacher should be aware of the standards. Also, as professionals, teachers may choose to follow or not follow these standards, but, at the very least, they should be aware of them and understand the ethical thinking behind them. Their fellow professionals have given a lot of thought to the behaviors suggested in the *Standards for Educational and Psychological Testing*, and they make good sense, so most professionals follow these guidelines.

Much of the *Standards* focus on standardized testing and the use of testing information to make high stakes decisions about individuals. Some of these standards, and other ethical issues surrounding these tests, are presented in Chapter 13. There are several standards, however, that are more relevant to classroom assessment and teacher-made tests. The "official" numbers for these ethical standards are taken from the *Standards* book:

- **5.10 When test information is released to (students or parents), those responsible . . . should provide appropriate interpretations . . . (including) what scores mean . . .**

  This means that students and parents may make all sorts of assumptions about what a test score means, what grade it's equivalent to, how it reflects knowledge or skill level, and so on. An ethical teacher will always explain how to interpret a score when sharing it.

- **11.4 The test user should have a clear rationale for the intended uses of a test . . . in terms of its validity and contribution to the assessment and decision-making process.**

As Chapter 3 presents in great detail, assessments do not exist in a vacuum; they are usually not given just for the sake of giving a test. Professionals design an assessment for a specific purpose. They identify an assessment target, often an instructional objective, and work backward from that target to design an assessment.

- **11.7 Test users have the responsibility to protect the security of tests . . .**

It is tempting to use the same test each year or each semester. It takes a lot of work to create a good assessment and it saves a lot of energy and time to reuse it with a new group of students. If students have been allowed to keep the test, though, it is possible, and perhaps likely, that it will be shared among students. Professional teachers either keep completed tests (after sharing results with students) or they create new assessments each time, perhaps from a larger pool of items or tasks that they develop on one occasion and then draw from over time.

- **11.2 A test taker's score should not be interpreted in isolation . . .**
- **13.7 A decision that will have a major impact on a student should not be made on the basis of a single score.**

Even the most reliable assessment represents a small sampling, only a few observations, of a student's knowledge and abilities. "Big" scores like grades should be based on many observations, many assessments that cover a wide variety of approaches and instructional objectives.

THINGS TO THINK ABOUT

1. How are reliability and validity related to each other?

2. Which type of test, *norm-referenced* or *criterion-referenced*, is "best"? How does the intended purpose of the test matter?

3. How does the choice of objective or subjective scoring rules affect reliability? How does it affect validity?

4. List six *constructs* from the world of education or psychology that are not mentioned in this chapter.

Looking Back in This Chapter

- Quality assessment is **valid**, which means it really does measure what it is supposed to, and it is **reliable**, which means it produces performances that represent typical performance for each student.
- Assessments can be scored **objectively**, which means the correct score is determined by a clear rule, or **subjectively**, which means that there is some judgment required in awarding points.
- Scoring can be **norm-referenced**, which means that the grade or score a student gets depends on how other students performed, or **criterion-referenced**, which means that the grade depends on some standard or criterion that is unrelated to how students actually perform.
- Teachers and other test professionals have established a set of ethical standards that guide them in the socially responsible use of classroom assessment.

ON THE WEB

A handy guide for using Excel spreadsheets to analyze data in general
http://www.sagepub.com/liustudy/chapters/08/UsingExceltoAnalyzeData.pdf

A variety of online calculators for figuring out correlation coefficients
http://www.easycalculation.com/statistics/correlation.php

Instructions for using SPSS software to do item analyses

http://www.spsstools.net/Syntax/ItemAnalysis/UsingSPSSforItemAnalysis.pdf

Free online utility for computing coefficient alpha
http://www.wessa.net/rwasp_cronbach.wasp

Analyzing tests using spreadsheets like Excel
http://languagetesting.info/statistics/excel.html

STUDENT STUDY SITE

Visit **www.sagepub.com/frey** to access additional study tools including eFlashcards, web quizzes, web resources, additional rubrics, and links to SAGE journal articles.

REFERENCES

American Educational Research Association, American Psychological Association, & National Council on Measurement in Education. (1999). *Standards for educational and psychological testing*. Washington, DC: American Educational Research Association.

Crocker, L. (2003). Teaching for the test: Validity, fairness, and moral action. *Educational Measurement: Issues and Practice*, *22*(3), 5–11.

Cronbach, L. J. (1951). Coefficient alpha and the internal structure of tests. *Psychometrika*, *16*, 297–334.

Kane, M. T. (2008). Terminology, emphasis, and utility in validation. *Educational Researcher*, *37*(2), 76–82.

Lissitz, R. W., & Samuelsen, K. (2007). A suggested change in terminology and emphasis regarding validity and education. *Educational Researcher*, *36*(8), 437–448.

Messick, S. (1989). Validity. In R. L. Linn (Ed.), *Educational measurement* (3rd ed., pp. 13–103). New York, NY: American Council on Education/Macmillan.

Radford, B. (2010). *Scientific paranormal investigation*. Boston, MA: Rhombus.

Thorndike, E. L. (1904). *An introduction to the theory of mental and social measurements*. New York, NY: Science Press.

CHAPTER 3

BASIC ASSESSMENT STRATEGY

Categories of Learning, Objectives, and Backward Design

Looking Ahead in This Chapter

This chapter presents traditional and more contemporary systems of classification for possible levels of student learning, including the simple but very useful old standby, *Bloom's Taxonomy*. Methods and suggestions for producing measurable, observable objectives are provided, and a useful approach to making assessment choices, which focuses on what a teacher decides are the most important things to teach, called backward design, is explored.

———— ❧❧❧ ————

Objectives

After studying this chapter, you should be able to

- List the stages of Bloom's Taxonomy of levels of understanding
- List the stages or categories of other frameworks for classifying understanding
- Create high quality instructional objectives that are linked to high quality classroom assessment
- Describe the Common Core standards, which most states have adopted
- Apply the steps of *backward design*, which creates a logical chain of objectives to assessment to instruction

———— ❧❧❧ ————

Ms. Andreas Gets Strategic

Another start to the school year was just around the corner, and it was time to head back and start planning. As a second year teacher, Ms. Andreas had a fairly good idea of what she was doing regarding lesson plans. She pulled out the folders of Earth Science lessons, worksheets, activities, and labs. Keeping all that paperwork from last year was one of the best decisions Ms. Andreas made during her first year, and she quickly wrote out the first 2 weeks of plans. Mr. McWilliams, the principal, popped his head into the room and said, "Welcome back Ms. Andreas. I am glad you are here. I wanted to speak with you about this school year."

"Well, I don't know if I like the sound of that," Ms. Andreas said smiling. "What can I do for you?"

"Mr. Coutu has been transferred to another school in the district because they needed his certification to fill the spot. You know that he was going to be team leader, but now I was wondering if you would take over that role. It comes with a small stipend and a few additional fun meetings. What do you think?"

"Wouldn't that also mean that I would work with everyone on lesson plans and integrating curriculum?"

"Yes, and the main focus I need is for you to work on the alignment of lesson plans with objectives. That's a goal of ours this year; making the fit between the two more precise and obvious."

"Most of my lesson plans are based on the textbooks," she said.

"As are most teachers, but I need you to think about how this team can prepare for any changes that might come about next year with new textbooks and then help your team implement it. Can you do that?"

Ms. Andreas accepted. And she was pretty confident that she knew how to tackle the assignment . . .

(To Be Continued)

"If you don't know where you are going, you will probably end up somewhere else."

Lawrence J. Peter, Educator (1919–1990)

Teaching is tough to do well. The classroom is a complex environment with so many different participants, goals, expectations, pressures, and possibilities. It is useful to try to simplify the educational aspects of the classroom (at least) by focusing on what a teacher hopes to make happen regarding student learning and the strategies for helping make those things happen. In the modern classroom, assessment is a crucial component, perhaps *the* crucial component in those strategies. This chapter explores traditional and modern ways of categorizing the different types of student learning that can occur in the classroom, suggests tactics for defining teachers' expectations in useful and concrete objectives, and presents the modern strategy of "backward" design to promote student learning through close connections between objectives and assessment.

CATEGORIES OF LEARNING

Assessment in the modern classroom is driven by a teacher's objectives for his or her students. Those objectives can be classified in helpful ways that guide choices of both teaching and testing strategies.

Bloom's Taxonomy

Most teachers, when thinking about the types or levels of learning they wish for their students, apply a well-regarded theory that describes knowledge regarding levels or categories (a *taxonomy*). This classic theory was developed by educational researcher Benjamin Bloom and colleagues who suggested six different cognitive stages in learning (Bloom, 1956; Bloom, Hastings, & Madaus, 1971). The categories were designed to guide teachers when they develop instructional objectives. Bloom's cognitive domains are presented below in order from lowest to highest (or deepest) understanding. Yes, somewhat confusingly in this original version, the lowest level of knowledge is something called *knowledge*.

1. **Knowledge.** Involves the simple recall of information; memorization of words, facts, and concepts

2. **Comprehension.** The lowest level of real understanding; knowing what is being communicated

3. **Application.** The use of generalized knowledge to solve a problem the student has not seen before

4. **Analysis.** Breaking an idea or communication into parts such that the relationship among the parts is made clear

5. **Synthesis.** Putting pieces together so as to constitute a pattern or idea not clearly seen before

6. **Evaluation.** Use of some standard of appraisal; making judgments about the value of ideas, materials, or methods within an area

The appropriate level of understanding depends on the nature of the teaching. At introductory stages, a lower level of learning is usually the goal (*Knowledge* or *Comprehension*). For advanced classes or units, higher levels are expected (*Analysis* or above).

Bloom's Taxonomy Revised

For decades, this simple breakdown of knowledge has been found to be very useful. It presents a reasonable way of thinking about the continuum of learning that makes sense and matches real-world experience. There were some quibbles, though, that researchers, theorists, and educators had with the original six stages. These concerns focused on the order of the stages, their names, and describing the levels in observable ways. Early in this century, Anderson and Krathwohl (2001) presented a modern version of Bloom's framework. They changed the order a bit (the product creation stage, *synthesis*, is now considered the highest form of learning), described the stages as types of cognitive processing (using verbs instead of nouns), and presented many examples of how those processes actually occur in observable classroom behavior. The modern version of Bloom's Taxonomy looks like this:

1. **Remembering.** Retrieving relevant knowledge from long-term memory. It is demonstrated by recognizing and recalling information.

2. **Understanding.** Constructing meaning through interpretation, classification, and summarization. It is demonstrated by explaining, comparing, or contrasting.

3. **Applying.** Carrying out a procedure. It is demonstrated by implementing.

4. **Analyzing.** Breaking ideas or content into parts and pieces. It is demonstrated by indicating how the parts relate to one another or to an overall structure.

5. **Evaluating.** Making judgments. It is demonstrated by producing critiques or investigating the value of content or ideas.

6. **Creating.** Putting elements together to form a meaningful whole. It is demonstrated by planning or organizing pieces into a new pattern or product.

A second dimension was also added by differentiating between different kinds of knowledge. The Anderson and Krathwohl model describes four types of knowledge:

1. **Factual.** Knowledge of what is true or exists
2. **Conceptual.** Knowledge of ideas and the abstract
3. **Procedural.** Knowledge of how to do something
4. **Metacognitive.** Knowledge about one's own knowledge

So, if one wished, one could choose learning goals so specific that they apply to a specific level of learning *and* a specific type of knowledge, producing 24 different types of potential learning outcomes.

Values as Objectives

Good Question!

Q. I have all sorts of goals for my students, some of which are not about learning anything in the typical sense. For instance, I may want my students to "learn" to appreciate classical music. How do I apply schemes like Bloom's Taxonomy for that sort of learning?

A. Just as there are ways to classify knowledge, there are also some useful ways to categorize attitudinal and affective learning. In fact, Bloom's Taxonomy was part of a set of classification systems that included a taxonomy for the "affective domain." A few years later, Krathwohl, Bloom, and Masia (1964) suggested this set of levels for learning goals having to do with *attitude change*, *appreciation*, or supporting some *value*:

1. **Receiving.** Awareness of the existence of certain ideas
2. **Responding.** Committing in small ways to the value
3. **Valuing.** Supporting or favoring the idea
4. **Organization.** Relating the view to those already held
5. **Characterization.** Behaving in ways consistent with a view

Other Classification Systems

There are other useful but less generalizable organizational schemes for identifying instructional objectives and designing classroom assessments. For older students who are preparing for jobs, the skills necessary for learning a craft or occupational behavior have been broken down by Dave (1970) in this way:

1. **Imitation.** Copying the actions of others

2. **Manipulation.** Reproducing activity from memory

3. **Precision.** Executing consistently without help

4. **Articulation.** Applying expertise to meet a nonstandard objective

5. **Naturalization.** Applying skills automatically, without thinking

Two organizational approaches to the stages of psychomotor skill development are presented by Simpson (1966), for general physical body control skills for young students, and Harrow (1972), for the sort of skillful body movement used by dancers, gymnasts, actors, and public speakers. Simpson's Taxonomy has seven stages:

1. **Perception.** Awareness

2. **Set.** Readiness

3. **Guided Response.** Attempt

4. **Mechanism.** Basic proficiency

5. **Complex Overt Response.** Expert proficiency

6. **Adaptation.** Adaptable proficiency

7. **Origination.** Creative proficiency

Harrow's Taxonomy is a set of categories, not necessarily a sequence of stages:

- **Reflex Movement.** Involuntary reaction
- **Basic Fundamental Movements.** Basic simple movement
- **Perceptual Activities.** Basic response
- **Physical Abilities.** Fitness
- **Skilled Movements.** Complex operations
- **Nondiscursive Communication.** Meaningfully expressive activity

INSTRUCTIONAL OBJECTIVES

"A straight path never leads anywhere except to the objective."

Andre Gide, Nobel Laureate (1869–1951)

Standard training for teachers includes learning ways to identify the hoped-for outcomes for their students and ways to express those outcomes in observable, measurable ways. These student outcomes are typically labeled *instructional* objectives (because they shape teachers' lesson plans and instructional choices), and they are usually written as behaviors (so they can be observed and measured). In fact, if an objective cannot be assessed, it is probably not a very useful objective, at least in terms of planning how one will teach to that objective.

Goals and Objectives

Good Question!

Q. Is a learning *goal* the same as an instructional *objective*? Do I have to choose my words carefully when I talk about goals instead of objectives?

A. You can use whatever words you want when thinking about the learning outcomes you want for your students. There are some customary ways of defining those terms in education, though. Typically the word *goal* is used for broad, abstract outcomes, and the word *objective* is used for narrow, more concrete outcomes.

You can think of a goal as generating a whole bunch of objectives. Meeting those objectives provides evidence that a goal is being met. This is similar to the scientific method where support for many narrow hypotheses provides support for the broad theory that generated them. Objectives are like hypotheses, and goals are like theories.

"All my students will learn basic beginning reading skills" is a goal.
"All my students will learn the 26 letter alphabet" is an objective.
"All my students will be able to recite the 26 letter alphabet with no errors" is an observable instructional objective.

Good instructional objectives have these characteristics:

A behavioral action must occur: The student will . . . name, compare, decide, indicate, write, mark, sing, answer, and so on.

An observable outcome or product is identified: Assessment results, compositions, birdhouses, performances, and so on.

The criterion for success is identified: List three examples, recite without error, complete 70% of the steps on a checklist, and so on.

The conditions under which the behavior must be performed are often described (or assumed): When asked, on a quiz; when questioned, in front of the class, at the science fair, and so on.

Because the most valuable instructional objectives are, well, *objective*, the wording matters. Words that aren't open to interpretation are best. So it is best to avoid abstract words such as *knows*, *understands*, and *appreciates*. Better words are *solves*, *builds*, and *writes*. A good objective communicates your intent well and leaves little wiggle room.

Objectives, Assessment Formats, and Bloom's Taxonomy

The move during the last 50 years toward more explicitly considered instructional objectives in the classroom was driven by Bloom's Taxonomy, which was designed to generate quality objectives. Consider Table 3.1, which lists each level using the revised categories and suggests words that are useful in describing behaviors consistent with each level.

Table 3.1 Bloom's Revised Taxonomy and Observable Behaviors

Level	Useful Verbs
Remembering	Name, define, match, outline
Understanding	Classify, summarize, explain
Applying	Demonstrate, solve, compute
Analyzing	Separate, diagram, order
Evaluating	Support, judge, interpret
Creating	Revise, compose, construct

Just as different objectives can be matched with different levels of Bloom's Taxonomy, the choice of the different approaches to assessment can be driven by the cognitive level of learning for which a teacher has aimed instruction. Each approach often suggests different expectations of learning. Although each assessment philosophy can be designed to assess at any level, the most common levels of learning for each approach are listed here:

- Traditional Paper-and-Pencil Assessment

  Formats such as multiple-choice and matching are very efficient ways of measuring learning at the relatively low levels of *Understanding* and *Remembering*. In fact, other formats, such as performance-based assessment, may make assessing these levels a bit more complicated.

- Performance-Based Assessment

  This approach is often taken when teachers wish to assess higher levels of Bloom's Taxonomy such as *Creating, Evaluating, Analyzing*, and *Applying*. Though not impossible, it is often difficult to assess at these levels using objectively scored selection items such as true-false and multiple-choice items.

- Formative Assessment

  Any level of Bloom's Taxonomy can be assessed formatively and most any item format can be used. If the formative assessment system focuses on collecting quantitative data (e.g., to chart progress), the use of traditional paper-and-pencil tests can work well. If the focus is for students to judge the depth and clarity of their own understanding, the well-detailed scoring rubrics used in performance-based assessment can be very useful.

- Authentic Assessment

  Real-world evaluations are usually based on performance or production and seldom based on traditional paper-and-pencil test scores. Consequently, it is likely that the most authentic assessment strategies are based on performance-based formats. Regarding Bloom's Taxonomy, authentic assessment tends to value higher levels of knowing such as *Application* and above.

- Universally Designed Assessment

  The principles of universal test design apply to any assessment formats. Many of the research-based suggestions for developing assessments fair to all students, however, focus on traditional paper-and-pencil formats. Choosing tasks that are meaningful to all students and providing instructions that can be processed and understood equally well by all students are important universal test design goals, and those goals make sense regardless of the level of learning expected or item format used.

Modern Classroom Objectives

Since the time of Bloom (1950s and 1960s), teachers have moved a bit from mainly expecting memorization and recitation of basic facts as student outcomes to expecting more complex and higher level (in Bloom's terms) outcomes. Today's teachers tend to have instructional objectives that describe outcomes that are consequently more complex. The constructivist approach, which values student-driven learning, tends to result in objectives that are less standardized and sometimes less concrete. Because objectives still should drive both instruction and assessment, most teachers still produce concrete behavioral objectives for their students. Today, they are often created and determined through a collaboration between students and teacher.

Another modern aspect of classroom objectives is that often, maybe even usually, they are broadly predetermined by school, district, or state policy. There are likely broad goals or objectives spelled out by state or district boards of education, and individual classrooms are expected to have instructional goals that are aligned or are consistent with those goals. Even in these cases, though, teachers typically have the freedom and obligation to specify instructional objectives that are relevant to the teacher-chosen activities and learning strategies.

A third way that modern classroom objectives may differ from those explicitly chosen in the past is in the kinds of learning that a teacher expects. Some objectives are not easily derived from traditional Bloom or Bloom-type classification systems (Bissell & Lemons, 2006). Fink (2003) lists some of these contemporary types of objectives: leadership, interpersonal skills, communication, ethics, learning how to learn (metacognitive skills), tolerance, and "character." The *Taxonomy of Significant Learning* defines learning in terms of significant change that affects students' lives. Instructional objectives that can have lasting benefits beyond the classroom, according to Fink, focus on

Foundational Knowledge. Understanding and remembering

Application. Skills

Integration. Connecting new knowledge and skills to what came before

Human Dimension. Knowing yourself and others

Caring. Developing feelings, values, and attitudes

Learning How to Learn. Teaching students to be self-directed

Tables of Specifications

Many teachers, when designing a classroom assessment, will organize their instructional objectives into rows and columns and create a table of what is to be assessed. Commonly referred to as a **table of specifications**, this organizational scheme provides a mental blueprint of what should be covered in a test. Often these tables include information on the different importance or weighting of each content area, piece of knowledge, or specific skill or ability to be demonstrated. Very detailed tables sometimes even include the Bloom's level of knowledge to be assessed. Chapter 4 describes *Tables of Specifications* in greater detail and provides examples of what these look like in real-world classrooms.

Common Core Standards

A recent initiative is having an effect on state, district, and classroom objectives. The Common Core Standards are coordinated by the National Governors Association Center for Best Practices (NGA Center) and the Council of Chief State School Officers (CCSSO). This standardized set of principles, goals, and objectives was developed in collaboration with teachers, administrators, and educational researchers to provide a single broad framework for critical skills and areas of knowledge that students need for success in future education and in the real world. Since 2009, a series of federal grants have provided motivation for states to adopt these objectives as their own.

The standards have been divided into two categories:

1. College and career readiness standards, which address what students are expected to learn when they have graduated from high school, and

2. K–12 standards, which address expectations for each grade level.

At this point, 45 states have adopted the common core, which means that they are planning to implement this initiative by 2015 and base at least 85% of their state curricula on the Common Core.

There are principles for each major content area and for each grade level. The principles are further broken down into standards and assessable specific objectives. To give a sense of what we are talking about, a couple of examples are provided below that were taken from the Common Core's web-based center at http://www.corestandards.org.

Common Core Reading Standards for Kindergartners

Key Ideas and Details

1. With prompting and support, ask and answer questions about key details in a text.

2. With prompting and support, identify the main topic and retell key details of a text.

3. With prompting and support, describe the connection between two individuals, events, ideas, or pieces of information in a text.

Craft and Structure

4. With prompting and support, ask and answer questions about unknown words in a text.

5. Know and use various text features (e.g., headings, tables of contents, glossaries, electronic menus, icons) to locate key facts or information in a text.

6. Name the author and illustrator of a text and define the role of each in presenting the ideas or information in a text.

Integration of Knowledge and Ideas

7. With prompting and support, describe the relationship between illustrations and the text in which they appear (e.g., what person, place, thing, or idea in the text an illustration depicts).

8. With prompting and support, identify the reasons an author gives to support points in a text.

9. With prompting and support, identify basic similarities in and differences between two texts on the same topic (e.g., in illustrations, descriptions, or procedures).

Range of Reading and Level of Text Complexity

10. Actively engage in group reading activities with purpose and understanding.

Common Core Mathematics Objectives (Ratios and Proportional Relationships) for 6th Graders

Understand ratio concepts and use ratio reasoning to solve problems.

1. Understand the concept of a ratio and use ratio language to describe a ratio relationship between two quantities. *For example, "The ratio of wings to beaks in the bird house at the zoo was 2:1, because for every 2 wings there was 1 beak." "For every vote candidate A received, candidate C received nearly three votes."*

2. Understand the concept of a unit rate *a/b* associated with a ratio *a:b* with *b* ≠ 0, and use rate language in the context of a ratio relationship. *For example, "This recipe has a ratio of 3 cups of flour to 4 cups of sugar, so there is 3/4 cup of flour for each cup of sugar." "We paid $75 for 15 hamburgers, which is a rate of $5 per hamburger."*

3. Use ratio and rate reasoning to solve real-world and mathematical problems, e.g., by reasoning about tables of equivalent ratios, tape diagrams, double number line diagrams, or equations.

   a. Make tables of equivalent ratios relating quantities with whole number measurements, find missing values in the tables, and plot the pairs of values on the coordinate plane. Use tables to compare ratios.

   b. Solve unit rate problems including those involving unit pricing and constant speed. *For example, if it took 7 hours to mow 4 lawns, then at that rate, how many lawns could be mowed in 35 hours? At what rate were lawns being mowed?*

   c. Find a percentage of a quantity as a rate per 100 (e.g., 30% of a quantity means 30/100 times the quantity); solve problems involving finding the whole, given a part and the percentage.

   d. Use ratio reasoning to convert measurement units; manipulate and transform units appropriately when multiplying or dividing quantities.

The Politics of a Common Core

As you might expect, a national set of standards has been controversial. Those in favor of establishing a common set of expectations argue that

- It will provide a common understanding of what students are expected to learn.

- It will create benchmarks that can be applied wherever a student attends school.
- It will lead to higher quality education regardless of which state a family lives in.
- Common standards will provide a greater opportunity to share experiences and best practices within and across states that will improve our ability to best serve the needs of students.
- Its focus on both skills and conceptual understanding will prepare students for future success.

Those who oppose moving toward the proposed common core believe that

- The standards were written too quickly without enough careful thought and analysis.
- Requiring that the same content be taught to every child in a specific grade ignores the notion of individual development.
- The traditional emphasis on local control of schools may be weakened.
- Schools with standards more advanced than those of the common core may "lower" their standards.

Regardless of the controversies surrounding the Common Core, almost all states have moved toward developing state standards that are consistent with the Core and, consequently, the modern classroom does or will include similar assessment objectives across the country.

BACKWARD DESIGN

> *"The road leading to a goal does not separate you from the destination; it is a part of it."*
>
> Charles DeLint, Author and Musician

In *Understanding by Design*, a book on the power of "backward design" for instruction and assessment by Grant Wiggins and Jay McTighe (2005, 2011, 2012), the authors describe a common (and, as they would deem it, old-fashioned) approach to designing instruction and assessment. A teacher might

1. Begin with the textbook or an activity that has been used before.
2. Derive objectives from the content of that book or activity.

3. Use a test from the textbook or from a school resource that appears to be the fairest way to assess the hoped-for outcomes.

Sometimes, there may not even be an assessment. There may be the assumption that engaging in the activity or reading the book will result in learning, but it is not assessed. An example of how this process might work, modifying an example given by Wiggins and McTighe, involves the novel *To Kill a Mockingbird*.

1. A decision is made to "teach" the novel in a 9th grade class.

2. Instructional objectives include demonstrating knowledge of the plot, main characters, and so on. Meeting these objectives will provide evidence that the book was read and understood.

3. A multiple-choice test available from a website is chosen because the items seem to validly cover the objectives.

This is a somewhat simplified description of the process, of course. Real-life teachers give more thought to the objectives of their instruction and the teaching strategies they use than is shown here, but the general approach and sequence (which is the point being made by Wiggins and McTighe) may be fairly common. The assessment is decided at the end and the objectives are derived from the instructional activity.

The backward design philosophy changes the order in this sequence. Objectives are determined first. Ways of validly and reliably assessing those objectives are then designed. These assessment strategies focus on making the outcome *observable* in concrete ways. Last, a strategy for instruction is devised, which is meant to result in learning. The activity is chosen last, not first. That is why this process is called *backward design*.

Our *To Kill a Mockingbird* example would look much different if subject to backward design. It might look something like this:

1. A decision is made to increase students' understanding of prejudice and class in America. Objectives are developed, which include being able to identify the act of stereotyping, appreciate the danger of generalizations, evaluate the irrationality of bias, and so on.

2. An assessment strategy is developed, which includes essays, or critical analyses of media, or debates and speeches, or short-answer tests, and so on.

3. An instructional activity designed to increase understanding of prejudice and class in America is chosen, the reading and discussion of *To Kill a Mockingbird*.

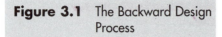

Figure 3.1 The Backward Design Process

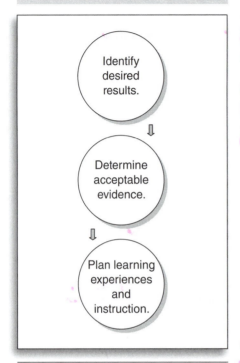

Source: Adapted from Wiggins & Tighe, 2005.

In both examples, students read the same novel.

Notice the potential strengths of the backward design approach, though. More meaningful objectives are chosen (outcomes that matter), and the assessment is closely tied to the objectives in ways that will likely result in assessment with greater validity and reliability. The close relationship between the assessment and the objectives will surely lead to greater validity, and the observable, concrete nature of the assessment outcomes should lead to greater reliability.

Figure 3.1 shows the three simple steps in the backward design process.

Identifying What Should Be Taught

Part of the process of backward design as advocated by Wiggins and McTighe (2005) is identifying the really important stuff that should be taught. What are the big ideas or skills that will have "enduring value" (p. 10) long after much of the lesson is forgotten. One way to decide on priorities among potential instructional objectives is to categorize everything that seems to be relevant to a topic, everything that might be a reasonable objective, into one of three nested groupings. The largest group contains everything that seems relevant. These are the bits of knowledge, concepts, and skills that are, to use Wiggins and McTighe's phrasing, at least *worth being familiar with.* This broad set of possibilities is driven by the state or district standards. Within that large group of potential objectives is a somewhat smaller grouping, which includes only knowledge that is *important to know and do.* The teacher thinks about what is most essential in a unit; what would make the teaching of a topic or domain incomplete if it were absent? These are the skills and required knowledge for students to competently perform or meaningfully comprehend a subject. Finally, there is the third group within the other two, and it is even smaller. This is the category of enduring value. These are the big ideas and underlying concepts that allow for understanding everything else and can transfer to future learning and the real world.

A very relevant example of these three categories and the elements that might belong in them is given by the authors. They use the illustration of an imaginary college course on classroom assessment. I'll share it here because it is similar to the organizational strategy of this textbook and helps make clear distinctions among the groupings. For a course on classroom assessment, the topic of standardized tests is certainly in the category of *worth being familiar with*. Teachers need to know about them and understand their development and scoring, but they typically don't work directly with them very often. In the *important to know and do* category, we might find information on different formats for assessments and items, guidance on assessment construction, distinctions between norm- and criterion-referenced philosophies, and so on. It is important that teachers *know about and can do* these things. Finally, the most crucial aspects of the topic of classroom assessment, those important for *enduring understanding*, likely include the concepts of *validity* and *reliability*. Understand those concepts and you can learn most anything about classroom assessment.

Backward design starts by picking the big ideas you want your students to understand.

The Big Rocks

When teachers consider all that could be covered in a unit or course, it is clear that there is a lot that could be forced into the allotted time for any topic. How can a teacher decide which are the elements with "enduring value" that should provide the focus for instruction? An analogy that compares a course with a glass jar helps clarify the role of these big ideas in making choices.

Imagine a glass jar about the size of a jar of peanut butter. It's been cleaned out and the label has been removed, so it is a clear empty container just waiting to be filled up. How much can it hold? To find out, you might grab some rocks off the ground and fill the jar with them until they reach the top. Now the jar is full and can hold no more. How many rocks are in the jar? Let's say there are 12 rocks. So the jar holds 12 rocks. Maybe that answers the question of how much the jar can hold.

But you realize the jar is not really full. Notice those pebbles at your feet? There's room in the jar for a couple handfuls of pebbles to fill the spaces left by the bigger rocks. Pour those in all the way to the top.

Is the jar full now? Not really. Grabbing some sand, you can easily pour quite a bit of sand into the jar. So it was not full before, really. But, surely, it is full now.

Aha, spotting a nearby pitcher of water, you realize there is plenty of room in the jar to pour some water in. It can hold a lot more than you thought.

So a jar can hold a lot of stuff—big rocks, pebbles, grains of sand, and drops of water. It's just a matter of scale. At this point, of course, the original big rocks aren't even visible. You could fit a lot of objectives into a course and cover a lot of content, but the really important parts might get lost among all the pebbles and sand. To identify the critical enduring ideas, though, start by emptying that jar of everything, except for those original few rocks. Focus on teaching the big rocks. You can surround those rocks with other important things to know and do, like the pebbles, and many grains of basic facts and concepts, like the sand. But it is those big rocks that should be the foundation of your teaching and assessment.

Determining Acceptable Evidence

"I think I tend to test what is easy to test, instead of assessing what is most important."

5th Grade Teacher (Wiggins and McTighe, 2005, p. 16)

Assessment is a critical piece of backward design. The evidence produced should be credible and have "social validity." *Social validity* means that to those who care from an educational perspective (teacher, student, parents, administrators, policymakers) the assessment activity makes sense as a clear way of making understanding or ability visible. If you want to know if students understand science, have them do science. To find out if students can drive a car, assess them while they drive a car. If you want to know if students can identify colors, ask them to identify colors.

Different assessment formats work well as opportunities to display knowledge, understanding, or ability. In backward design, the appropriate assessment format depends on the nature of the instructional objective. Each of those three levels or categories of importance have associated types of assessment that would work best. Table 3.2 shows how the nature of each category of objective suggests a particularly valid type of assessment. Notice that the types of assessment are among the five approaches to modern classroom assessment featured in the chapters ahead. There also is some overlap as to how real-life teachers use various assessment approaches for the different types of objectives they work with. Most, maybe all, authentic assessment is performance-based, for example. Additionally, sometimes, well-written, traditional, objectively scored assessment formats (such as multiple-choice or matching) can measure at the application level necessary for those objectives which are important to know and do.

Table 3.2 Backward Design: Matching Assessment Formats to the Relative Importance of Objectives

Priority	Corresponding Assessment Format
Worth being familiar with	**Traditional Paper-and-Pencil Tests** Basic introductory and background information can be assessed reliably and efficiently with these objectively scored formats.
Important to know and do	**Performance-Based Assessment** Skills and the application of important concepts should be assessed in ways that demonstrate mastery.
Enduring understanding	**Authentic Assessment** Assessments that encourage long-term learning should be engaging and intrinsically meaningful for students.

Ms. Andreas Gets Strategic (Part II)

Mr. McWilliams sent out an e-mail later that afternoon to all teachers on the team followed by an e-mail from Ms. Andreas. Through the e-mails, the first team meeting was arranged. They discussed their summers a bit, and Mr. Johnson spoke about a training he attended this summer. The main focus of the training was on the Standards and how teachers need to understand which objectives require more depth of understanding and which objectives have fewer expectations.

Ms. Andreas started. "As you all know, it's not clear which textbooks the district will be selecting this year. Mr. McWilliams has asked that we start planning, though, based on the instructional objectives we know will be important. I am proposing that this year we use backward design."

Mr. Jenkins said, "Explain that a little bit more; I think I know what you mean but . . ."

"Well, to me, it is like if you were going to travel; pick the destination first and then find the different ways to get there. First, we pick big ideas that are important to learn; these are the major objectives of understanding that we want for our kiddos. So the Standards define our big ideas. This is the end destination for the students. Once we have that we can determine how to assess whether we have reached that point. Next, we plan the lessons to teach the skills or concepts that are central to our assessments. I have been preparing my lessons this way for the last couple of days just to get my head around the idea of backward design. Here is an example.

"For my class, one big idea is that life on Earth has a history of change, and the clues to understanding those changes are in the rocks. I have assessments already that cover different types of rocks, the rock cycle, some vocabulary, and so on," she said.

Mr. Johnson said, "So your lesson plans came *last* in this process. That's why you call this backward design? Ok, we have to make our own tests because the textbook, whatever it is, isn't likely to include everything we want to cover."

"Exactly. If we need to, we can build assessments that are super closely tied with our objectives. This also ties in to the depth of understanding issue that Mr. Johnson talked about from his training. When I was planning the assessments, I followed Bloom's Taxonomy basically, so some assessments just try to get at basic understanding, and the project-based ones attempt to uncover their ability to analyze and evaluate the information."

Ms. Atalmis sounded a little excited. "I think this might be easier to integrate in my lessons. I won't be restricted to the textbook near as much. I am just sitting here thinking of more ways to include Math and Science into my Social Studies lessons. And if you guys share your 'big ideas,' I can incorporate those a little in my specific lesson plans. For example, I think a big idea for me would be how people lived in the past. Different regions had influencing land and weather factors that effected how they lived, like the rocky North was not great for farming. I can infuse knowledge about those rock types, where they came from, what type they are, and the rock cycle. Or climate when you guys get to that in Science . . ."

Ms. Andreas loved it when a plan came together.

THINGS TO THINK ABOUT

1. Picking one of the common taxonomies, identify a few instructional objectives for a unit you will commonly teach.

2. How does your state use the Common Core standards? Or do they?

3. How well do teachers cover those aspects of a topic that have "enduring value"?

4. What are some examples of instructional activities or assessments you have experienced that seem unrelated to instructional objectives?

Depth of Knowledge

Looking Back in This Chapter

Bloom's Taxonomy, both the original version and more recent versions, classifies understanding as moving from relatively low levels of memorized knowledge to higher levels of deep understanding that involve evaluative and creative skills.

- While Bloom's Taxonomy is still front and center in the modern classroom, these days instructional objectives are more commonly determined by states and districts and less commonly chosen entirely by teachers.
- Good instructional objectives describe an expected observable outcome for students and the method of assessment that will be used.
- The *Common Core* is a set of principles, goals, and objectives to provide a single broad framework for critical skills and areas of knowledge that students need for success.
- Backward design starts with identification of an important student outcome, followed by choices about how to make that outcome visible, and ends with instructional strategies.

ON THE WEB

A list of verbs to use in instructional objectives
http://www.au.af.mil/au/awc/awcgate/edref/bloom.htm

A handy chart to generate assessments for Bloom's Taxonomy
http://www.cesa7.org/tdc/documents/Bloomswheelforactivestudentlearning.pdf

Apps for Bloom's Taxonomy
http://www.schrockguide.net/bloomin-apps.html

Guide for developing instructional objectives
http://www.jblearning.com/samples/0763740233/40233_ch03_final.pdf

Steps for creating an assessment plan using backward design
http://www.ascd.org/ASCD/pdf/books/mctighe2004_intro.pdf

Example of a backward design
http://www.slideshare.net/Soushilove/backward-design-unit-sample

STUDENT STUDY SITE

Visit **www.sagepub.com/frey** to access additional study tools including eFlashcards, web quizzes, web resources, additional rubrics, and links to SAGE journal articles.

REFERENCES

Anderson, L. W., & Krathwohl, D. R. (Eds.). (2001). *A taxonomy for learning, teaching and assessing: A revision of Bloom's Taxonomy of educational objectives: Complete edition.* New York, NY: Longman.

Bissell, A. N., & Lemons, P. P. (2006). A new method for assessing critical thinking in the classroom. *BioScience, 56*(1), 66–72.

Bloom, B. S. (1956). *Taxonomy of educational objectives: The classification of educational goals* (1st ed.). Harlow, Essex, England: Longman.

Bloom, B. S., Hastings, J. T., & Madaus, E. F. (1971). *Handbook on formative and summative evaluation of student learning.* New York, NY: McGraw-Hill.

Dave, R. H. (1970). Psychomotor levels. In R. J. Armstrong (Ed.), *Developing and writing educational objectives.* Tucson, AZ: Educational Innovators Press.

Fink, L. D. (2003). *"What is significant learning?" Excerpt from Creating Significant Learning Experiences.* San Francisco, CA: Jossey-Bass.

Harrow, A. J. (1972). *A taxonomy of the psychomotor domain: A guide for developing behavioral objectives.* New York, NY: McKay.

Krathwohl, D. R., Bloom, B. S., & Masia, B. B. (Eds.). (1964). *Taxonomy of educational objectives: Handbook 2, affective domain.* New York, NY: McKay.

Simpson, E. J. (1966). *The classification of educational objectives: Psychomotor domain*. Eric Document Reproduction Services ED 010 368.

Wiggins, G., & McTighe, J. (2005). *Understanding by design* (2nd ed.). Alexandria, VA: Association for Supervision and Curriculum Development.

Wiggins, G., & McTighe, J. (2011). What is backward design? In *Understanding by Design* (pp. 7–19). Alexandria, VA: Association for Supervision and Curriculum Development.

Wiggins, G. P., & McTighe, J. (2012). *The understanding by design guide to advanced concepts in creating and reviewing units*. Alexandria, VA: Association for Supervision and Curriculum Development.

CHAPTER 4

FORMATIVE ASSESSMENT

Looking Ahead in This Chapter

This chapter examines the powerful potential of formative assessment, exploring in detail why this style of assessment is now best practice. We also discuss the characteristics of validity and reliability most relevant to formative assessment and present a set of "how-to" guidelines with examples for using it in the classroom. Finally, we show how to assess the quality of formative assessment.

— ❧❧❧ —

Objectives

After studying this chapter, you should be able to

- Define formative assessment
- Describe why self-directed learning and feedback are the primary advantages of formative assessment in the classroom
- Outline what we know about formative assessment and how it works
- Explain how to design a classroom environment appropriate for formal and informal assessment
- Describe how to assess the quality of your own formative assessment with a scoring rubric

— ❧❧❧ —

Ms. Lee Doesn't Like Surprises

As the 5th grade teachers came together for their weekly team meeting, Ms. Lee was hoping they wouldn't discuss the dismal results of the common science unit exam they all gave. But, of course, Mr. Rivera, as team leader, began the meeting with the first item on the agenda being the science exam results. He started with, "Were your scores as bad as mine?"

Ms. Jackson responded, "Unfortunately, yes. I only had about a third of the class 'pass' but even those scores were not very good."

"Okay, but what should we do?" Mr. Rivera asked. "Because the district pacing guide and the grade level lesson plans do not allow very much time to reteach topics, let alone the entire unit!"

Ms. Lee had done some analysis. "I broke down my scores by question and what percentage of students selected the right answer," she said. "More than 70 percent of my students missed questions 4, 18, and 24."

Ms. Scott Jackson added, "I also had a high percentage of students miss those questions; they're about solutions and mixtures. I wonder if they missed those because they don't understand the concept of dissolving properties."

Ms. Lee realized that there *was* specific information that the students were missing, some things they didn't quite get yet. But what bothered her most was that it would be nice to not be surprised every time she gave a test. She'd like to know *before* she was done teaching a lesson or unit how, or if, learning was happening. And, she bet, there must be ways that students can know how they're doing long before they take some final exam. Because, of course, by then it was too late. After the meeting, Ms. Lee went back to her room to start thinking about assessment plans for the next unit . . .

(To Be Continued)

For millions of students over the years, the sole purpose of classroom assessment has been to serve as an achievement test to measure how much they have learned. Teachers must report how well their students have done. They must assign grades, so therefore they must test. What do students know? What skills do they have? Has the teaching worked? Though a well-designed exam at the end of a lesson or unit can accurately answer these questions about whether learning *has* occurred, it doesn't provide any information about learning *while* it is happening. The traditional purpose of classroom assessment has long been *summative*, a reporting of what has come before. The modern classroom teacher, though, is equally interested in *formative* assessment, gathering data while teaching and learning are occurring.

DEFINING FORMATIVE ASSESSMENT

Some might think it obvious that testing is summative, that it happens at the end of learning to differentiate good students from bad and rank their performance so grades can be assigned. After all, in popular media and in the experiences of past generations, this is what it meant to take a test. This historic image of the role of classroom assessment and the inevitable anxiety that can go along with it is clear in this vintage description from the long-running Hardy Boys juvenile adventure book series:

> "A week went by, a week in which the Hardy boys and their chums again wrestled with refractory Latin phrases and geometrical problems, as the examinations drew near. There was little time for fun, even outside school hours. The boys were all overcome by that helpless feeling that comes with the approach of examinations, the feeling that everything they had ever known had somehow escaped their memory and that as fast as they learned one fact they forgot another."
>
> *The Secret of the Old Mill*, 1927, Franklin W. Dixon
> (In Connelly, 2008)

Classroom assessment still helps us assign grades, but it can do so much more today. The biggest recent change in our thinking about modern classroom assessment is the realization that assessment can provide information to students during a unit, *before* instruction has been completed, so they can judge their own ongoing learning and progress. Students can now monitor, control, and improve their own learning. Teachers too can gather information to modify their instruction, change course, or alter strategy while learning is still taking place. Students and teachers both can change their ways of behaving and thinking "on the fly."

This modern use of classroom assessment is called **formative assessment**. It provides useful feedback while learning is forming, while concepts and knowledge bases are still being developed. It is not meant to be summative, and performance and scores are not counted toward grades. Indeed, the teacher may not even see these raw results.

Formative assessment gives information directly to students while instruction is still going on, not at the end of a unit. It allows them to judge their level of understanding or gauge the effectiveness of their practice or study efforts. With that feedback, they can change the way they think about a concept, study harder or differently, and apply their learning in better and more meaningful ways. Formative assessment is the only type of educational testing that is designed to directly affect and accelerate learning (Nicol & Macfarlane-Dick, 2007). In a manner of speaking, assessment can *become* instruction.

To push this idea a bit further, think of formative assessment as reversing "teaching to the test" formulas, because in some ways the test *is* the teaching. With **scoring rubrics**, like those used in performance-based assessment and constructed-response items, teachers prepare a detailed set of components, skills, or aspects of an assigned performance or product. (See Chapter 6 for more on scoring rubrics.) They assign descriptions to ratings to indicate in concrete ways how the quality of responses will be judged.

For example, if several instructional days are planned for teaching students how to write a good haiku poem, a rubric can be constructed with teacher-identified criteria for quality haikus. As students work on different drafts of their poems, they can apply the rubric themselves to their own work as a guide for improvement. The most effective way of using rubrics is to share them with students during instruction and to actually base teaching on those components identified for the rubric development process. In this way, the test *becomes* the instructional plan. That's how formative assessment can potentially work as effectively as direct instruction.

A straightforward definition of formative assessment is provided by Airasian and Russell (2007): "Observations and feedback intended to alter and improve students' learning while instruction is taking place" (p. 6). However, the field uses the term inconsistently to mean a variety of things. A recent review of many dozens of scholarly writings catalogued the various purposes for formative assessment as understood by different authors (Frey & Schmitt, 2007). Some authors emphasize how formative feedback can be useful to teachers. Others identify feedback to students as the primary purpose. Figure 4.1 summarizes this range of views. Most researchers today focus on the power of formative assessment as a means for students to apply feedback to controlling and improving their own learning. While teachers certainly alter their own instruction based on the results of formative assessment, the approach is most powerful because of its unique and direct benefits to students.

Figure 4.1 Sampling of Differing Definitions of Formative Assessment

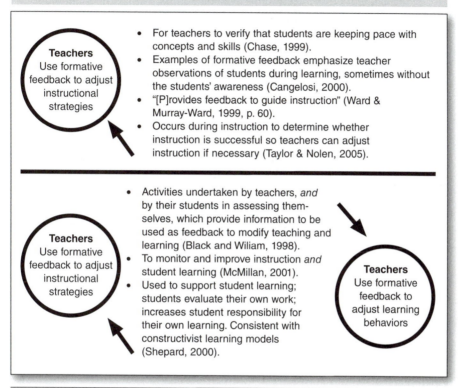

Source: Adapted from Frey & Schmitt, 2007.

Note: As shown above the line, formative assessment is viewed by some as benefitting the teacher only. Below the line, we see how many have expanded their definition of formative assessment to include direct benefits to student learning, not only improvement of instruction.

Formative vs. Summative Assessment

"When the cook tastes the soup, that's formative assessment. When the customer tastes the soup, that's summative assessment."

—Paul Black, Formative Assessment Scholar

Teachers choose between formative and summative tools depending on their assessment goals. If it is the end of the term and a science teacher, like Ms. Lee in the opening and closing story in this chapter, must determine the level of achievement for her students because she must assign a grade, then she will likely choose to use a traditional summative assessment such as a final exam. If, on the other hand, she is interested in the effectiveness of her teaching during instruction, or wants students to know how well they are learning along the way, she might choose any of the various formative assessment techniques.

Here's a brief list of the differences between formative and summative assessment and how their purposes differ:

Formative Assessment	Summative Assessment
Feedback is for the teacher or student or both	Feedback is for the teacher
Assessment directly affects teaching and learning	Assessment indirectly affects teaching and learning
Assessment uses criterion-referenced scoring	Assessment often uses norm-referenced scoring
Grade is not affected	Grade is affected
Stakes are low	Stakes are high

THE ROLE OF FORMATIVE ASSESSMENT IN THE MODERN CLASSROOM

"Holding students responsible for their learning progress is a major mind-shift for many teachers. We frequently hear people say, 'If only Ms. Smith would change . . .' or 'teachers need to . . .' or 'If we had different students we might try . . .' Real Change, however, begins with the individual. It all begins with you. Even if it is only one teacher at a time making the changes, the potential for contagion is greater when there is at least one teacher showing what is possible."

Arthur Costa and Bena Kallick, 2004

Table 4.1 Teachers' Use of Formative Assessment

Question	Mean
Of all your assessments, what percentage are given: during instruction after instruction	25% 75%
Of all your assessments, what percentage: do not affect students' grades affect students' grades	12% 88%

Source: Taken from Frey and Schmitt (2010).
Note: N = 139.

In a recent survey (Frey & Schmitt, 2010), teachers were asked a series of questions about the nature of the assessments they make themselves and how frequently they use them. Among other assessment practices, the study (which is discussed in more detail in Chapter 5) investigated the extent to which real-life teachers use formative assessment in their classrooms. As shown in Table 4.1, formative assessment is used only occasionally. Of course, it is possible that the teachers surveyed frequently engage in all sorts of formative assessment classroom activities, but they may not think of those activities as assessment. They may consider them just good old-fashioned teaching. As the quotation heading in this section suggests, however, treating assessment as a process that can directly influence learning might require a systematic change in thinking, a change in the perspectives of teachers and administrators, and a change in the classroom environment. Still, today's classroom teacher can create formative assessments that are meaningful and produce reliable information.

Think about the three different purposes of assessment summarized in Table 4.2. All assessment provides feedback, data that describes the present state of some variable, but the way the feedback is used and the intended audience for it differs across these different purposes. The value of formative assessment as an approach becomes clear when one realizes that it efficiently meets the needs of both the second and third purposes of assessment. It occurs during instruction to give feedback to both students and teachers, *and* it can work as assessment for learning by allowing students to control their own development. Traditional *summative assessment* only provides feedback for teachers to evaluate the present state of their students' learning in order to assign grades. We should not be too tough on summative assessment as a way to affect teaching and learning. Many teachers, of course, use summative feedback in a formative

Table 4.2 Possible Roles for Assessment

Purpose	Example	Affects Grade?	Who Gets Feedback?
Summative Assessment	A unit quiz	Yes	Teacher
Assessment During Instruction	During a lecture about modern classroom assessment, the teacher asks students to explain why a test cannot be valid if it is not reliable.	No	Teachers and Students
Assessment for Learning	Students regularly fill out self-reflection forms identifying chemistry concepts that they "don't get yet" or "need more practice with."	No	Students

way, learning from the results of this semester's teaching how to improve the teaching for next time, and, conceivably, students might reflect on performance in the past to affect their approach to the next topic that comes along.

Assessment during instruction has a long tradition in the classroom and is consistent with the spirit of formative assessment. Teachers frequently pause for questions or informally collect information while lecturing or during demonstrations. In this way, they get a sense of where students are in the development of their understanding.

Assessment for learning has become a term with a specific technical definition describing a preliminary diagnostic stage, collaborative student-teacher involvement, and frequent formative assessment. It describes feedback systems that are student-centered and allow students to modify and control their own learning. The focus of this chapter is on this approach to formative assessment.

You may have noticed that Table 4.2 is a bit simplified and shows that sometimes feedback can be for students only, while in real life, assessment for learning data meant for students is frequently seen and interpreted by teachers as well. What we've tried to emphasize in the table is that the power of feedback comes mostly from the students' understanding of it, not the teacher's. Feedback is powerful because it fuels self-directed learning. Let's think about that process.

Self-Directed Learning

In an environment chock-full of formative evaluation opportunities and practice, children, especially young children, can become the most successful kind of students: self-directed learners. Costa and Kallick (2009) define **self-directed learners** as students who are self-managing, self-monitoring, and self-modifying. Here's what those traits mean:

- *Self-Managing* Able to approach tasks understanding their relative importance and likely outcomes. Self-managers make use of their own experiences.
- *Self-Monitoring* Able to use metacognitive strategies. Self-monitors know themselves, their skills, and their work patterns. They can tell when a strategy is not working and plan new approaches.
- *Self-Modifying* Able to reflect on experience and alter an approach. Through reflection, self-modifiers can apply learning to future problems.

Formative assessment provides exactly the structured and meaningful data that builds self-directed learners. By learning from past experience, formative assessment creates self-managers. By getting frequent and relevant information about their performance, students learn to self-monitor. Finally, as students get used to a regular schedule of formative assessment that they can interpret themselves, they develop the skills needed to modify their behaviors.

Feedback offered by formative assessment helps students become self-directed learners, but some types of feedback are more helpful than others.

The Power of Feedback

Behavioral theories about how feedback affects learning go back at least 100 years to discoveries of basic scientific laws about how positive or negative experiences influence performance (Thorndike, 1913). Theories specific to learning and performance that help us identify which types of formative assessments best affect learning in educational settings are much more recent.

In a review of hundreds of psychological studies, DeNisi and Kluger (2000) noted that contrary to common assumption, feedback, defined as information about how well someone did, did not always improve performance on a learning task. In fact, about one third of the time, it actually hurt it! To try to clarify this surprising realization, the authors developed a model for understanding feedback that centers on where the attention is focused when someone gives feedback. Three key points of their **feedback intervention theory** are the following:

1. Feedback that focuses attention on the specific task and increases motivation for that task tends to increase performance.

2. Focusing on the broader aspects of performance tends to interfere with the potential benefits of the feedback at best and decrease performance at worst.

3. Evidence of success and evidence of failure are, in general, equally effective types of feedback. *Negative feedback* is defined as evidence that the student has not mastered a skill yet or has not yet learned with deep understanding; *positive feedback* is evidence that the student has improved.

Parallel implications for designing formative *assessment for learning* in the classroom are these:

1. The feedback from formative assessment should be specific to the task, and the formative assessment system should create an environment that increases motivation.

2. Feedback designed to inform students about general abilities or broad goals is less effective and may interfere with specific task performance.

3. Because effective feedback can be negative or positive, teachers can use self-scoring assessments such as concretely detailed scoring rubrics. When formative assessments focus on specific tasks, any level of performance

(any score) can be useful as feedback. Students don't need to focus on strengths and weaknesses; they just need specific feedback on the performance of specific tasks.

The power of feedback is the central force in formative assessment. Frequent, meaningful, and specific data for students on the current state of their own understanding and skill development allows for the development of self-directed learning.

WHAT WE KNOW ABOUT FORMATIVE ASSESSMENT

Formative assessment is probably the most thoroughly studied modern classroom assessment approach. A massive amount of research suggests it can actually improve student outcomes. It increases motivation, self-efficacy, and academic interest, and can increase student learning (Black & Wiliam, 2003, 2009; Shepard, 2005, 2009; Stiggins, 2010). Five characteristics of classroom assessment have been found to influence learning: frequent use, learning goals that are valued by students, self-assessment, student reflection on assessment data, and low emphasis on grades (Black & Wiliam, 1998). Formative assessment includes them all.

Value of Formative Assessment Compared With Other Approaches

Q: Of the five classroom assessment approaches described in this book—traditional, performance-based, formative, authentic, and universal test design—formative assessment is the only one found to actually increase learning. So are the other methods not as good?

A: All five perspectives described in this book, when applied appropriately, will increase the *validity of scores* from assessments. That is, all five can correct systematic errors that have penalized or benefitted students in invalid assessments, so *test scores* might increase (or decrease). Also, of course, anytime students or teachers see a score on a test, it allows them to consider their past behaviors and contemplate changing for the future. Only formative assessment, though, has been shown through research to increase *learning*.

Good Question!

That is not the same as saying that learning occurred *because of* the assessment, but it is reasonable to assume that a formative assessment system should result in improved achievement.

Black and Wiliam's Study

When we listed five aspects of formative assessment that have been shown to affect learning, we used a summary produced by a groundbreaking piece of research. The Black and Wiliam study is the most cited research article in support of formative assessment and has been very influential in shaping our views of the value of this approach. So it's worth taking the time to explore their findings and methods.

Black and Wiliam's 1998 comprehensive review of the effectiveness of formative assessment on student performance summarized about 250 different studies. Some of the studies were themselves summaries of studies, or meta-analyses, which statistically combine the results of many similar studies (see the **Closer Look** box for a description of meta-analysis). The article reported gains from a half to a full standard deviation, with low-achieving students making the largest increases (see Chapter 11 for a discussion of the **standard deviation**, a common indicator of variability among student scores). A connection of such strength between a cause (formative assessment) and an effect (student learning) is rare in educational research. That such a strong relationship seems to exist between a type of assessment and student performance accounts for formative assessment's rise to the top of the list of instructional best practices.

A Closer Look

What Is a Meta-Analysis?

Even if they have the time to explore scientific research findings, teachers who want to apply them in their classrooms often rely on grand summaries of many studies, or meta-analyses. The term *meta-analysis* suggests that the small truths within many scientific studies have been combined to produce a big truth, such as Black and Wiliam's finding that formative assessment affects student performance. So what is a meta-analysis?

Meta-analysis is a mathematical, statistical way of taking the quantitative results of many different studies and combining them into a single quantitative estimate of the "truth." That single estimate is usually formatted as a number representing the relationship between two variables, such as the use of formative assessment and learning. Meta-analyses are very difficult to do, and in education there are very few of them because several criteria must be met before one is possible.

First, each study to be included must use the same two variables, and they must be defined and measured in very similar ways. Second, the published results of the study must report the quantitative results in the same format, so they can be combined (or at least the results should provide enough information for another researcher to calculate the values needed). Finally, while there are accepted ways that meta-analyses can be done, there is not yet full agreement on a variety of methodological issues. These include the right way to combine or average all the findings, for instance, and whether to weight all studies equally or make adjustments based on quality.

Kingston and Nash's Study

The Black and Wiliam review is scholarly and well regarded, but it is not without its critics. The main concern is primarily about the actual level of effectiveness of formative assessment, not whether formative assessment can affect learning (Dunn & Mulvenon, 2009). (See the **There's a Stat for That** box for a definition of **effect sizes**.) For example, Bennett (2011) argued that the hundreds of studies included in the review could not be meaningfully combined into a single analysis that summarized or combined effect sizes, and that the sources of the effect sizes summarized were not given. Shepard (2009) worried that it is primarily (or only) these effect sizes that other researchers, essayists, and policymakers cite, while the many studies themselves have been forgotten and the fundamentals behind how formative assessment works have been jumbled.

Clearly there are difficulties inherent in doing a meta-analysis on formative assessment, and we know that the Black and Wiliam study did not produce a statistically precise estimate of the effect size of the formative assessment and learning relationship. This was discussed in a 2011 study by Kingston and Nash, one of the few rigorous meta-analyses conducted on the topic. While they began with more than 300 studies to review, by the time the authors narrowed the group down to those that defined the two variables in similar ways and provided enough information to combine results in a standard quantitative way, only 13 studies remained.

Their grand estimate of the effectiveness of formative assessment on learning was .20 standard deviations. This is roughly equivalent to saying that a student at the 50th percentile would learn enough using formative assessment to move to the 58th percentile on some learning objective or test, all things being equal. This amount of growth is considered on the small side, but still meaningful.

There's a Stat for That!

Effect Sizes

One of the most persuasive and widely reported findings of the Black and Wiliam (1998) paper on the effectiveness of formative assessment is that "effect sizes" range from .5 to 1.0. What is an effect size, and is .5 or 1.0 big, small, or somewhere in between?

An *effect size* is a standardized, quantitative way of reporting the strength of the relationship between an intervention or treatment (here, an assessment approach) and some outcome of interest (classroom performance). Because every study uses different variables measured in different ways, we report effect sizes in a uniform way to make comparisons and meta-analyses easier. For example, imagine we want to compare the performance of two groups of students in some experiment. The math involved is to first subtract one mean from the other. This mean difference between the groups is then divided by the average standard deviation in the groups of scores. Jacob Cohen (1969) called the resulting value *d*.

$$d = \text{Mean of Group 1} - \text{Mean of Group 2} \,/\, \text{Average Standard Deviation in the Groups}$$

Scholars have suggested that an effect size of .2 should be considered small, .5 medium, and .8 large. So the "effect sizes of .5 to 1.0" reported by Black and Wiliam mean that many formative assessment studies found medium to large differences in learning between classrooms that used formative assessment and those that did not.

A Closer Look

Applying Research and Theory to Formative Assessment in the Real World

A basic tenet of research design is that if you wish to demonstrate that one variable affects another, you need to rule out all the other possible causes for the outcome under investigation. When you are using the validity framework for judging whether an assessment acts in a formative way, for example, you must have a causal chain of steps. The variables are defined here as "exposure to the formative feedback" and "learning," and the feedback is supposed to affect the learning. For this claim to be reasonable, the feedback must be specific, narrow, and accurate, and—here's where the cause-and-effect part happens—there must be some mechanism by which the student can change. So first, of course, it must be possible for the feedback to cause a change. Second, we must rule out other possible factors that could cause a change.

To convince researchers that one variable causes another, the most persuasive approach is to compare how much learning occurred in groups of students who differ in only one way—that is, one group received the feedback and the other did not. The easiest way to equalize groups on all variables except one is to randomly assign students to those groups. In that way, we ensure that the groups are roughly equal on other potential causal variables, so these causes cannot reasonably be responsible for any differences in group outcomes.

There is not much real-world research, especially in education, that can achieve this random assignment, so often we are left with believing that cause-and-effect relationships exist because it makes sense that they should. Much of what we consider educational best practice is theoretical, with very little experimental research that speaks to it. While there is experimental support for the general value of narrow and accurate feedback, there is not likely to be a study that focuses on every teacher's particular context, environment, variables, or instructional objectives. Teachers thus use theory, such as Nichols, Meyers, and Burling's validity framework, to judge whether it *makes sense* that their formative assessments will work.

WHAT FORMATIVE ASSESSMENT LOOKS LIKE IN THE CLASSROOM

There is both science and art to much of what teachers do. Assessment is no exception. The science of formative assessment is in the application of the various theories of why formative assessment works and in the research that has led to best practice suggestions for effective assessment. The art comes in finding meaningful assessment opportunities in the context of each teacher's unique lesson plans, curriculum, and classroom environment. There also is art in choosing formal and informal times to assess. Some assessment is formal, such as quizzes, tests, and scored performances. These assessments usually result in a formal evaluation by the teacher and are sometimes saved as part of student portfolios and other records of learning. Formative assessment can be informal, as well. Questioning, observing, listening, and checking student work while learning is occurring are ways that teachers can use formative assessment informally. Both formal and informal assessment can provide feedback to teachers and students, and the theories of formative assessment guide them both.

Designing Formative Assessments That Work

Teachers can structure formative assessment in their classrooms in many valid ways. To be most useful, formative assessment must meet two goals:

1. Provide meaningful and accurate feedback

2. Allow students to control their own learning

Nichols, Meyers, and Burling (2009) argue, however, that we should go further and say that formative assessment cannot be considered valid unless there is evidence, real or theoretical, that it does what it is intended to do: increase learning. Classroom teachers aren't in a position, of course, to gather data or apply detailed theoretical criteria to all the assessments they produce (especially when they are creating and administering assessments, both formal and informal, all the time), but these authors provide a framework for determining whether a formative assessment will serve its intended purpose of allowing students to monitor and control their own learning through meaningful and accurate feedback.

The validity framework begins by assuming that any formative assessment task is part of a system or series of many such opportunities, and that these opportunities are coordinated and directly related to instruction. We can think of what happens in a classroom as having three phases: an *assessment phase*, an *instructional phase*, and a *summative phase*. The formative part of learning occurs in the first two phases. Initial feedback provides information to the teacher, who adjusts instruction based on it, and to the students, who moderate or frame their behavioral and cognitive responses to instruction based on it. For example, a teacher can give a quick quiz or some informal questions to the class as a group before starting a new unit to get a sense of where the students are regarding their current knowledge or skill level, and then spend more or less time on different portions of a lesson based on this information. The summative phase occurs when any results of the formative assessment could be expected to be seen. This could be reflected in test scores, improved performance, or any evidence of learning.

For a formative assessment to be valid, Nichols et al. (2009) point out that during the formative phases:

1. The assessment feedback must provide information about a student's current level of achievement (knowledge, skill level, conceptual understanding).

   This comes from formal or informal assessment and should be similar in purpose to the eventual summative evidence of learning.

2. The information must be narrowly related to the learning goal (the construct of interest, a skill, an objective).

   For example, if the instructional objective is that students will be able to build a birdhouse, the formative assessment should focus on whether they can build a birdhouse, not on an unrelated but important skill (such as workshop safety) that is not part of the intended objective.

3. Interpretations of the feedback must allow for progress to be made (behavioral changes, a change in motivation, adapting to new learning strategies).

   Students need to know exactly what behaviors they need to change or what aspects of a concept they are misunderstanding. For example, instead of a comment on a draft of a composition such as "poorly organized," a more specific comment such as "place the concluding paragraph at the end of the composition, not in the middle" works best.

If classroom teachers can reasonably assume that each of these links in the chain exist, then they can conclude that their formative assessment has validity.

Scoring Formative Assessments

For feedback to work it must be accurate and, theory suggests, it must be precise. Precision is a function of reliability, and the types of reliability most relevant for formative assessment are inter-rater reliability and internal reliability (both discussed in Chapter 2).

Inter-rater Reliability

When students use rubrics to assess their own work or performance, their subjectivity may be in question. Students do not (at first) have the experience and wisdom that teachers have to judge the quality of their work. They may therefore subjectively apply descriptors assigned to points on a scoring scale in a rubric that seems concrete and objective to the experienced teacher. To increase inter-rater reliability, teachers should write scoring rubrics meant to be used by students at an appropriate developmental level. Ideally, students should be trained to use them.

Internal Reliability

Internal reliability may be a concern when the assessment consists of several steps on a checklist. If the points earned at each step are totaled as an indicator of progress, the steps should represent strongly related items that work together to help the student achieve a skill or meet a learning objective. If they do not, the formative assessment may suffer from low internal reliability.

How to Use Informal Formative Assessment

Formative assessment has been in use for quite a long time, at least in the form of informal data collection and feedback. Part of the art of teaching is the ability to judge whether a student or classroom full of students is "getting it" or is "with" you. Thus, teachers ask questions during instruction, observe student behaviors in the classroom, and so on.

Airasian (2005) describes these sorts of behaviors as *assessment during instruction* (described earlier) and argues that, when teachers teach, they really are doing two things simultaneously: delivering instruction as planned and continuously judging the success of that instruction so they can change plans as needed. In this view, instruction amounts to a continuous process of assessing progress. This is formative assessment designed to benefit the teacher primarily, so he or she can adapt teaching on the fly.

Some assessment targets for teachers evaluating their teaching while they teach are

- Interest level of the students
- Appropriateness of the instructional strategy
- Students to call on
- Pace of instruction
- Level of understanding reflected in students' answers to questions
- Best time to start or stop an activity

To do this sort of "live" assessment well, Airasian has several suggestions. First, use a broad sample of students. Avoid observing or calling on only the most active, vocal, and highest-achieving students. When asking a question of the whole class, scan the whole room; check out the eyes of many students. Are they looking at you or looking away? Get a sense of whether most students seem ready and willing to respond.

Second, to fully judge instructional success, supplement or verify your informal conclusions with more formal assessment by combining review exercise, homework, and the sorts of formal assessment described later in this chapter with assessment during instruction. Finally, ask questions, lots of questions. Oral questioning is the most efficient form of data collection during instruction. Some teachers ask students hundreds of questions every day. Airasian describes the asking of questions as the second most common form of teaching, after the tried-and-true lecture format. Good questions reinforce important points, identify misconceptions, keep students' attention, and promote deeper processing of information.

Technology

Clickers

Audience response systems (ARS), or clickers, are handheld wireless signaling devices that allow students to choose a button and anonymously send their answers or choices to a central computer display so teachers—and all the other students—can see what the class as a whole thinks or knows about a topic. Clickers are a quick and efficient method of informal formative assessment that collects data from, and shares data with, the whole classroom almost instantly. Students can report how they feel, indicate what they think the answer to a multiple-choice question is, and provide a variety of check-ins to show how well learning is occurring. The data not only provides feedback to the teacher; it can also let students know when their answer differs from that of other students.

Research on the use of clickers suggests some good ways they can be used as formative assessment (Caldwell, 2007; Kenwright, 2009). Useful questions should

- be related to specific learning goals or beliefs,
- help students be aware of others' views,
- seek out misconceptions or "gray" areas,
- act as advance organizers (to activate areas of knowledge or thought at the start of instruction),
- be fairly difficult,
- include distractors that represent common errors, and
- allow an "I don't know" or "I'm not sure" option.

The brief, teacher-student interactions that happen all the time during class time can also function as powerful formative assessment, especially when they are in the form of purposeful conversation that centers on student products or performance. In Table 4.3, Torrance and Pryor (2001) provide examples of these common classroom moments and point out how they could affect student learning or motivation.

Table 4.3 Classroom Formative Assessment Opportunities

Teacher-Student Interaction	Potential Student Benefit
Teacher observes students while they work.	Enhanced motivation
Teacher examines students' work.	Enhanced motivation
Teacher negotiates quality criteria with students.	Enhanced self-monitoring skills
Teacher asks "substantial" questions; students respond.	Rehearsal of understanding; articulation of understanding
Teacher asks for clarification of the steps of a process.	Enhanced reflection, speculation, and self-awareness
Teacher asks students why they took a specific step or made a specific choice while problem solving.	Enhanced metacognition and deepened understanding
Teacher critiques student products.	Articulation of quality criteria; enhanced self-monitoring skills
Teacher invites students to critique their own work.	Articulation of quality criteria; enhanced self-monitoring skills
Teacher negotiates with students about what to do next.	Deepens understanding of process

Source: Adapted from Torrance & Pryor, 2001.

Kipling's Six Questions

"I keep six honest serving men,
They taught me all I knew;
Their names are What and Why and When
And How and Where and Who."
Rudyard Kipling (1865–1936)
Just So Stories (1902)

There are so many types of questions teachers can choose to ask students. Which types are best? Rudyard Kipling's poem suggests six powerful types

Real-World Choices Teachers Make

of questions that can serve teachers well as ways to judge the level of understanding of their students during instruction. They might sound like this in the classroom:

> Questions are a powerful and simple type of formative assessment that keeps students engaged.

What? What do you think happens next? What is 2+2? What is the next step?

Why? Why did that happen? Why is this important?

When? When did that happen? When will we add the acid?

How? How do you feel? How should we do this? How much do you know about this?

Where? Where would we go next? Where was the Declaration of Independence signed?

Who? Whose idea was this? Who was our first president?

How to Use Formal Formative Assessment

There are many ways to use formative assessment in the classroom. Some formats that appear to be valid, based on theory and the criteria established through research, include the following:

- *Quizzes* or exams that do not affect grades. These are most effective when they are closely tied to the skills or content being taught and students score them themselves. Feedback about why any answers were wrong is particularly useful.
- *Conferences* in which work plans and strategies are discussed. These conferences are one-on-one collaborative planning sessions with each student

and the teacher to identify useful approaches and goals specific to the task.

- *Performance control charts* on which students have a numeric criterion for success on an assignment. Teachers and students often collaborate on what level of performance they would like to a reach. Alternatively, the goal might simply be growth or progress. These data displays might include all students (sometimes identified by a code name or user ID) and hang on a bulletin board for all to see, or they might be private between the teacher and each student.
- *Practice exercises* in textbooks. This is perhaps the oldest and most traditional formal approach to formative feedback.
- *Guided interviews* of students. The format is similar to *conferencing*, but the purpose is different. Guided interviews are designed to explore student comprehension of concepts and then help correct any misunderstandings.
- *Self-reflection worksheets* to identify areas of struggle or difficulty. Students will ask themselves, What do I understand well? What do I still have questions about? What do I need to practice more?
- *A written statement of specific academic goals*. Students can frequently compare the written goals with data they've collected to evaluate progress. Student motivation to learn increases when they have goals and see progress toward those goals.
- *Self-scoring rubrics* for quality, skills, or abilities. Students can use the scoring rubrics developed to assess performance tasks, if these are objective enough, as they develop products, write drafts, or practice procedures.
- *Letters to parents*. One authentic use of knowledge is to explain to others what you have learned or are learning. Asking students to write letters that will be shared with parents about what they are studying allows for reflection. Teachers can evaluate the letters for understanding.
- *Checklists* with steps or objectives and options like "sometimes" and "not yet." Students and teachers can collaborate on the steps, and students then can assess their own progress toward meeting a learning objective or goal.

How to Create a Formative Assessment Environment

Formative assessment is concerned with the creation of, and capitalization upon, "moments of contingency" in instruction for the purpose of regulation of learning processes. . . . While this focus is narrow, its impact is broad, since how teachers, learners and their peers create and capitalize on these moments . . . entails considerations of instructional design, curriculum, pedagogy, psychology and epistemology. (Black & Wiliam, 2009, p. 9)

It is one thing to develop a stand-alone formative assessment for the benefit of students or to guide instruction, but formative assessment works most powerfully when it defines a whole environment. As the quotation above suggests, we could apply the assessment for learning approach to all aspects of teaching and learning. With some planning, teachers can create formative assessment *classrooms*, in which the formative approach is the common way of doing things. Students who grow up in these environments become skilled learners and skilled self-evaluators.

Black and Wiliam describe a formative classroom assessment environment as one in which

evidence about student achievement is elicited, interpreted, and used by teachers, learners, or their peers, to make decisions about the next steps in instruction that are likely to be better, or better founded, than the decisions they would have taken in the absence of evidence that was elicited. (2009, p. 9)

This description envisions a data-driven, assessment-rich world where students and teachers expect and interpret a constant stream of feedback to guide their teaching and learning. Such classrooms are possible and effective, especially when students grow accustomed to this way of learning at an early age. Three key components of a comprehensive formative assessment system are the design of lesson plans, the role of the teacher, and the creation of feedback opportunities.

Lesson Plans

Some lesson plans work better than others in integrating formative assessment. When new or advanced concepts are introduced, one lesson plan strategy that works well is the "big question" approach (Shulman, 2005). The lesson begins with a big question chosen to lead students through a problem-solving process toward an objective. Students discuss the question in pairs, in groups, or as a whole class with the teacher guiding them through an analysis of the ideas and facts. The conversations among students, with the teacher, and among the whole class allow students to clarify their own thinking, compare their understanding with that of others, learn through observation, and practice the methods of self-assessment and problem-solving.

For example, a big question at the start of a physics unit might be "Why do heavy objects fall at the same speed as lighter objects?" Group activities might include first verifying whether this is true through experimentation. Then, students can suggest hypotheses or guesses as to why this might be true. The class can choose the most likely hypotheses and then search on the Web, in the library, or in their textbook for any laws or principles that might account for this. During all these stages, the teacher is observing and listening and asking questions to make student thinking visible throughout the process. Students are also evaluating their own understanding as they interact with other students and the teacher.

Role of the Teacher

The teacher is in charge of the formative assessment classroom. His or her role is to identify the learning objectives, design activities that promote learning, and provide opportunities for feedback. In the formative assessment environment, teachers generally have two broad goals for their students: learning and developing the skills to control their own learning. Consequently, teachers focus on engaging students, guiding and clarifying understanding, and modeling and demonstrating self-evaluation skills. So within a lesson implementing the big question approach, for example, the teacher attempts to structure the conversation, allowing for any answers and questions students produce, while always providing supportive critiques of the ideas and suggestions offered. The teacher advances the learning goal by applying student contributions to the question of the moment; the specificity of the learning goal determines how tight a hand a teacher chooses to keep on the discussion. In our physics question illustration from earlier, the teacher has chosen the question, predetermined the steps and stages in the learning process (experiment, pick a guess to explain results, hunt for scientific principles to support the guess), and deals with all questions and guesses by guiding the class as a large group toward solutions. Notice that learning occurs whether students come up with the "right" answer immediately or need some help from the teacher.

Feedback Opportunities

Feedback opportunities are those "moments of contingency" that Black and Wiliam referred to in the quotation at the start of this section. If we observed a formative assessment classroom, we would notice evidence of frequent formal assessment (such as performance control charts, public displays of student work, self-reflection worksheets) and a continuous flow of informal formative assessment (frequent questions and answers with teachers and peers, focused problem-centered discussions, collaborative work groups). These two types of feedback create a powerful combination, a one-two punch that molds self-directed learners. Recall that the best feedback gives specific guidance on how to perform a task correctly. Thus, the most effective formative assessment classrooms focus on feedback that relates to the task at hand and the quality of the work produced. It makes sense to also include some feedback designed to foster error detection and other self-monitoring strategies. Sticking with our physics-based big question example about the speed of falling objects, the teacher would guide students through modeling or direct instruction on the right way to conduct an experiment, how to evaluate a hypothesis, how to judge the authority of reference sources, and how to talk and collaborate like a scientist.

FORMATIVE ASSESSMENT WITH YOUNG CHILDREN

Formative assessment is most useful when students receive information about their own thinking and learning and are able to self-evaluate using *metacognitive* strategies (thinking about thinking). Young children below the age of 8 or 9 have difficulty thinking in abstract ways, though, and one might be skeptical of their ability to benefit from formative assessment.

Preschool children and other young students, however, do benefit from formative assessment environments, especially when they have experienced this style of conversation with teachers and adults from the start of their schooling. Remember that formative assessment teaches, among other things, that performance on assessments is not a measure of one's self-worth or value. Assessment feedback can be used to control and change your behaviors and ways of doing things; it does not define you. Children, even young children, can learn to think that way. In some ways, it is a more natural way of thinking about school performance. We might all intuitively treat assessment that way if we were not taught otherwise.

There are many things teachers can do to create an environment of useful, instructive formative assessment for younger students (Puckett & Black, 2008):

- develop reasonable expectations for performance that are still appropriately challenging,
- empower students,
- promote respect among students,
- create a climate free from embarrassment and ridicule, and
- encourage risk taking and the freedom to make mistakes.

Other aspects of formative assessment that work well with even young children include talking with students about characteristics of quality that are important and that they have control over, and familiarizing them with judgment tasks (such as assigning "scores" on rubrics). Providing stress-free experiences that involve assessing themselves using standards helps create students who become master self-assessors.

ASSESSING THE ASSESSMENT

Any successful approach to formative assessment should be based on student-understood learning goals and student self-assessment and should promote student reflection. Research and theory suggest several criteria for quality when it comes to the design of formative assessment. Table 4.4 presents those characteristics, along with recommendations from the National Council of Teachers of English (2010), in the format of a scoring rubric. The form includes

Table 4.4 Rubric for Assessing the Quality of Formative Assessments

Characteristic			
Role of Assessment	0 Summative	1 Guide Teacher	2 Guide Student
Goal of Assessment	0 Increase Basic Knowledge	1 Increase Understanding	2 Increase Understanding and Self-Assessment Skills
Focus of Assessment	0 Quantity of Work	1	2 Quality of Work
Specificity of Feedback	0 Not Specific to Task	1 Specific to Task	2 Specific to Sub-task
Interpretation of Performance	0 Norm-Referenced	1	2 Criterion-Referenced
Contribution to Grade	0 High	1 Low	2 None
Frequency	0 Low	1	2 High

those criteria that are the most concrete and directly observable. You can use this instrument to evaluate the validity of the formative assessments you design or use, and it also acts as a handy summary of the key components for quality formative assessment.

Ms. Lee Doesn't Like Surprises (Part II)

Ms. Lee went back to her classroom knowing that she needed to plan ways of using assessment to provide feedback to her and, perhaps more important, to her students while learning was still going on, not just after it was over and it was too late to do anything about it. Remembering some concepts from her college course on classroom assessment, she pulled out her old textbook and also Googled *formative assessment*. She quickly found some suggestions for formative assessment in her classroom. The ideas included spending 15 minutes per day guiding students through a self-directed process, a clicker unit so students can know where they stand, and a lab where the students can create the rubrics they will use to grade their labs. Deciding she would take a couple of days to spend a bit more time on the topic, Ms. Lee gathered all the information that afternoon and was ready for her experiment in formative assessment.

Ms. Lee began by reading aloud the questions on the *clicker unit*; then the students were given time to think about the answer and select from multiple-choice options. When everyone had answered, the "correct" answer was revealed. Depending on the number of students who missed the question, Ms. Lee had the students present arguments for both sides, paired students and asked them to discuss the concept further, or decided that she would reteach the concept, maybe using a different approach. One question fostered a particularly strong debate between students. When asked to identify a mixture between four choices, half the students selected sand in water while the other half selected sugar in water.

Escobar started the conversation by saying, "You cannot ever combine sand and water!"

"Well you can see the sugar at the bottom of the Kool-Aid because those don't mix either, so we are both right," rebutted Alyssa.

Ms. Lee asked, "What role does *dissolving* play in this argument?" Nobody raised their hand. Ms. Lee had discovered a vocabulary word, and a process, that was missing in their understanding of mixtures and solutions. She told the class that tomorrow's activity would help define and apply vocabulary words.

The following day, Ms. Lee passed out construction paper. She informed the students they would be making *Frayer Models* for the four most important words related to mixtures and solutions. Ms. Lee put two example models on the over-head and asked the students, "Which of these is better?" She followed with, "Why?" After allowing for some good wait time, Ms. Lee called on a few students to check for understanding. Explaining more about how to write a good Frayer Model, the students were broken into groups of four. While the students worked to determine which words they would use, Ms. Lee walked around clarifying vocabulary words.

Throughout the year, the 5th grade students worked in multiple labs, including one over mixtures and solutions. Ms. Lee wrote one assignment on the board: "Make a list of what makes a lab activity *good*." The students were instructed to take out any labs that they had completed from their science folders and skim through the directions, activities, and requirements for the written report at the end of the lab. A few minutes had gone by when Ms. Lee asked students to find a partner to create a new list of what makes a good lab. After 5 minutes, the students again were asked to find a different partner and do the same process. One day, students were asked to create a lab based on the previous two activities. Ms. Lee instructed, "Select one of the vocabulary words from the Frayer Models you created. Think of ways you could create a lab for other groups to complete that would give those other students a *concrete* understanding of that vocabulary word. Remember to agree on the points that make a good lab." As an example, Ms. Lee selected one vocabulary word, *dissolving*, and then walked through the process with the class to create a lab. Students selected materials, procedures, and what should be discussed in the report. During this process, Ms. Lee continued to question the students, eliciting discussion, discovering misconceptions, until the students created high quality first drafts of a lab plan.

Over the next couple of days, student groups developed and revised their lab plans. Students would use a 2 + 2 model, in the scoring rubrics they designed for labs, where they would evaluate another group's lab write-up and provide two strengths and two weaknesses. When students found it difficult to provide two of each, Ms. Lee would question every aspect of their rubric and the connection to the vocabulary word.

When the next unit test approached, students felt more confident going into the test compared with last time, because the activities helped them guide their learning. They already knew what they knew and did not yet know. Ms. Lee was even happier than her students because she knew that, while there would still be students struggling in some areas, she had a good idea about where their strengths and weaknesses would be. There would be fewer surprises this time, which was a good thing. Because Ms. Lee doesn't like surprises.

THINGS TO THINK ABOUT

1. How might you use formative assessment in your classroom?

2. Who do you think might be resistant to formative assessment? Teachers, administrators, parents, students? Why?

3. Are there circumstances in which feedback might hurt performance?

4. Do you remember a teacher who was especially good at providing students with helpful feedback that encouraged growth and learning? What sort of tactics did he or she use when providing feedback?

Looking Back in This Chapter

- Formative assessment provides meaningful feedback to students and teachers.
- Teachers use formative assessment to improve their teaching during instruction.
- Students use formative assessment to evaluate their own learning and adjust their understanding during instruction.
- Classrooms can be designed as formative assessment environments where students view feedback as useful information, not as an evaluation of their abilities or worth.
- Quality formative assessment is frequent, specific, and student-centered.

ON THE WEB

Techniques to check for understanding
http://daretodifferentiate.wikispaces.com/
file/view/03+-+Formative+Assessment+Stra
tegies.pdf

Key strategies for formative assessment
http://www.nctm.org/news/content.aspx?
id=11474

A flow chart of formative assessment
http://datause.cse.ucla.edu/fa_strats.php?
node=0

Self-directed learning
http://www.selfdirectedlearning.com/
teaching-self-directed-learning-tools.html

Providing feedback
http://evaluate.curtin.edu.au/local/docs/5
providing-feedback-for-student-learning.pdf

STUDENT STUDY SITE

Visit **www.sagepub.com/frey** to access additional study tools including eFlashcards, web quizzes, web resources, additional rubrics, and links to SAGE journal articles.

REFERENCES

Airasian, P. (2005). *Classroom assessment: Concepts and applications* (5th ed.). New York, NY: McGraw-Hill.

Airasian, P., & Russell, M. (2007). *Classroom assessment: Concepts and applications* (6th ed.). New York, NY: McGraw-Hill.

Bennett, R. E. (2011). Formative assessment: A critical review. *Assessment in Education: Principles, Policy, & Practice, 18*(1), 5–25.

Black, P. J., & Wiliam, D. (1998). Inside the black box: Raising standards through classroom assessment. *Phi Delta Kappan, 80*(2), 139–148.

Black, P., & Wiliam, D. (2003). 'In praise of educational research': Formative assessment. *British Educational Research Journal, 29*(5), 623–637.

Black, P., & Wiliam, D. (2009). Developing the theory of formative assessment. *Educational Assessment, Evaluation and Accountability, 21*(1), 5–31.

Caldwell, J. E. (2007). Clickers in the large classroom: Current research and best-practice tips. *CBE-Life Sciences Education, 6,* Spring, 9–20.

Cangelosi, J. S. (2000). *Assessment strategies for monitoring student learning.* New York, NY: Addison Wesley Longman.

Chase, C. I. (1999). *Classroom assessment for educators.* New York, NY: Addison-Wesley.

Cohen, J. (1969). *Statistical power analysis for the behavioral sciences.* San Diego, CA: Academic Press.

Connelly, M. (2008). *The Hardy Boys mysteries, 1927–1979: A cultural and literary history.* Jefferson, NC: McFarland & Company.

Costa, A. L., & Kallick, B. (2009). *Habits of mind across the curriculum: Practical and creative strategies for teachers.* Association for Supervision & Curriculum Development.

DeNisi, A. S., & Kluger, A. N. (2000). Feedback effectiveness: Can 360-degree appraisals be improved? *The Academy of Management Executive, 14*(1), 129–139.

Dunn, K. E., & Mulvenon, S. W. (2009). A critical review of research on formative assessment: The limited scientific evidence of the impact of formative assessment in education. *Practical Assessment, Research & Evaluation, 14*(7), 1–11.

Frey, B. B., & Schmitt, V. L. (2007). Coming to terms with classroom assessment. *Journal of Advanced Academics, 18*(3), 402–423.

Frey, B. B., & Schmitt, V. L. (2010). Teachers' classroom assessment practices. *Middle Grades Research Journal, 5*(3), 107–117.

Kenwright, K. (2009). Clickers in the classroom. *TechTrends, 53*(1), 74–77.

Kingston, N., & Nash, B. (2011, Winter). Formative assessment: A meta-analysis and a call for research. *Educational Measurement: Issues and Practice, 30*(4), 28–37.

McMillan, J. H. (2001). *Classroom assessment: Principles and practice for effective instruction* (2nd ed.). Needham Heights, MA: Allyn and Bacon.

National Council of Teachers of English. (2010). *Fostering high-quality formative assessment.* Urbana, IL: Author.

Nichols, P., Meyers, J., & Burling, K. (2009). A framework for evaluating and planning assessments intended to improve student achievement. *Educational Measurement: Issues and Practice, 28*(3), 14–23.

Nicol, D. J., & Macfarlane-Dick, D. (2007). Formative assessment and self-regulated learning: A model and seven principles of good feedback practice. *Studies in Higher Education, 31*(2), 199–218.

Puckett, M. B., & Black, J. K. (2008). *Meaningful assessments of the young child* (3rd ed.). Upper Saddle River, NJ: Pearson.

Shepard, L. A. (2000). *The role of classroom assessment in teaching and learning.* Los Angeles, CA: Center for the Study of Evaluation.

Shepard, L. A. (2005). Linking formative assessment to scaffolding. *Educational Leadership, 63*(3), 66–70.

Shepard, L. A. (2009). Commentary: Evaluating the validity of formative and interim assessment. *Educational Measurement: Issues and Practice, 28*(3), 32–37.

Shulman, L. S. (2005). *The signature pedagogies of the professions of law, medicine, engineering, and the clergy: Potential lessons for the education of teachers.* Paper presented at the National Science Foundation Mathematics and Science Partnerships Workshop, Irvine, CA.

Stiggins, R. (2010). Essential formative assessment competencies for teachers and school leaders. *Handbook of Formative Assessment,* 233–250.

Taylor, C. S., & Nolen, S. B. (2005). *Classroom assessment: Supporting teaching and learning in real classrooms.* Upper Saddle River, NJ: Pearson.

Thorndike, E. L. (1913). *Educational psychology: Vol. 1. The original nature of man.* New York, NY: Columbia University Teachers College.

Torrance, H., & Pryor, J. (2001). Developing formative assessment in the classroom: Using action research to explore and modify theory. *British Educational Research Journal, 27*(5), 615–631.

Ward, A. W., & Murray-Ward, M. (1999). *Assessment in the classroom.* London, England: Wadsworth.

CHAPTER 5

SUMMATIVE ASSESSMENT

Traditional Paper-and-Pencil Tests

Looking Ahead in This Chapter

Objectively scorable item formats designed to measure knowledge are still the most common approaches to assessment in today's classrooms. These formats include multiple-choice, matching, true-false, fill-in-the-blank, and short answer. Research suggests some good rules for writing traditional test questions, but most of our guidance comes from consulting experts. Many examples of real-world tests are provided and critiqued, and an assessment for assessing the quality of traditional tests is provided.

Objectives

After studying this chapter, you should be able to

- Identify the relative frequency with which teachers use the various approaches to classroom assessment
- Describe the various formats of paper-and-pencil assessment questions
- Apply recommended guidelines for composing traditional paper-and-pencil test items
- Analyze the quality of real-world paper-and-pencil assessments

Mr. Kilmer Is Troubled

Mr. Kilmer's last statement was cut short by the ring of the bell and the students shutting their books in unison. They were already headed out the door. After the students had left, Mr. Kilmer followed them out to monitor the hall. A 7th grade student approached Mr. Kilmer asking for help with his locker, which was the most common problem Mr. Kilmer faced in between periods. While he helped the student, he overheard a conversation taking place:

Austin laughed. "I got the same grade you did and didn't study at all. I guessed on almost all of the answers! Don't you feel dumb for spending time studying?"

"Well at least I know something about the Revolutionary War; you didn't even read the chapter. You won't be able to guess on everything. Besides, you just got lucky this time whereas I can do it every time," retorted Jamaya.

As Mr. Kilmer walked back to greet his next class, he reflected on the last test he gave and had spent so much time working on. He wanted to take a look at the grades to see if there actually was something to what the students were discussing in the hall. He noticed that test grades tended to be higher than normal for some of his otherwise lower-scoring students. Maybe they had studied extra hard (some of them), but maybe there were clues in the test itself, or some other hints that allowed students to guess the right answers. He weighted test scores the heaviest of all in his grading plan, so the thought that the test scores might not really reflect learning was troubling.

Ms. Rivera passed by and he asked her if she ever worried about such things. She told him that most of her test items were in the same format as those on the state tests, so she had no worries about that. Multiple-choice items, matching, true-false, and especially fill-in-the-blank questions are also so easy and quick to write. Did she ever wonder if people could get the right answer without actually knowing it? Sometimes, sure, but she didn't think it could happen that often.

Mr. Kilmer was even more troubled now. How could Ms. Rivera or he have any confidence about their test questions? They were in the traditional format, so surely they were, at least, "evidence-based." There must be some rules about what makes a good test question. There must be some guidelines for making sure that a good old-fashioned multiple-choice test measures what it is supposed to. He wondered . . .

(To Be Continued)

There is a long list of customs in classroom assessment, most of them having to do with questions being asked and answers being chosen and scored. This chapter presents these well-established question-and-answer formats. They are formats such as the multiple-choice question with which we are all familiar. Another custom, as well entrenched in the tradition of American education as structured questions and answers, is the assumption that assessment should be **summative**. That is, the purpose of testing is often assumed to come after instruction has ended with the purpose of measuring what has already been learned. Summative assessment is what most students and parents picture when they hear the word *test*. In Chapter 4, we compared summative assessment with **formative assessment** and we emphasized the power of assessment *while* instruction is going on and *while* learning is happening. As we'll see, using assessments as summative is still the most common purpose of teacher-made tests. Here are the defining characteristics of summative assessment:

- It assesses student learning at the end of a period of instruction.
- It is typically very formal with defined test-taking rules and scoring procedures.
- Points are awarded based on what students know, understand, or can do.
- It provides data primarily for the teacher's benefit.
- Its main purpose is to determine grades.

The traditional paper-and-pencil test approach is almost *always* used for summative purposes. Likewise, if a teacher plans to base a course or term grade on test results, it is likely that he or she is relying on traditional paper-and-pencil assessment. Performance-based assessment is used as well for assigning grades, but the most common grading plan, research suggests, is still built around the traditional approach. This chapter and Chapter 6 cover the traditional and common test item formats that are designed to measure student knowledge and understanding.

The term **traditional paper-and-pencil assessment** is the usual (if somewhat vague) label given to multiple-choice questions, matching items, true-false questions, fill-in-the-blank items, and short answer questions—any question format where there is one predetermined correct answer.

Traditional paper-and-pencil tests can be

- scored **objectively** or **subjectively**. With objectively scored items, there is one correct answer and no judgment is required when assigning scores.

With subjectively scored answers, there are different ways to produce a correct answer and teacher judgment affects the scores.

- selection items or supply items. With selection items, the answer is provided to students and they must simply select it or indicate it (like circling the answer on a multiple-choice test). With supply items, the answer is not on the test, and students must supply it (like with a short answer question or essay question).

Here is an example of a traditional selection test question:

1. With which art movement is the painter Goya associated?

   A Cubism
   B Baroque
   C Impressionism
   D Romanticism

The correct answer is D.

Here's a similar question in a supply format:

1. Goya is considered a leader of the art movement known as _____.

Objectively scored items are explored in this chapter regarding whether they use selection or supply formats. It's worthwhile to take a second to explain the organization of the next few chapters. The specific type of supply item where students are required to build a complex answer, *constructed-response items*, though, are covered in their own chapter, Chapter 6. Another type of assessment format, *performance-based* assessment, that, broadly speaking, is a supply item format, is presented in Chapter 7. Some performance-based formats rely on constructed responses, so there will be some overlap between the ideas and techniques discussed in Chapters 5 and 6. The primary distinction between performance-based assessment and other supply formats is that the intent of performance-based assessment is usually to measure *skill* or *ability*, not *knowledge* or *understanding*. Dividing traditional paper-and-pencil assessment, constructed response items, and performance-based assessment into three different chapters is a bit arbitrary. But this three-chapter sequence of *traditional paper-and-pencil approaches*, *constructed-response items*, and *performance-based assessment* is a useful way to organize the material and explore these approaches.

Good Question!

Categorizing Item Types

Q: You have a tendency to use qualifiers when classifying item types (e.g., short answer items are *usually* objectively scored, essay questions might be performance-based *or* traditional assessment). As an instructional strategy, such wishy-washiness leaves something to be desired. Can you clarify?

A: The correct label or category for an item or assessment approach partly depends on the intended *purpose* of the assessment and how it is scored. If a supply item (such as a short answer question) has only one correct answer (or a short list of correct answers), it is objectively scorable. If the teacher is waiting to see what answer a student gives and then evaluates it for correctness, then there is subjectivity there. To use your other example about essay questions, if the essay question is designed to assess *knowledge* (such as facts about the life of Abraham Lincoln), then, under our definitions, it is *traditional* assessment. If the essay question is designed to assess writing *ability* (such as a composition about how you spent your summer vacation), then it is *performance-based* assessment. The distinction is based on what the teacher wishes to assess—knowledge or ability.

It might seem odd that a book with *modern* in its title that promises up-to-date training on all the useful contemporary perspectives on classroom assessment would begin with traditional approaches that have changed little in 100 years. There are a couple of reasons why this makes sense, though. First, these traditional approaches, when done right, can produce scores with high degrees of validity and reliability. They are fairly easy to compose, they are efficient, and students and teachers are fairly comfortable with them. Second, it turns out that the modern classroom still tends to rely on these traditional methods.

CLASSROOM TEACHERS' USE OF TRADITIONAL PAPER-AND-PENCIL ASSESSMENT

Traditional classroom assessment, with its questions and one-and-only-one correct answers, has long been a common part of the student experience. Here's an example from Lewis Carroll's *Alice in Wonderland* book *Through the Looking Glass* (1871):

"Do you know Languages? What's the French for fiddle-de-dee?"

"Fiddle-de-dee's not English," Alice replied gravely.

"Who ever said it was?" said the Red Queen.

Alice thought she saw a way out of the difficulty this time. "If you'll tell me what language 'fiddle-de-dee' is, I'll tell you the French for it!" she exclaimed triumphantly.

But the Red Queen drew herself up rather stiffly, and said, "Queens never make bargains."

"I wish Queens never asked questions," Alice thought to herself.

"Don't let us quarrel," the White Queen said in an anxious tone. "What is the cause of lightning?"

"The cause of lightning," Alice said very decidedly, for she felt quite certain about this, "is the thunder—no, no!" she hastily corrected herself. "I meant the other way."

"It's too late to correct it," said the Red Queen; "when you've once said a thing, that fixes it, and you must take the consequences."

As Alice knows, asking questions and scoring responses based on an answer key that provides the only acceptable answers has been a popular educational assessment format for centuries. With educational researchers and teacher educators promoting modern approaches, such as performance-based assessment, formative assessment, and authentic assessment, though, one might think that the use of traditional paper-and-pencil tests today would be minimal, with an emphasis on the new ways. A survey of teachers in a midwestern state, designed to get an idea of what goes on in today's classrooms regarding the assessment choices teachers make, however, shows that the tried-and-true traditional approach is still the most common (Frey & Schmitt, 2010). The survey posed questions covering six characteristics of classroom testing asking teachers to estimate the "percentage of the time" they use various approaches to assessments. They were told to only think about their "own testing, not mandated standardized tests."

Teachers' responses are shown in Table 5.1. Traditional paper-and-pencil testing remains the most common classroom assessment experience. Notice, also, that summative assessment is much more common than formative. Relatively few tests do *not* affect student grades, and 75% of tests are given *after* instruction is completed, so there is little formative assessment going on. Teachers do frequently design their own classroom assessments to measure the effect of their own teaching, but they still rely on tests or items written by others, presumably from textbooks or commercially produced worksheets,

Table 5.1 Teachers' Classroom Assessment Practices

Question	Mean
About what percentage of the time do you use:	
traditional tests	60%
performance-based tests	28%
One assessment that combines both	12%
When you use traditional assessments, about what percentage of the time do you use:	
multiple-choice	24%
matching	14%
true-false	10%
short answer/fill-in-the-blank	27%
essay	15%
other formats	11%
Of all your assessments, what percentage are given:	
during instruction	25%
after instruction	75%
Of all your assessments, what percentage:	
do not affect students' grades	12%
affect students grades	88%
About what percentage of the time do you use:	
tests you made yourself	55%
tests made by others	35%
one assessment that combines both	9%

Source: Adapted from Frey and Schmitt (2010).

Note: N = 139.

much of the time. (Items that appear in test banks that accompany textbooks or prepackaged curricula are, often, notoriously poor.)

Little has changed since the 1980s in the classroom assessment environment, at least regarding relative emphasis on the various assessment approaches and the still common use of tests as mostly summative. A survey given more than 25 years ago found similar results (Gullickson, 1985). Then, teacher-made objectively scored traditional paper-and-pencil tests were the most common method used across all levels and subjects taught.

Using the numbers in Table 5.1, one can figure out the overall relative frequency of a variety of more specific assessment formats. Table 5.2 shows these estimates. Writing assignments are the most common type of classroom assessment

Table 5.2 Frequency of Classroom Assessment Formats

Assessment Format	Percentage of All Assessments
Essays or writing assignments	19
Short answer/fill-in-the-blank items	16
Multiple-choice items	14
Group projects	9
Matching items	9
Presentations (e.g., speeches, debates)	8
True-false items	6
Concept mapping	2
Other performance-based formats	7
Other traditional paper-and-pencil formats	6

Source: Adapted from Frey and Schmitt (2010).

Note: N = 139; total does not sum to 100% because of rounding.

reported, followed by short answer/fill-in-the-blank and multiple-choice items. If your childhood memories of classroom assessments are mostly recollections of essay assignments and lengthy multiple-choice tests, well, things are still pretty much like that. Indeed, it is possible that your college classes are that way, too.

Paper-and-Pencil Tests and Young Children

Good Question!

Q: How young can I go? Should I give something like a multiple-choice test to a preschooler or kindergartner?

A: The short answer is No. Young children must be assessed differently than older children (above, let's say, the age of 7). This is true for several reasons. First, the instructions for what a student is supposed to do on a paper-and-pencil test are pretty complex and sometimes abstract. Developmentally, preschool children and those in the early grades would likely struggle with complex directions. Second, young children learn differently, and how they can show their learning is different. They construct knowledge through hands-on experience and not through paper-and-pencil activities (Guddemi & Case, 2004). Using paper and pencil to demonstrate learning, then, is a mismatch with the nature of their learning. Third, administering traditional tests takes time. The attention span of young children is notoriously short. For these reasons, assessment of very young children is usually done informally, through direct observation, or with intrinsically "fun" performance-based strategies.

ITEM FORMATS

Most traditional objectively scorable, paper-and-pencil questions are classifiable under one (or a combination) of just a few formats. The formats are *multiple-choice*, *matching*, *true-false*, *fill-in-the-blank*, and *short answer*.

Multiple-Choice Items

Technically, matching items, true-false items, and a variety of other specific item types where correct answers are available and students select the correct answer are all multiple-choice questions. In this book, though, the term *multiple-choice item* will refer to those questions that are comprised of a *stem* followed by a small set of answer options associated with that stem. Students circle, mark, write in, or otherwise indicate their answer. That is typically the format that is thought of as a multiple-choice question. A multiple-choice question looks like this:

1. Which superhero was born on another planet?	*Stem*
A. Batman	*Distractor*
B. Spider-man	*Distractor*
C. Superman	*Correct Answer ("Keyed" Answer)*
D. Wonder Woman	*Distractor*

(By the way, as we compare the various formats for objectively scorable test questions, we will use the same content over and over [in this case, comic-book characters] to make the point that any given instructional objective can be assessed using many different item formats.) The stem is the part of the item that asks the question or directs the student to provide a correct answer. So stems can be questions like "Who wrote *Harry Potter and the Sorcerer's Stone?*" or instructions like "Circle the term that best describes the cause of evaporation." Stems can end in question marks or periods (or, I suppose for very exciting tests, exclamation points). Wrong answers are called *distractors*, not because they are meant to fool or trick students, but because they are plausible answers and a student must really have knowledge to pick the correct answer instead of it. The correct answer is called, sensibly, the *correct answer*, or sometimes the *keyed* answer because it is the answer that is on the answer key (the list of correct answers that makes scoring so simple).

Real-World Choices Teachers Make

A Beautiful Shape

It can be a daunting task for a teacher to start with a blank page and have to compose a multiple-choice test while trying to remember, juggle, and apply all the best practices /she has learned. One easy rule of thumb regarding at least the *look* of a multiple-choice item is that its basic shape should be based on a stem that is longer than any of the answer options. Indeed, some stems are half a page and provide material from which one or many questions will be derived (e.g., maps, charts, pictures, lengthy scenarios, geometric designs, passages of text). Following this guideline alone gets teachers well on the way to producing a solid test and results in a general look of quality, even from a distance. Aesthetically speaking, a good multiple-choice item should look like this:

1. _____
   _____
   _____

   A _____
   B _____
   C _____
   D _____

Or your left hand held out in front of you pointing to the right:

Matching Items

The matching items format is, essentially, a way of combining many potential multiple-choice items into one small, tidy space. The components of matching items are typically arranged into two columns. The first column usually contains a variety of numbered items, terms, descriptors, or phrases—these act as the stems for matching items, though they are usually brief and not complete sentences or questions. The second column has a variety of lettered answer options (also brief) that might match any of the stems in the first column. The correct match is indicated next to the question in the first column. For each stem on the left, students must scan all the possible answer options on the right. Because well-written matching items allow answer options to be used more than once or not at all, there are potentially many distractors for each question. The hardest part of writing matching items is to make all the possible answer options plausible distractors for each stem. It is difficult to have a large group of answer options that all match conceptually and grammatically. Another acceptable difference between multiple-choice questions and items using the matching format is the relative length of stems and answer options. Because matching items work together as a single, somewhat complex assessment activity, it is less important regarding efficiency that stems be longer than answer options. Matching items look something like this (see how five matching questions can fit in the space of about one multiple-choice item?):

1. _____ Batman	A. Royalty
2. _____ Spider-man	B. Born on another planet
3. _____ Superman	C. Believes criminals are a "cowardly lot"
4. _____ Wonder Woman	D. Feels guilt over death of his Uncle Ben
5. _____ Aquaman	E. Powers due to absorption of gamma-rays
	F. Transforms by speaking the word "Shazam!"

By the way, the correct answers are 1 = C, 2 = D, 3 = B, 4 = A, and 5 = A. Notice the same answer, A, is used more than once, and E and F are not used at all.

True-False Items

True-false questions, and other two-answer option formats, are popular because they are simple to compose and, theoretically, have a clearly correct answer. Teachers like these questions because they are a breeze to write. As we discuss later, though, they are difficult to write well. True-false items are statements that are objectively true or false, and students indicate which it is with a customary mark of *T* or *F*. Many of these items can be put in a fairly compact space, and students can answer them very quickly. True-false items look like this:

1. _____ Spider-man received his powers by absorbing gamma-rays.

2. _____ Billy Batson transforms into Captain Marvel by speaking the word "Shazam!"

3. _____ Batman believes criminals are a "cowardly lot."

4. _____ Wonder Woman is an Amazonian princess.

In case the characteristics of comic book superheroes are still not in your knowledge base, the answers are 1 = F, 2 = T, 3 = T, and 4 = T.

Fill-in-the-Blank and Short Answer Questions

Fill-in-the-blank or short answer questions can be objectively scored, but they still require that students supply the correct answer, as opposed to selecting it from a list of possibilities. Guessing blindly, then, is not really possible, and this format makes it easier to measure at a higher level of Bloom's Taxonomy (see Chapter 3 for a review of these levels of understanding). A fill-in-the-blank item has an incomplete sentence with one or more blanks that the student must "fill." (As the research reviewed later in this chapter advises, good fill-in-the-blank items have only one blank, at the end.) Short answer questions differ from fill-in-the-blank in that they are complete questions or sentences and students write in the correct answer to the question. As the term *short answer* suggests, these questions expect a brief response of only a word or two. Items with these formats look like this:

1. The Incredible Hulk received his powers by absorbing _____.

2. Billy Batson transforms into Captain Marvel by speaking the word _____.

3. Which superhero believes criminals are a "cowardly lot"?

4. Which superhero is an Amazonian princess?

The correct answers are 1 = gamma-rays, 2 = Shazam, 3 = Batman, and 4 = Wonder Woman.

Item Difficulty

To find the difficulty of a test question, calculate the percentage of students who got it right. The lower that percentage, the harder the question.

Individual questions from objectively scored classroom assessments can be analyzed statistically for a variety of characteristics. One way to find out if an item is "working" is to see how hard it is to answer correctly. Easy items are questions that most students answered correctly; difficult items are questions that most students missed. The **item difficulty index** shows the proportion of students who got an item right. It is easy to compute, and real-world teachers often use this information to make decisions on whether to use the same question again in the future or to change it in some way.

The item difficulty index is calculated by dividing the number of students who got an item correct by the total number of students who took the test:

$$\text{Item Difficulty} = \frac{\text{Number Who Got the Correct Answer}}{\text{Total Number of Students Taking the Test}}$$

As a proportion, the item difficulty index will always be between .00 and 1.00. The higher the value, the easier an item is. If an item is too hard, and you conclude that you must not have taught the item well enough, you can "remove" the item from the test. By not computing that item as part of the total score, some believe that the test becomes a fairer measure of student learning. (In practice, simply giving every student credit for a correct answer on the item is the simplest solution mathematically. This is almost, but *not quite*, the same thing.) If you do make some change in your assessment

(Continued)

(Continued)

and your scores in this way, consider sharing the decision with your students. Teachers of high school and college students sometimes share a complete item analysis of each test with their students. This works well as a way of identifying tough areas and areas that the class has mastered.

   Of course, another way, other than as an estimate of difficulty, to interpret the same number is that it shows how many students know something or have met a specific objective. Philosophically, teachers differ on whether they decide an item was too hard, students just haven't met an instructional objective, or the teacher did not do a good job teaching something. So when faced with a low difficulty index, some teachers change the item, and others change the way they teach. As a professional, you get to decide your own perspective on what this number means. You be the judge.

WHAT WE KNOW ABOUT TRADITIONAL ASSESSMENT

> *"It appears that assessment is an example of a subject where there are two camps; one full of well meaning, earnest teachers and researchers immersed in the language and culture of assessment practice (validity, generalizability, psychometrics are examples of the words they commonly use); the other full of well meaning, earnest teachers facing the day to day practical problems of running assessments in full awareness of what should be done, but only too aware of what can be achieved in their circumstances."*
>
> John Bligh, Editor, *Medical Education*, 2001

   Traditional classroom assessment centers on a simple theory: by asking people questions, we can find out what they know. That isn't a theory, really, under the strict scientific definition; it is a commonsense strategy for assessing something that cannot be seen directly, the invisible construct of interest, learning. There are theories from the broader world of measurement that can suggest smart ways of doing things in the classroom, but there often is found to be a gap between theory and practice, between the science and the art of classroom teaching. The world of educational research is missing a strong basic theory of its own underlying traditional, objectively scored classroom assessment, unless one counts the concepts of *validity* and *reliability* and their applications as theories (Brookhart, 2003; Moss, 2007; Moss, Girard, & Haniford, 2006).

There are some theoretical perspectives that inform multiple-choice testing and the like, however. For example, the classic, and a bit stodgy, *Bloom's Taxonomy* approach of categorizing levels of knowledge has recently been subjected to proposed revisions and expansions that alter the six levels of understanding somewhat and place them within a context of cognitive processes (*remember, understand, apply, analyze, evaluate, create*; see Chapter 3). Further, knowledge is distinguished in the proposed approach into four types—factual knowledge, conceptual knowledge, *procedural* knowledge, and *metacognitive* knowledge (knowing about one's knowledge and thinking). The suggestion is that assessment is useful when it is aligned together in the same "cell" with objectives and instruction (Airasian & Miranda, 2002; Amer, 2006). So a multiple-choice question could be valid for assessing the application of conceptual knowledge, for example, if the item, its related instructional objective, and the instructional strategy are all tied to conceptual knowledge at the application level. If an objectively scorable format does not work for a relevant type of knowledge, such as, say, procedural knowledge, then this theoretical perspective suggests it would not be a valid choice. Chapter 3 details the modern taxonomies for classifying items and levels of learning.

Quality traditional paper-and-pencil, objectively scored classroom assessments should be designed, one would reasonably assume, following best practice guidelines, or empirically validated item-writing rules. Unfortunately, for those who wish a research-based set of best practices, real-world studies establishing the "right" way to do things with traditional assessment are rare. Even when one conducts a true experimental study by manipulating some aspect of item design (e.g., three answer options or four for a multiple-choice item; should one include "All of the Above" as an answer option?) to see its effect on some outcome variable of interest, such as validity, reliability, or scores, the results are often inconclusive. Consequently, even among the most comprehensively well-trained teachers, "item-writing rules are based primarily on common sense and the conventional wisdom of test experts" (Millman & Greene, 1993, p. 353), and "item writing is still largely a creative act" (Haladyna, Downing, & Rodriguez, 2002, p. 329).

To get some wise guidance, then, on the "rules" to follow when writing multiple-choice items, matching items, and the other traditional formats, the best we can do is identify the guidelines that are most recommended by experts, those educational researchers who do a lot of thinking and writing about classroom assessments. Haladyna, Downing, and Rodriguez (2002; Downing & Haladyna, 2006; Haladyna & Downing, 1989a, 1989b; Rodriguez, 2005), for example, have cataloged guidelines for traditional item formats by examining what the authors of textbooks offer as advice, as well as pulling

Table 5.3 Top 40 Item-Writing Rules

1.	"All of the Above" should not be an answer option.
2.	"None of the Above" should not be an answer option.
3.	All answer options should be plausible.
4.	Order of answer options should either be logical (e.g., shortest to longest) or random.
5.	Items should cover important concepts and objectives.
6.	Negative wording should not be used.
7.	Answer options should include only one correct answer.
8.	Answer options should all be grammatically consistent with stem.
9.	Specific determiners (e.g., *always*, *never*) should not be used.
10.	Answer options should be homogeneous.
11.	Stems must be unambiguous and clearly state the problem.
12.	Correct answer options should not be the longest answer option.
13.	Answer options should not be longer than the stem.
14.	Items should use appropriate vocabulary.
15.	In fill-in-the-blank items, a single blank should be used, at the end.
16.	Items should be independent of each other.
17.	In matching, there should be more answer options than stems.
18.	All parts of an item or exercise should appear on the same page.
19.	True-false items should have simple structure.
20.	True-false items should be entirely true or entirely false.
21.	There should be three to five answer options.
22.	Answer options should not have repetitive wording.
23.	Point value of items should be presented.
24.	Stems and examples should not be directly from textbook.
25.	Matching item directions should include basis for match.
26.	Answer options should be logically independent of one another.
27.	Directions should be included.
28.	Questions using the same format should be together.
29.	Vague frequency terms (e.g., *often*, *usually*) should not be used.
30.	Multiple-choice stems should be complete sentences.
31.	There should be an equal number of true and false statements.
32.	True-false statements should be of equal length.
33.	Individual items should be short.
34.	In matching, answer options should be available more than once.
35.	For matching tests, the number of answer options should be less than 7 for elementary students.
36.	For matching tests, the number of answer options should be less than17 for secondary students.
37.	Complex item formats ("a and b, but not c") should not be used.
38.	All items should be numbered.
39.	Test copies should be clear, readable, and not handwritten.
40.	Stems should be on the left, and answer options on the right.

Source: Adapted from Frey et al. (2005).

Note: A few textbooks supported the use of "None of the Above" as a way of increasing difficulty.

from the few experimental studies that exist. A review of 20 classroom assessment textbooks developed a list of item-writing guidelines that were supported by multiple experts (Frey, Petersen, Edwards, Pedrotti, & Peyton, 2005). The top 40 most frequently supported item-writing "rules" that were found in the review are presented in Table 5.3. They are shown in order of support. For example, the most common advice was to avoid the use of *All* (or *None*) *of the Above* as an answer option, so that's first on the list, followed by using plausible distractors, avoiding predictable answer option order (e.g., so that *C* is not always the right answer), and so on.

A Closer Look

Best Practice and the Real World

We have mentioned before that there is often a disconnect between educational research, theory, best practice, and the way real-life teachers behave. A good example is with our scholarly-based, expert developed, item-writing guidelines. Real-world teachers violate many of these guidelines all the time.

The teacher-made tests collected as part of the survey of teachers' assessment practices summarized earlier in this chapter were analyzed as to whether their tests followed those *Top 40* rules. They did not. Out of about 1,500 different questions used by the sample of real-world teachers on real-world assessments, more than 90% of them were in "violation" of at least one guideline. For example, 34% of tests had items with incomplete stems (e.g., *The 16th U.S. President was:*), 21% of tests included items (such as matching items) where not all the answer options were grammatically consistent with the stem (e.g., gender, plurals, a/an), and 24% of all tests used fill-in-the-blank items with more than one blank or a blank that was not at the end. Seventeen percent of all tests had misspellings, grammatical errors, or typos.

From the perspective of classroom assessment researchers and instructors, the results may appear bleak, but considering the lack of empirical support for many rules, it might be more reasonable to identify most *rules* as *guidelines* or, even less prescriptive, *suggestions*. It also is reasonable to not treat the potential harm to validity as uniform across all rule violations. Consider a test that does not number all items or indicate point values (which was the case with 70% of the tests) when students assume correctly that all items are worth one point, but is otherwise of high quality. Compare that test with one that does number items and indicates point values, but provides all manner of unintentional clues, such as distractors that do not match the stem grammatically or are implausible. One might feel fairly secure in trusting the validity of scores from the first test, but not the second. Aggregated summaries across items indicating total numbers of rule violations or tests with errors are less informative than guideline-specific data.

(Continued)

(Continued)

It is possible that teachers are aware of these item-writing guidelines but choose not to apply them. Some rules require a substantial amount of extra work and time (e.g., producing enough plausible distractors, avoiding the use of negatively worded stems), and teachers might see the extra effort as producing little benefit. It is certainly likely, though, that one reason teachers do not apply most item rules is because they have not been taught them.

TABLES OF SPECIFICATIONS

For most of the approaches to modern classroom assessment, the key aspect of validity that concerns teachers most is *content validity*. That is certainly the case with traditional assessment. Content validity is the characteristic of a test that covers what it is supposed to; the items on the test are a fair representation of all the items that could or should be on the test.

A common method of ensuring valid representation across the many questions on a teacher-made test is to use a **table of specifications**. A table of specifications is often literally a table (a matrix with columns and rows), or it can be an organized list, outline, or "blueprint" of the items that will be on the test. Tables of specifications are designed by teachers to set out in black-and-white what content (e.g., domains, categories, topics, concepts, skills) will be covered on an assessment and the relative weight for each component regarding the proportion of questions and their point values on an assessment. Simple tables cover those bare basics, but more complex tables can indicate the level of the question (in terms of some framework like Bloom's Taxonomy), the format of the item (multiple-choice, short answer, etc.), the matching instructional objective, and any other characteristics that are important to the teacher as he builds the assessment.

A simple table might look like Table 5.4.

Table 5.4 Simple Table of Specifications

Quiz 2: The Great Gatsby

	Facts About the Book (e.g., Author, Influence)	Characters and Events	Thematic Elements
Number of Questions	2	5	3

A more detailed table might look like Table 5.5.

Table 5.5 Complex Table of Specifications

Unit 1 Exam: *The Great Gatsby*

Bloom's Taxonomy Cognitive Level	Knowledge	Application	Analysis	Total
Plot	3			3 (12%)
Theme	5	6		11 (44%)
Character Motivation	4	2	5	11 (44%)
Total	12 (48%)	8 (32%)	5 (20%)	25 (100%)

The purpose of a table of specifications is to identify the achievement domains being measured and to ensure that a fair and representative sample of questions appears on the test. Teachers cannot measure every topic or objective and cannot ask every question they might wish to ask. A table of specifications allows the teacher to construct a test that focuses on the key areas and weights those different areas based on their importance.

Tables of specification typically are designed based on the list of course objectives, the topics covered in class, the amount of time spent on those topics, textbook chapter topics, and the emphasis and space provided in the text. In some cases, a great weight will be assigned to a concept that is extremely important, even if relatively little class time was spent on the topic. Three steps are involved in creating a table of specifications: (1) choosing the measurement goals and domain to be covered; (2) breaking the domain into key or fairly independent parts—concepts, terms, procedures, applications; and (3) constructing the table. Teachers have already made decisions (or the district has decided for them) about the broad areas that should be taught. So the choice of what broad domains a test should cover has usually already been made. A bit trickier is to outline the subject matter into smaller components, but most teachers have already had to design teaching plans, strategies, and schedules based on an outline of content. Lists of classroom objectives, district curriculum guidelines, and textbook sections and keywords are other commonly used sources for identifying categories for tables of specification. When actually constructing the table, teachers may want only a simple structure, as with the first example above, or they may be interested in greater detail about the types of items, the cognitive levels for items, the best mix of objectively scored items, open-ended and constructed-response items, and so on, with even more guidance than is provided in the second example.

A table of specifications benefits students in two ways. First, it improves the validity of teacher-made tests. Second, it can improve student learning, as well. A table of specifications helps to ensure that there is a match between what is taught and what is tested. Classroom assessment should be driven by classroom teaching, which itself is driven by course goals and objectives. In this logical chain, tables of specifications provide the link between teaching and testing.

$$\text{Objectives} \rightarrow \text{Teaching} \rightarrow \text{Testing}$$

Tables of specifications can help students at all ability levels learn better. By providing the table to students *during* instruction, students can recognize the main ideas, key skills, and relationships among concepts more easily. The table of specifications can act in the same way as a *concept map* to analyze content areas. Teachers can even collaborate with students on the construction of the table of specifications—what are the main ideas and topics, what emphasis should be placed on each topic, and what should be on the test? Open discussion and negotiation of these issues can encourage higher levels of understanding, while also modeling good learning and study skills.

THE "RULES"

The item-writing suggestions shown in Table 5.3 are a good start to ensure the aspect of validity known as *construct validity*. By reviewing the 40 guidelines, you might notice that almost all reflect the overriding concern for the validity of the item responses. Indeed, perhaps the most basic obligation for classroom assessment is that one should assess the key instructional objectives, and that is covered in "Rule" 5. *Items should cover important concepts and objectives.* Recalling the types of validity (Chapter 2), this clearly is a content validity issue and is supported by a good table of specifications. The reasoning behind other guidelines as a group can be summarized as construct validity concerns because they guard against situations where students can get a question correct without having the requisite knowledge or miss a question when they do have the knowledge.

Potentially Confusing Wording or Ambiguous Requirements

If some respondents understand a question or a set of instructions, and others do not, their responses may vary as a result of that difference, not as a result of different underlying levels of knowledge or skill. Some of the rules that make sure that items are not measuring the ability to figure out the instructions or clarity in what is being asked are the following: *1. "All of the Above" should not be an answer option; 2. "None of the Above" should not be an answer option; 6. Negative wording should not be used; 7. Answer options should include only one correct answer; 11. Stems must be unambiguous and clearly state the problem; 14. Items should use appropriate vocabulary; 15. In fill-in-the-blank items, a single blank should be used, at the end; 19. True-false items should have simple structure; 20. True-false items should be entirely true or entirely false; 25. Matching item directions should include basis for match; 27. Directions should be included; 29. Vague frequency terms (e.g., often, usually) should not be used; 30. Multiple-choice stems should be complete sentences;* and *37. Complex item formats ("a and b, but not c") should not be used.*

Guessing

If respondents choose a correct answer by chance, instead of knowing the correct answer, there is no information in that response (and reliability, of course, will decrease). Consequently, some guidelines are designed to decrease the chance of guessing correctly by encouraging as many plausible answer options as is reasonable. These include the following: *3. All answer options should be plausible; 17. In matching, there should be more answer options than stems; 21. There should be three to five answer options; 34. In matching, answer options should be available more than once; 35. For matching tests, the number of answer options should be less than 7 for elementary age tests;* and *36. For matching tests, the number of answer options should be less than 17 for secondary age tests (in matching).*

Rules Addressing Test-Taking Efficiency

A large set of item-writing rules are designed to make the test-taking process as focused and free from distraction as possible. These rules all deal with formatting options: *13. Answer options should not be longer than the stem; 18. All parts of an item or exercise should appear on the same page; 22. Answer options should not have repetitive wording; 23. Point value of items should be presented; 28. Questions using the same format should be together; 33. Individual items should be short; 38. All items should be numbered; 39. Test copies should be clear, readable, and not handwritten;* and *40. Stems should be on the left, and answer options on the right.*

Rules Designed to Control for Testwiseness

In a somewhat interesting "post-modern" way, many of these item-writing guidelines exist as ways of counteracting testwise respondents. Some students (maybe you used some of these tricks back in the day) have mastered the ability to recognize patterns in answer options, identify unintentional clues, or use other skills unrelated to the level of knowledge or ability that is the intended target of a test. Being "good at taking tests" is a useful school skill, but it is a validity concern for classroom teachers because it is rare that "being good at taking tests" is the construct of interest. Rules designed to prevent "testwiseness" from affecting scores include these: *4. Order of answer options should be logical or vary*; *8. Answer options should all be grammatically consistent with stem*; *9. Specific determiners (e.g., always, never) should not be used*; *10. Answer options should be homogeneous*; *12. Correct answer options should not be the longest answer option*; *16. Items should be independent of each other*; *24. Stems and examples should not be directly from textbook*; *26. Answer options should be logically independent of one another*; *31. There should be an equal number of true and false statements*; and *32. True-false statements should be of equal length*.

Rules, Guidelines, Best Practices, and Suggestions

Good Question!

Q: When you talk about the Top 40 "rules" for item writing, you insist on putting quotation marks around the word *rules*. Seems like these rules should either be presented as best practice or just what some people think, but not somewhere in between. Which is it?

A: Most of the guidelines suggested here are not backed up by real-world research. It's not that there have been studies and the results oppose these guidelines; it's that there are not studies at all for the most part. So most of these guidelines are provided because they are supported by people who give these things a lot of thought. Most of them make sense on their face. As professionals, teachers need to be aware of the "rule" (there go those quotes again), understand the reason for it, and then decide whether to apply it. The professional part comes not in the accepting or rejecting of the suggestion but in being aware of its existence and the thinking behind it, and then deciding to accept or reject it.

Technology

Item Analysis Online

There are several useful websites and software packages that provide free and (somewhat) simple tools for analyzing test items regarding validity and other characteristics:

- http://www.hr-software.net/cgi/ItemAnalysis.cgi
  - This analysis site is maintained by a human resources software company. One can enter test data and get reliability estimates and difficulty and discrimination indices (using correlations). A nice feature of the reports generated is that they include the actual formulas that were used. It is a bit complicated to enter data, but use the samples provided to get the hang of the format they prefer.
- http://deltasigmasoft.com/
  - This software company, Delta Sigma Soft, provides a free copy of their analytical software that works with small-scale data sets. It works for tests of 25 items or less, but if you have a longer assessment, you could create two files and still get some useful information.
- http://www.itemanalysis.com/index.php
  - J. Patrick Meyer, a professor at the University of Virginia, created this free software. Provided is a downloadable program for classical item analysis and the more complex "item response theory" procedures, which not only provides the basic indices and reliability information, but also uses an approach called *differential item functioning* to suggest items that may be biased or invalid for subgroups or populations.

RELIABILITY OF TRADITIONAL ASSESSMENT

One relative strength of traditional objectively scored assessments compared with other approaches (such as performance-based assessment) is that reliability of these assessments tends to be great. Inter-rater reliability, for example, should be high because the scoring is objective and there should be very little randomness or judgment in the scoring. So that source of poor reliability shouldn't be a problem. Internal reliability is fairly simple to ensure, as well, because lengthy tests that have many items designed to measure knowledge of a single topic or domain, or a small number of related topics, tend to have high internal reliability. (The randomness associated with responses to any single item is likely to "cancel" itself out across many observations or questions.)

The main reason for low reliability of traditional paper-and-pencil tests is that students will guess at answers they don't know for sure. So-called *educated* guessing, where students have some idea or have narrowed down the answer options to just a couple of possibilities, is less of a worry because there is less randomness there, but pure guessing adds an element of luck to a student's performance on any single occasion that can't help but lower reliability. Recall that many of the item-writing rules suggested in this chapter are designed to limit guessing, so that is a good place to start when designing traditional assessments with high reliability. Increasing the number of answer options should help, as well, though there is a limit to how many answer options one can have before many of them stop operating as plausible distractors.

There's a Stat for That!

Guessing

The fewer answer options there are, the easier it is to get a question right just by chance.

Chance alone would give anyone a 25% chance of getting a four-answer option multiple-choice item correct. Right? One out of 4 answer options are correct, so you can guess the right answer to that question 1 out of 4 times. A 100-question multiple-choice test shouldn't produce a score less than 25% correct. Similarly, I wouldn't expect an item difficulty index (see the *There's a Stat for That* earlier in this chapter) below .25. Consequently, one can assume that some of the points any student gets on an objectively scored traditional assessment are due to chance, just lucky guessing. A **corrected score** that has been adjusted for guessing can be computed, which gives a purer indication of student knowledge. The equation is

$$\text{Corrected Score} = \text{Number of Items Right} - \frac{\text{Number of Items Wrong}}{\text{Average Number of Answer Options} - 1}$$

The corrected score makes it easier to appreciate really high levels of performance that are far removed from chance and to identify students who did not perform better or much better than chance.

WHAT TRADITIONAL ASSESSMENT LOOKS LIKE IN THE CLASSROOM

"In theory, there is no difference between theory and practice. But, in practice, there is."

Yogi Berra (NY Yankees baseball manager)

It is one thing to know what is labeled best practice and quite another to apply those practices when teaching. Earlier, we considered that most classroom assessments gathered from actual teachers violate all sorts of guidelines about how things *ought* to be. Practicing teachers, especially those who are well trained, simply do the best they can to translate the rules of good practice into the classroom assessments they design and rely on. They keep validity and reliability in mind but must mold those expectations into the time and logistics of their instructional days.

What follows are real-world examples of the various types of traditional paper-and-pencil items and assessments. As we define this type of assessment in this chapter, their purpose is to measure knowledge using objectively scored items such as multiple-choice, matching, true-false, and short answer or fill-in-the-blank. The real classroom assessments presented in this chapter are not chosen because they are perfect or even that they follow all the sage advice in these pages, but instead because they are pretty good and are used by real teachers. Many violate some of the "rules" presented here, and we have pointed that out in some cases. Rest assured, though, that all the examples are classroom assessments that likely produce valid and reliable data. Readers can use their own wisdom, the material in this book, or the "meta-assessment" at the end of this chapter to make judgments as to the ultimate quality of these examples. We have provided our own evaluation of these assessments, as well.

By the way, these examples are based on real tests donated for research studies on teachers' assessment practices. We have changed them a bit so that we are not using another's work without giving them credit, but because they were contributed anonymously, we cannot even thank them by name.

You also may notice that the real-life use of the basic formats often combines them together into hybrid formats (e.g., asking students to mark true or false next to each possible answer option in a multiple-choice question) or use formats that look different, but still fit into the four broad types (e.g., asking students to list steps in order, which functions as a collection of short-answer items; providing a word bank from which to choose fill-in-the-blank items, which turns the questions into a bunch of matching items).

Figure 5.4

Phoenix Rising

Answer each question by selecting the one correct answer. Circle the letter that best answers the question.

1. Where did the nuclear power plant accident happen?
   a. Cookshire
   b. North Haversham
   c. Manchester
   d. Boston

2. What name does Ezra give the puppy?
   a. Spot
   b. Shep
   c. Tyrus
   d. Caleb

3. Who is the antagonist in the novel?
   a. Nyle
   b. Ezra
   c. Muncie
   d. Ripley

4. Who is the protagonist in the novel?
   a. Nyle
   b. Ezra
   c. Muncie
   d. Ripley

5. What illness does Ezra have at the end of the novel?
   a. Leukemia
   b. Sickle Cell Anemia
   c. Parkinson's Disease
   d. Carbon Dioxide Poisoning

Multiple-Choice Tests

Figure 5.4 is from an 8th grade literature test.

Most of the *Top 40* item-writing rules are followed here. It is a good strategy to use the same key set of answer options on multiple-choice items (e.g., 3 and 4); this prevents the unintentional giving of clues as to the right answer. Though it is not listed in our Top 40, it is also a good idea to use uppercase letters (A, B, C, D) instead of lowercase (a, b, c, d) to label answer options (as this test does). Students with visual or perceptual difficulties can more easily see differences among capital letters.

Matching

1. The example in Figure 5.5, from the 3rd grade, is labeled as "Fill in the blank" but actually uses a *word bank*, which is a common matching format.

There are a few "rule" violations in this fill-in-the-blank quiz. Fill-in-the-blank items should have a single blank, and it should be at the end. Also, there are some grammatical clues in several items. For item 4, for example, the answer must be a plural word, and there is only one plural word in the word bank.

Figure 5.5

Fill in the blank. Use a word from the following list.

transparent	matter	colored	bubbly
opaque	viscous	solid	gas
liquid	water	mixture	screen
layers	flexible	rigid	separate

1. Most of the matter on our planet is a _____, _____, or _____.

2. Two properties of soda are _____ and _____.

3. _____ is a transparent liquid.

4. _____ are formed when water and oil are mixed.

2. Figure 5.6 shows an example from a high school cooking class.

Figure 5.6

Matching

Match each ingredient with its function when baking bread. (7 points)

1. _____ Eggs   A. Color, flavor, and nutrients
2. _____ Fat   B. Flavor, texture, and browning
3. _____ Flour   C. Moistens the protein and starch
4. _____ Leavening agent   D. Regulates the yeast
5. _____ Liquid   E. Produces gas so the bread will rise
6. _____ Salt   F. Provides structure
7. _____ Sugar   G. Makes the bread soft

The stems are on the left and the answer options are on the right, which is consistent with the guidelines for item writing. Also, the number of points possible is provided. What is missing here are directions indicating that some answer options may not be used and some may be used more than once. Additionally, matching items should have *more* answer options than stems or questions.

True-False

1. The example in Figure 5.7 is from a middle school classroom language arts test.

Notice how the multiple-choice format becomes essentially a *true-false* (two answer options) format because there may be more than one correct answer to each question. It might help students to know about the scoring rules. For instance, is everything worth 1 point (i.e., are there eight questions here or two)? The structure of items follows good true-false guidelines, however. All statements are roughly equal length, and only one thought or statement is expressed in each.

2. An elementary classroom assessment about drugs used by the D.A.R.E.: *Drug Abuse Resistance Education* program (D.A.R.E. elementary curriculum pretest, n.d.).

Figure 5.7

Answer each question.

Because there may be more than one right answer, mark a *Yes* or *No* for each answer!

Which of the following is characteristic of nonfiction?

1. It is all about real events and real people.	Yes	No
2. It tells stories that are made up.	Yes	No
3. Events happen in chronological order.	Yes	No
4. It tells about things that never happened.	Yes	No

Which of these are the author's purposes when writing nonfiction?

5. Inform	Yes	No
6. Express	Yes	No
7. Persuade	Yes	No
8. Entertain	Yes	No

D.A.R.E. ELEMENTARY CURRICULUM
PRETEST

TRUE OR FALSE: Read each statement below. Decide whether it is true or false. Place an X on the answer sheet for the response that best answers the question.

True or False:

1. Marijuana is not harmful.

2. Marijuana is safer than tobacco.

3. Tobacco smoking only affects your lungs.

4. There are safe and responsible ways to get out of risky situations.

5. Peer pressure only comes from people who are your friends.

6. Most teens drink alcohol.

7. Inhalants are a serious risk to young people.

8. Television and magazine ads try to get people to smoke and drink alcohol.

9. There are healthy and responsible ways to refuse an offer of illegal drugs.

10. Sometimes, alcohol can help the brain work better.

This quiz is used as a "pretest" to reflect student knowledge and attitudes before presentations. Though these items may function well to assess student attitudes about drug use, they do not work well as objectively true or false statements. Words such as *safe*, *safer*, *responsible*, *serious*, and others don't work well as part of true-false statements because there is subjective meaning to these terms. Also, there are negatively worded statements (e.g., Item 1, which is a violation of one of the guidelines on our Top 40 list).

Fill-in-the-Blank

Figure 5.8 shows an example taken from a high school chemistry test.

The fill-in-the-blank format allows for efficient assessment of knowledge basic facts. In this example, all the items have only one blank, which is a good

Figure 5.8

Fill in the Blank

1. A substance that is made up of one or more elements that have been chemically combined is a/an _____.

2. Two atoms of hydrogen and one atom of oxygen when chemically combined form the compound called _____.

3. A chlorine atom, which has 17 electrons, has _____ valence electrons.

4. The only element that does not follow the "Rule of 8" is _____.

5. In the molecule H_6C_2O, there are _____ atoms.

rule to follow. Strictly speaking, Items 3 and 5 do not place the blank at the end, which violates one of our guidelines, but the structure of the sentences is such that the few words after the blank probably do not create confusion as to the intended answer.

Short Answer

Here's a quiz on *The Adventures of Huckleberry Finn*:

1. What astronomical event happened the same year the author was born and the year he died?

2. What is Mark Twain's real name?

3. Where did Tom and Huck get the $6,000?

4. Who had made the mark in the snow?

5. Why does Huck go live with his father again?

Short answer items work best when the correct response is one word or just a few words that can be objectively scored as the right answer. Most of the items in this example have an expected very short answer that can be clearly wrong or right. Item 5, though, allows for a variety of correct answers (because "why" is open to so many interpretations) and would likely need to be treated as a *constructed response* item and scored with a rubric. Chapter 6 explores the constructed response format.

ASSESSING THE ASSESSMENT

This chapter presents some best practice suggestions for construction of quality traditional paper-and-pencil test items. Teachers can use this set of guidelines to judge the quality of their own classroom assessments. The extent to which items on a test violate the "rules" presented here speaks to the validity of the assessment to some degree. There are other aspects of validity, of course, that cannot be evaluated just by looking at the questions and tasks on a teacher-made test, but these criteria provide good basic standards against which to compare. A Top 40 set of rules was offered based on the collective wisdom of classroom assessment experts, but many of them are not directly observable by

Table 5.6 Form to Evaluate the Technical Validity of a Traditional Paper-and-Pencil Assessment

Number of Objectively Scored Items:	Number of Items With Errors:	Number of Rules Violated:	
Rule		**Specific Items With This Error**	**Number of Items With This Error**
General Rules			
1. Test copies should be clear, readable, and not handwritten.			
2. All items should be numbered.			
3. Directions should be included.			
4. Point values of items should be presented.			
5. Questions using the same format should be together.			
6. All parts of an item or exercise should appear on the same page.			
Multiple-Choice and Matching			
7. Options grammatically consistent with stem (gender, plural, vowel).			
Multiple-Choice and True-False			
8. Vague frequency terms (e.g., *often*, *usually*) should not be used.			
9. Specific determiners (e.g., *always*, *never*) should not be used.			
Multiple-Choice			
10. Answer options should be homogeneous.			
11. All answer options should be plausible.			
12. Answer options should not have repetitive wording.			
13. Multiple-choice stems should be complete sentences.			
14. Complex item formats ("a and b, but not c") should not be used.			
15. There should be three to five answer options.			
16. "All of the Above" should not be an answer option.			
17. "None of the Above" should not be an answer option.			
18. Order of answer options should be logical (e.g., quantity, length).			
19. Negative wording should not be used.			
20. Stems must be unambiguous and clearly state the problem.			

Number of Objectively Scored Items:	Number of Items With Errors:	Number of Rules Violated:	
Rule		**Specific Items With This Error**	**Number of Items With This Error**
21. Items should be independent of each other.			
22. Answer options should not be longer than the stem.			
Matching			
23. In matching, there should be more answer options than stems.			
24. Matching item directions should include basis for match.			
25. In matching, answer options should be available more than once.			
26. Number of answer options should be less than 7 for elementary age.			
27. Number of answer options should be less than 17 for secondary age.			
28. Matching stems should be left, answer options right.			
Fill-in-the-Blank			
29. In fill-in-the-blank items, one blank should be used, at the end.			
True-False			
30. True-false items should have simple structure.			
31. Any misspellings, typos, or grammatical errors? (Copyright Bruce Frey, 2011)			

examining the physical test form itself. Thirty of them, though, are fairly concrete and could be used as a somewhat scholarly set of guidelines through which to evaluate traditional paper-and-pencil objectively scored classroom assessments. Table 5.6 presents the scoring form that was used for the study on the quality of teacher-made tests described in this book. It lays out the 30 item-writing guidelines that are observable through examination of a classroom assessment and allows for data collection that speaks to its technical quality. The number of items that violate rules, the rules that are violated, and the percentage of the overall group of items that violate one guideline or another can be calculated.

Mr. Kilmer Is Troubled (Part II)

The next chapter in Mr. Kilmer's class was over the Federalist Era. Mr. Kilmer had the assessment he had made last year, but he realized now that he had not followed the guidelines he had learned back in college.

He first wanted to ensure that the questions being asked on the test matched what was being taught during the lesson. On a separate sheet of paper, Mr. Kilmer wrote down his instructional objectives for the lesson (these were based on the state objectives and were in his district pacing guide) and verified that those topics were represented on the test. Next, he flipped through the chapter, writing down additional topics that seemed important. When this was completed, he compared his rough table to the lesson plans for the next couple of weeks.

Mr. Kilmer was pleased that almost everything aligned from the lesson plans to the state objectives and began examining the questions on the test. Having read a bit about how to write quality paper-and-pencil tests, he came across a passage about how guessing lowers reliability, and he knew his tests hadn't been designed to limit guessing. Although the true-false section was simple to create and easy to score, Mr. Kilmer knew he needed to rely on other formats to decrease the guessing element.

Looking back at the rough table he created, he began writing questions about each topic in a different format. Mr. Kilmer started by writing the multiple-choice questions. The stems were not that hard to write, but coming up with distractors was a bit trickier. He needed to make sure all the distractors were plausible to limit a student's ability to eliminate and guess the right answer. Finding one distractor was simple, but the second and mainly the third were a bit more complicated for some of the questions. Next, he added a section of matching questions based on the important historical figures highlighted in the chapter. He listed brief descriptions of the individuals on one side and then all the names on the other. The true-false section was next, and he made a few changes, including increasing the number of questions so that guessing would be less of a factor. The statements were short and clearly true or false. Finally, Mr. Kilmer wanted to add short answer questions to finish the test. He was able to look back over the test and find a couple of topics not yet covered and wrote questions that required a brief answer that could be objectively scored right or wrong. He wrote a quick scoring guide for the section that listed the few acceptable answers.

Pretty proud of his new test, Mr. Kilmer turned to his classroom assessment textbook to where he remembered the "40 Rules" were located. The first five rules seemed just fine, but there were a few problems with Rules 6, 17, 22, 25, 27, and 34. Writing the directions to each part was corrected first. Then Mr. Kilmer went back to the matching section and added more answer options than stems with the possibility of using each answer option more than once.

When he thought it was finally finished, he printed a copy of the test and reviewed it against his objectives. Although every objective was covered, he thought that some objectives should be covered more because they were more important. He added a few more items for those objectives.

Now he was finally done. It was a lot of work this first time, but he knew he could keep track of student performance and fiddle with his questions each time to fine-tune things. The test was two weeks away, and Mr. Kilmer was actually excited about giving it. Jamaya, the student who had studied for the last test, would do just fine. In fact, this next test might even be fairer for him because it was so closely based on what was taught. Austin, though, wouldn't be able to guess his way to success this time. Mr. Kilmer was concerned as he thought about this, because he did care about Austin. But it wouldn't be exactly accurate to say that he found the thought *troubling*.

THINGS TO THINK ABOUT

1. Many states do not require training in classroom assessment as part of teacher education requirements. Why do you think that is?

2. In your experience, which of the Top 40 "Rules" are most commonly ignored? Why?

3. What test-taking strategies have you used as a student?

4. What are the weaknesses of multiple-choice tests?

Looking Back in This Chapter

- Traditional paper-and-pencil assessment is still the most common approach to classroom assessment.
- Popular formats for objectively scorable test questions include multiple-choice, true false, fill-in-the-blank, matching, and short answer.
- There are dozens of guidelines for composing traditional paper-and-pencil test items. They are reasonable and make sense but are mostly not research-based.
- The traditional tests that teachers make for their own classrooms can be evaluated for quality by, at a minimum, applying the accepted item-writing guidelines.

ON THE WEB

Utilities for computerized item analysis
www.hr-software.net/cgi/ItemAnalysis.cgi

Software for advanced item analysis
www.itemanalysis.com/index.php

Item-writing rules
http://www.nova.edu/hpdtesting/ctl/ forms/itemwritingguidelines.pdf

Using Excel spreadsheets to calculate item statistics
http://languagetesting.info/statistics/excel .html

STUDENT STUDY SITE

Visit **www.sagepub.com/frey** to access additional study tools including eFlashcards, web quizzes, web resources, additional rubrics, and links to SAGE journal articles.

REFERENCES

Amer, A. (2006). Reflections on Bloom's revised taxonomy. *Electronic Journal of Research in Educational Psychology*, 4(1), 213–230.

Brookhart, S. M. (2003, Winter). Developing measurement theory for classroom assessment purposes and uses. *Educational Measurement: Issues and Practice*, 5–12.

Downing, S. M., & Haladyna, T. M. (2006). *Handbook of test development*. Mahwah, NJ: Lawrence Erlbaum.

Frey, B. B., Petersen, S. E., Edwards, L. M., Pedrotti, J. T., & Peyton, V. D. (2005). Item-writing rules: Collective wisdom. *Teaching and Teacher Education*, *21*, 357–364.

Frey, B. B., & Schmitt, V. L. (2010). Teachers' classroom assessment practices. *Middle Grades Research Journal*, *5*(3), 107–117.

Guddemi, M. P., & Case, B. J. (2004). *Assessing young children* (Assessment report). San Antonio, TX: Pearson.

Gullickson, A. R. (1985). Student evaluation techniques and their relationship to grade and curriculum. *Journal of Educational Research*, 79(2), 96–100.

Haladyna, T. M., & Downing, S. M. (1989a). A taxonomy of multiple-choice item-writing rules. *Applied Measurement in Education*, 2(1), 37–50.

Haladyna, T. M., & Downing, S. M. (1989b). Validity of a taxonomy of multiple-choice item writing rules. *Applied Measurement in Education*, 2(1), 51–78.

Haladyna, T. M., Downing, S. M., & Rodriguez, M. C. (2002). A review of multiple-choice item writing guidelines for classroom assessment. *Applied Measurement in Education*, 15(3), 309–334.

Millman, J., & Greene, J. (1993). The specifications and development of tests of achievement and ability. In R. L. Linn (Ed.), *Educational measurement* (3rd ed.). Phoenix, AZ: American Council on Education.

Moss, P. A. (2007). Reconstructing validity. *Educational Researcher, 36*(8), 470–476.

Moss, P. A., Girard, B. J., & Haniford, L. C. (2006). Validity in educational assessment. *Review of Research in Education, 30*, 109–162.

Rodriguez, M. C. (2005). Three options are optimal for multiple-choice items: A meta-analysis of 80 years of research. *Educational Measurement: Issues and Practice, 24*(2), 3–13.

CHAPTER 6

CONSTRUCTED-RESPONSE ITEMS AND SCORING RUBRICS

Looking Ahead in This Chapter

Constructed-response items require students to supply an original answer they create themselves. While this is the common approach for all performance-based assessment, in this chapter we focus on using it to measure knowledge and understanding, not skill or ability, by focusing on essay questions and writing assignments. We conclude with a modern way to assess essay answers and indeed all constructed-response items, the scoring rubric.

Objectives

After studying this chapter, you should be able to

- Describe constructed-response items
- Identify some advantages of constructed-response items for assessment
- Identify the characteristics of a good essay question
- Describe scoring rubrics and how to create them

Ms. Merz Gets a Call From a Parent

Angie got her test back, but she already knew the score would not be good. Her feelings were confirmed when she saw the big red numbers at the top: 17/30. Her mom was going to be so disappointed because they had actually studied together to prepare for this test. Angie was confused about so many of the questions, and she quickly glanced over her test to see what she could ask Ms. Merz to help her understand where she went wrong. She talked with Ms. Merz after class and started with, "What was the answer to question 3, because I put A?"

"B, but why did you think A?"

"Well, I narrowed down my choices between A and B, but both seem true so I just guessed. Really in *B*, Johnny was motivated by his attraction to Sylvia during some points of the book. *A* could also be true because money drove his decisions, too."

Ms. Mertz frowned. "Yes, that is how I wrote the answers, but in the questions it says choose the *best* answer. So both could be true but only A is the best answer." Angie didn't ask any more questions about the test.

Later, Ms. Merz got a phone call from Angie's mother. "Hello Ms. Merz, this is Angie's mom. I would like to discuss the last test over the novel the kids read. She brought home the test and did not do so well, but I know she read the book and knows the information. What do you think happened?"

"Well, Angie did have a few misunderstandings about the questions, which we went over in class. I assure you that this grade will not cause her to fail the class, and I am sure she will do better the next time," replied Ms. Merz.

"We studied together last night. I assure you that my daughter knows the material. She is just not good at taking those types of tests; she talks herself out of the correct answer a lot of the time."

Ms. Merz could hear the frustration in her voice and replied, "I've been thinking about that. I've been using this multiple-choice test for a while, and I really like it. But I have been wondering, not just with Angie, but some other students, too, whether I might try some different approaches that would really let them show me what they know. I have worried a bit that I am missing something. Thank you for calling! I have a plan for a different kind of test next time. Let's plan on talking again to see how the other format works for Angie."

(To Be Continued)

Classroom assessment practitioners have the tools to measure knowledge, especially basic knowledge of facts, very precisely. Traditional paper-and-pencil, objectively scored tests, when well designed, do a pretty good job of that. The problem is that teachers have objectives that go far beyond simple memorization and surface understanding at the low end of Bloom's Taxonomy. They often wish to assess deeper conceptual understanding for their students. When correctly designed, the traditional formats can also measure these constructs reasonably well, but it is usually easier and more direct to use an assessment format that asks students to *construct* an answer.

WHAT DO CONSTRUCTED-RESPONSE ITEMS LOOK LIKE?

Constructed-response items are assessment tasks that ask students to create a complex written answer or product such as a map or graph. The term also sometimes describes assignments such as essays and book reports. Constructed-response items are a type of *supply* item, as opposed to *selection* item, because students supply the answer rather than selecting it. Teachers can use constructed-response items to assess either knowledge and understanding or skill and ability.

As a matter of organization, this chapter focuses on using constructed-response formats for measuring knowledge and understanding, because Chapter 7 is all about evaluating skill and ability, the specialty of the performance-based assessment approach. Some might consider fill-in-the-blank and short-answer items to be constructed-response items because they are supply items, but they are usually scored objectively like other traditional formats (and do not produce complex answers). They are covered in Chapter 5. In this book we've grouped assessment approaches into chapters based on whether the scoring is objective or subjective and whether the measurement target is knowledge or ability.

Good Question!

Essay Questions and Performance-Based Assessment

Q: Aren't essay questions and other similar constructed-response items all performance-based items?

A: Some are and some aren't. If an assessment task requires constructing a product or giving a performance *and* its purpose is to assess skill or ability, then, by our definition, it is a performance-based assessment. If the constructed product is meant to demonstrate understanding or knowledge, then we would classify it as traditional assessment, not performance based. Using this definition, then, a book report that summarizes *A Separate Peace* to show the student understands the plot of the novel is not a performance-based assessment. On the other hand, a book report about *A Separate Peace* assigned to demonstrate that a student has compositional skills and the ability to write well is a performance-based assessment. The *purpose* of an assessment is often the key to both its classification and its validity.

As another example, think of the old-school assignment of "write a composition about what you did over summer vacation." The teacher is not assessing whether you have knowledge or understanding about what you did over summer vacation. The teacher is assessing how well you can write a composition. So *summer vacation* essays are performance-based assessments.

A Note on the Words Knowledge, Skill, and Ability

You may be wondering what the difference is between **knowledge**, **skill**, and **ability** as we use these terms in education. There *is* overlap. After all, someone can know the state capital and also know how to build a birdhouse. We use the word *know* in both cases, but clearly these are different kinds of knowledge. Psychologists call the first kind, knowing facts, *declarative* knowledge, and the second kind, knowing how to do something, *procedural* knowledge. For distinguishing the purposes of the different approaches to classroom assessment, it is useful to think of objectively scored formats as designed to measure the first kind of knowledge and performance-based assessment as best used in measuring the second kind. So when we describe traditional assessment as measuring "knowledge," think "declarative knowledge."

Likewise, we often use the words *skill* and *ability* to refer to the procedural knowledge exercised in the performance of some task. *Ability* typically means a broad, generalized example of procedural knowledge (writing ability, athletic ability, acting ability), while skill is a more specific application of that ability (writing haikus, skipping rope, timing a comic line). There is a third kind of knowledge, *knowledge by acquaintance* or the knowledge that something exists, but that is rarely an instructional objective. It is the kind of knowledge demonstrated in this exchange between elementary students in the TV show *The Simpsons*:

Martin: As your [class] president, I would demand a science-fic-
            tion library, featuring an ABC of the overlords of the
            genre: Asimov, Bester, Clarke!
Kid: What about Ray Bradbury?
Martin: [*dismissively*] I'm aware of his work.

Examples of Constructed-Response Items

As James Popham (2011) has pointed out, "the major payoff of all constructed-response items is they elicit student responses more closely approximating the kinds of behavior students must display in real life" (p. 164). So they tend to require students to demonstrate understanding by writing, designing, or other acts of "doing." Often, a moderately complex stimulus, something to respond to, provides the context for the task. Sometimes, a simple instruction is all that's needed. Here are some examples of constructed-response tasks with these criteria:

- You've just read *Huckleberry Finn*. Write a page to answer this question: What do you think Huck's motivations are for both running away and then coming home?
- Here is a map of Russia. Place each of the cities and geographic features shown on this list onto the map in their correct locations.
- Here is a bar chart showing the relative frequency of each score in a data set. Write a paragraph summarizing the findings.
- Draw two right triangles.

All these types of tasks require the student to construct a response and each student's "answer" will be unique in some way. That's why good constructed-response items that real teachers use require careful planning for scoring.

Here are some real-world examples of constructed-response items.

Example 1

Here, students have complete freedom to draw the human digestive system as they wish, with just enough structure provided to produce comparable responses (see Figure 6.1).

Example 2

"Explain in what ways a person's failure to apply step 5 of the seven-step path for making ethical decisions will impact his or her ability to make ethical decisions. Provide an example that illustrates this impact" (Reiner, Bothell, Sudweeks, & Wood, 2002, p. 8).

Draw and label as many parts of the human digestive system as you can. Draw right on top of this skeleton.

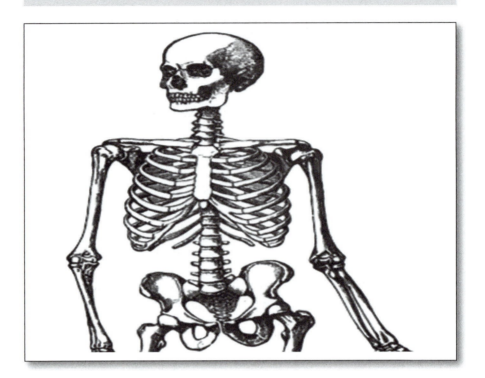

Students are given guidance as to the type of answer. While all responses will be different, each requires the application of the same skill, critical thinking.

Example 3

"Create a diagram that shows a classification arrangement of the following: quadrilateral, parallelogram, trapezoid, rhombus, rectangle, and square" (Faiz, n.d.).

Example 3 is another illustration of how students can have a nice balance of freedom and structured limitations in the response they can give.

Example 4

"Compare and contrast the following numbers: 3, 4, 6, 8, 9, 12, 15, 18. Place them in the appropriate spot on the Venn diagram. Be sure to add a title and labels to your diagram" (Faiz, n.d.).

There's a bit less freedom here than in Example 3.

Example 5

"The *Monroe Doctrine* had a positive impact on our country. Tell whether you agree or disagree with this statement. Give four specific reasons to support your answer" (Faiz, n.d.).

What makes these good examples of constructed-response items is that they all require deep understanding to produce high quality responses. The primary purpose in each case is to assess understanding.

WHAT WE KNOW ABOUT CONSTRUCTED-RESPONSE ITEMS

Research suggests that constructed-response items have certain advantages over selection items. They can serve as instruction to guide student thinking and learning in more positive ways than multiple-choice formats, they may make better use of instructional time, and they are often more valid than objectively scored approaches. Next we look at each of these advantages individually.

Constructed-Response Items vs. Multiple-Choice Items

The constructed-response format is a form of supply item that requires more than simply recalling or "knowing" an answer; it requires the construction or production of a response. Many performance-based assessments are constructed-response in their format, though some performance activities such as athletics and dance don't really fit well into the notion of a constructed response. It might be best to think of constructed response as the "producing a product" part of performance-based assessment.

Researchers in the late 1980s and early 1990s began to develop a body of evidence suggesting that assessment consisting of constructed responses had many advantages over objective item formats, such as multiple-choice, matching, and so on. Students often learn from multiple-choice testing that knowledge is not owned by them, there is only one right answer, the teacher is the one who knows the one right answer, and the students' obligation is to guess what that one right answer is (Shepard, 1991). School is all a game, and tests are the way we keep score. Deep learning is not the goal; consequently, students report that they prepare less for multiple-choice tests.

Constructed-response items, on the other hand, are different because while there are criteria for what makes for a "good answer," there is often not a single right way to respond. Students learn that their knowledge *is* their own. Constructed-response items are very consistent with a popular approach to teaching, the *constructivist* approach. Teachers who believe that students construct their own learning often design assessments which allow students to construct their own answers.

Constructed-Response Items as Timesavers

Another advantage of integrating constructed response assessment into the classroom is that the teacher and class do not lose instructional time to preparing and reviewing for the test. The teaching of the necessary skills or procedures through modeling, discussion, cooperative activities, demonstrations, and so on acts as review. No other review is necessary because the instruction is the assessment preparation. Smith (1991) found in her multiyear examination of two elementary schools that preparation and "recovery" for multiple-choice testing (that is, the tasks of analyzing test results, remediating, reviewing, self-evaluating, and getting instruction back up to speed) consumed as much as several weeks of instructional time. Perhaps the most troubling finding, though, was a drift in instructional strategies from more creative approaches toward lists of important facts that could be covered using a multiple-choice format.

Constructed-Response Items vs. Objectively Scored Items

There is also some evidence that the multiple-choice approach to assessment is intrinsically more troublesome for students with certain characteristics. We've known for some time that national standardized achievement tests, which are usually made up entirely of multiple-choice or objectively scorable items, often find large mean score differences among different genders, ethnicities, and races. Females frequently perform better on constructed-response tests than on those using multiple-choice approaches, and they can underperform compared with males on the multiple-choice portions of standardized tests while performing better on the constructed-response essay sections of those same tests (Hannon, 2012; Pope & Sydnor, 2010; Young & Fisler, 2000). So constructed-response tests may provide a fairer assessment of student understanding.

Student Preference

Teachers struggle to choose assessment approaches that are valid and reliable, but they also want the approach to be fair to their students and for their students to like it, or at least for the assessment not to increase student anxiety. Some believe that one of the disadvantages of multiple-choice tests is that students do not like them, and one of the perceived advantages of constructed-response assessments like essay tests is that students prefer them, perhaps because they feel trapped by objectively scored formats, or they are punished for their creativity, or some other negative perceptions.

A classic study suggests, however, that some students may in fact prefer multiple-choice tests over essay tests (Zeidner, 1987). Two hundred seventy-five Israeli junior high students were surveyed on a variety of dimensions about their preferences for multiple-choice exams compared with teacher-made essay tests. They were asked to rate the different formats in terms of perceived difficulty, complexity, clarity, interest, trickiness, fairness, value, success expectancy, anxiety evoked, and comfort level. As you might expect, students believed multiple-choice tests were more difficult, complex, tricky, and anxiety-causing than essay tests. Somewhat surprisingly, however, at the same time they liked multiple-choice exams more because of their clarity, interest, fairness, comfort level, and perceived likelihood of success. Overall, multiple-choice exams were a clear favorite.

The author of the study points out that student preference and motivation is one aspect of validity, so it may be useful for classroom teachers to take that into account. Of course, other characteristics of constructed-response formats speak positively to their validity. Essay tests may be the best way to observe deep understanding, for instance, and almost completely eliminate the possibility of guessing correct responses. Regardless of student preference, the constructed-response format still has strengths that are difficult to attain with multiple-choice tests.

ESSAY TESTS AND ESSAY ASSIGNMENTS

By far the most common constructed-response item type and the one with the longest history is the essay. Depending on the context and the decade, essays have been called themes, compositions, papers, and so on. While writing assignments are commonly used to assess the *ability* to write, in this chapter we focus on their use to measure understanding. Chapter 7 presents examples of scoring writing assignments as performance-based assessments to evaluate writing skill.

To assess whether a student understands the themes of a poem, the steps in the process of evaporation, or other areas of conceptual learning, a good essay question should have five characteristics (Battaglia, 2008; Reiner et al., 2002):

1. It is a supply item. By definition, an essay question does not allow students to select answers; they must compose them.

2. It requires lengthy answers, long enough to provide evidence of rich understanding of concepts and ideas. At a minimum, it should elicit answers longer than a single sentence.

3. It allows for creative and unique responses.

4. It is subjectively scored. The expertise of the teacher (and a reliable scoring system) produces valid and informative scores.

5. It has instructions that provide guidance as to the way of thinking and the form of the response.

When designing a good-quality essay question, a teacher should be clear about what a good answer is. What will a great answer look like? What will a pretty good answer look like? What are some possible forms that low-scoring answers will take? It is useful and perfectly appropriate to include in the directions what these requirements for a high-scoring response are. If a teacher has decided that a top-scoring answer in a U.S. history class will include three reasons the South chose to secede from the Union, then directions should cite that expectation.

Some recommendations for writing directions for essay questions are designed to keep the test fair for everyone regardless of their test-taking ability or how testwise they are. For example, it is useful to provide advice about how much time to spend on each question by specifying "20 minutes" or "1 page" or just by leaving a certain amount of space for answering the question on a test form. Most assessment experts also recommend not allowing students to select the questions they want to answer. Although this is a fairly common practice and likely reduces test anxiety by giving students more control over the assessment, it may create a relative disadvantage for students who do not have the advanced metacognitive skill of knowing what they know well and what they don't know as well. It also creates the uncomfortable situation in which the difficulty of the test varies by student and is ultimately unknown because students did not all take the same assessment.

Advantages of Essay Tests

As assessments and assignments, essays have several advantages over more objectively scored traditional formats such as multiple-choice tests. It is fairly simple to compose a good essay question, at least in comparison with producing quality multiple-choice items. For in-class exams, the question or prompt can be put on the board and students can answer using their own paper, saving a bit on resources. Most important, having students write answers in the form of organized sentences and paragraphs is a nearly direct way of observing student understanding. This approach is particularly suited for assessing at the higher levels of Bloom's Taxonomy (application, analysis, and above); for evaluating student attitude and appreciation; and for checking students' interpretation and understanding of connections in social studies, literature, science, and other subjects.

Disadvantages of Essay Tests

Soon after essay tests became popular in American schools in the late 1800s and early 1900s, textbooks began to point out some problems with them. For example, here is a list of concerns that has been around for almost a century:

> Lack of reliability of scores (has been) pointed out . . . as the first defect of the essay test. The reasons given for the unreliability of scores (is) the lack of objectivity and the influence of such factors as English construction, spelling, penmanship, neatness, arrangement of form, sympathy for the hard working but slow student, general improvement, and personal attributes on the grade. Other criticisms (are): (a) restricted usefulness with almost no opportunity for diagnosis; (b) encouragement of cramming; (c) little basis for comparison with other students or classes; (d) encouragement of bluffing; (e) consumption of an overshare of students' and instructor's time, (and) lack of any known formula for correction of guessing. (Weidemann & Morris, 1938, p. 517)

While it has always made sense that by asking people to write (or, less conveniently, talk) about their understanding of an idea or process we can get a good picture of what they know and how well they know it, the weakness has always been in the scoring.

RUBRICS

As we saw earlier, for a long time, essay tests and similar writing assignments were typically scored using a holistic approach. **Holistic** means this approach considers "the whole." Classroom teachers used to rate the essay in its entirety and subjectively judge whether it was *A* work or *B* work, worth 10 points or 8 points, and so on. Some teachers still use this scoring method. Of course, it is usually more objective than this simplified description makes it sound, because teachers often have, in their minds at least, some criteria or list of components that should be found in a high-quality answer, and they apply that set of criteria to the written work. In classroom assessment today, however, we have a new tool that makes teacher-chosen criteria for quality concrete and allows for a more objective scoring process. That tool is the scoring rubric, and it is invaluable for reliably assigning scores to assessments with constructed responses, not just essays. It is *the* assessment tool of choice for constructed-response items and, as Chapter 7 makes clear, for the broad category of performance-based assessment.

A **scoring rubric** is a written set of scoring rules, often in the form of a table. It identifies the criteria and required parts and pieces for a good-quality answer or product. It shows the relative weights of the criteria and the pieces, and the possible range of points for each. Three general scoring strategies for constructed-response items shape the design and use of rubrics. Teachers can choose any one or mix and match them. We have already discussed the *holistic* approach, which weighs the quality of the work in its entirety, often in comparison with the work of other students. This approach does not require a rubric at all. It is likely the weakest approach regarding validity, because it tends to be *norm-referenced*, not *criterion-referenced* (see Chapter 2), and regarding reliability, because only one score wholly determines the grade.

Another popular strategy and one that allows for objective scoring is the **analytic approach.** The rubric in this method commonly appears as a checklist of components that must be present in the product. Sometimes each component has a range of possible points that allow teachers to distinguish how well each component has been completed. Table 6.1 presents an example from the Rubistar website (see the Technology box), credited to "Mrs. Johnson." This rubric evaluates an imaginary diary entry for historical understanding.

It is written to be shared with *students* both before and after the assignment. It uses the analytic approach, with a list of elements that must be present and

Table 6.1 5th Grade—Diary Entry Written in the Voice of an Immigrant

Written from current point of view	Entire project is written from the point of view of an immigrant coming to the United States.	Project is mostly written from the point of view of an immigrant coming to the United States.	Project has some sentences written from the point of view of an immigrant coming to the United States.	Project is not written from the point of view of an immigrant coming to the United States.
Content - Journal 1- REQUIRED (see project list for required details)	Journal #1 is at least 1 page in length. A clear description of the arrival to America is written, along with a clear and vivid description of how you felt, how your family felt, and what is happening around you on the deck of the ship. Journal feels like it is a real person's diary. Lots of great details.	Journal #1 is 1 page in length. A description of the arrival to America is given, but does not give a lot of details about how you and your family were feeling. Journal feels like a real person's diary.	Journal #1 is less than 1 page in length. Some details about your arrival to America are present. Journal does not include how the rest of your family was feeling. Journal does not feel like a real person's actual diary.	Journal #1 is less than 1 page in length. Few details are present about your arrival to America. Journal does not include any details on your family. Journal does not sound like a real person's diary.
Grammar and Spelling	Sentences are complete, vary in length, and use perfect grammar. Spelling has no errors.	Sentences are complete, with few errors in grammar. Spelling has very few errors.	Some sentences are incomplete. Few grammar errors. Several spelling errors.	Choppy, incomplete sentences. Many grammar errors. No effort was made to use correct spelling.

a quantitative (objective) way of determining which one from a range of scores should be assigned to each piece. Table 6.2 presents an example of the analytic approach from Rubistar, credited to Mrs. Callwell. The assessment was for students to write a children's book about inventions of the U.S. industrial

Table 6.2 2IR Final Project—Children's Book

Book cover	The book cover is neat and attractive. The title and cover image are insightful and clever.	The book cover is neat and attractive. The title and cover image are relevant and expected.	The book cover is neat. The title and cover image are basic and mediocre.	The book cover is sloppy and unattractive. The title and cover image are subpar or unacceptable.
Introduction	The first page introduces the concept in a clever way and captures the reader's attention.	The first page is standard and expected. It introduces the assignment as opposed to the concept. There is some lure for the reader.	The first page is basic. It introduces the assignment and does not engage the reader.	The first page in unacceptable, subpar, or missing.
Inventions	The three inventions discussed in the book are unique inventions from the Second Industrial Revolution.	The three inventions discussed in the book are commonly recognized inventions from the Second Industrial Revolution.	The three inventions discussed in the book are basic or general inventions from the Second Industrial Revolution –or– one invention is missing.	Two or more inventions are missing from the book –or– inventions are not from the Second Industrial Revolution.
History	The history of each invention is thorough and well explained within the context of the Second Industrial Revolution.	The history of each invention is standard and explained within the context of the Second Industrial Revolution.	The history of one invention is missing –or– the inventions are not explained within the context of the Second Industrial Revolution.	Two or more histories are missing –or– the information is incorrect or unacceptable.
Evolution	The evolution of each invention is thorough and well explained from the Second Industrial Revolution to current.	The evolution of each invention is standard and explained from the Second Industrial Revolution to current.	The evolution of one invention is missing –or– the evolutions are not explained from the Second Industrial Revolution to current.	Two or more evolutions are missing –or– the information is incorrect or unacceptable.
Impact on Society	The impact on society for each invention is thorough and well explained within the context of the Second Industrial Revolution and current.	The impact on society for each invention is standard and explained within the context of the Second Industrial Revolution and current.	One of the impacts on society is missing –or– is not explained within the context of the Second Industrial Revolution and current.	Two or more impacts on society are missing –or– the information is incorrect or unacceptable.
Conclusion	The conclusion is summative; identifies the connection between the past, present, and future; and leaves the reader with a new perspective.	The conclusion is summative; identifies the connection between the past, present, and future; but does not leave the reader with a new perspective.	The conclusion is summative; but does not identify the connection between the past, present, and future; and does not leave the reader with a new perspective.	The conclusion is unacceptable, subpar, or missing.

revolution. Notice the rubric is primarily meant to assess knowledge and understanding (of inventions), but there also are some performance-based elements regarding writing a clever introduction and having an attractive cover.

A third strategy is to score the work based on key characteristics of quality. The **primary trait approach** is favored by many language arts teachers when scoring written essays and goes by names like *6 Traits of Writing* and the like. It is most appropriate when the written work is meant as a performance-based assessment to measure writing *ability*. (Chapter 7, the performance-based assessment chapter, describes this approach in detail.)

Other assignments and classroom activities that can be scored with rubrics include the following:

- **Group projects.** Students work together on a collaborative problem and can be assessed on discussions, group presentations, or group projects.
- **Writing assignments.** Students prepare written description, analysis, explanation, or summary.
- **Scientific experiments.** Teachers observe how well students can conduct scientific investigations.
- **Demonstrations.** Students perform, showing their mastery of content or procedures.
- **Portfolios.** Teachers make assessments based on collections of students' work. Typically, these portfolios are meant to evaluate development over time. Chapter 7 talks more about portfolios, a very common element of the modern classroom.

What's in a Name?

Teachers use the term *rubric* to describe the set of scoring rules for performance-based assessment. For some parents, however, the term has a religious connotation, and using it in a secular context can be controversial. Some districts prefer the term *scoring guide* for communications with parents.

"Rubric" is derived from *ruber*, Latin for red (Oxford English Dictionary, n.d.). In 15th century European monasteries, monks highlighted the beginning of important paragraphs with red lettering as they transcribed important religious works (Schmitt, 2007). The term *rubric* thus came to describe sacred rules for religious procedures, the numbering of biblical passages, and so on. In other contexts, the term is used to describe detailed lists of rules or procedures; it came into use for sets of performance-based assessment scoring rules beginning in the 1980s (Popham, 1997).

Characteristics of Quality Rubrics

There are generalizable criteria for what makes a "good" rubric (Allen & Knight, 2009; Jonsson & Svingby, 2007; Reddy & Andrade, 2010; Thaler, Kazemi, & Huscher, 2009). A review of the literature allows us to define the components of a "meta-rubric" (Schmitt, 2007, shown in Chapter 7) that identifies four components and 15 criteria by which we can judge teacher-developed scoring guides. According to this research-based set of standards, rubrics should have a purpose, criteria for identifying quality, a scoring system or scale, and general construction qualities. The purpose should align with clear, academic goals, and the activity should be cognitively complex and match the intended purpose. Criteria should be clear and positively worded, cover the objectives, and be grade-level appropriate. The scoring system should be precise, allow for a range or continuum of performance, and provide useful feedback. Regarding general qualities, rubrics should be organized, be free of mechanical errors, and reflect real-world expectations of performance. This final criterion suggests that constructed-response items are often authentic assessments (see Chapter 8).

How to Make a Rubric

What follows is a minimanual for designing and building your own rubrics:

Step 1. Identify the purpose of the assessment.

What is to be measured by the rubric? What will the score represent? If the assessment target is fairly simple or represents understanding at the lower levels of Bloom's Taxonomy, then a rubric may not be necessary or even the best method. Rubrics are most useful when the learning to be assessed is complex (Schmitt, 2007). So for the measurement of most skills and abilities, rubrics are recommended. They are also useful for assessing deep understanding. The greater the number of steps or pieces and the more abstract the learning goal, the greater advantage there is to breaking the learning goal into its critical characteristics or parts. That's what a rubric does best. On the other hand, if the assessment target is basic knowledge or not complicated, a more objective approach to scoring might be perfectly fine.

For example, imagine your measurement goal is to assess a student's knowledge of the letters of the alphabet. Sitting with the student one-on-one and showing different letters while asking the student to say out loud which letter it is makes sense and is a common strategy. To score that assessment, however, one is not helped by having a rubric that, perhaps, rates student accuracy from one end of a 5-point scale ("Not accurate") to the other end ("Very accurate"). This type of learning can be reliably and validly scored objectively by identifying correct and incorrect answers. No real judgment is required in this instance.

Step 2. Determine the criteria for success.

What will a good performance look like? What are the crucial indicators of quality in student "answers"? Here is where teacher expertise really comes into play. The teacher analyzes the assessment or performance task and decides what is most important. What are the key components, characteristics, or traits that determine quality in the answer, product, or performance created by the students?

These criteria can be affected by grade level expectations, cognitive complexity, level of student development, teachers' philosophies, and content coverage. Sometimes, in fact, the choice of standards for success is influenced by whether they can be observed and assessed fairly. Perfectly reasonable indicators of quality may not even make it onto a rubric if they cannot be concretely defined in ways that make them measureable.

In the next step to come (Step 3), the various scoring formats are discussed, but it is important to think now, in Step 2, of those scoring approaches when teachers choose their criteria. This is because if teachers will rate quality along some continuum from low scores to high scores, it is useful to concretely define each of the scores across that range. It's not always necessary to define every interval along the way, but the anchors (the points at either end), at least, should be defined. So teachers work to find explicit, directly observable (if that can be done), and as objectively interpretable as possible ways to put words around the score points. Will a score range of 2 points (which is really just a check of presence or absence of some characteristic), 3 points, 4 points, or 5 points or more work best to validly capture quality within the student's constructed response?

As an example of choosing quality criteria and defining them along a continuum, let's look at part of the scoring rubric used in real life by the SAT college admission test's judges (Schellscheidt, 2006). These days, for the SAT Writing section, students handwrite an essay responding to a topic provided by the exam. It is expected to be a personal essay, with test-takers supporting their own opinion.

The test developers have identified five crucial categories of quality for these essays. These are the criteria for success. They are

1. Development of position

2. Organization

3. Use of language

4. Sentence structure

5. Grammar and word usage

Each of these components or dimensions is scored along a range of scores from 1 to 6. (From a pure measurement perspective, by the way, it makes more sense to have ratings start at 0, not 1. After all, if there is complete absence of quality, or whatever the construct might be, why should someone receive any points at all? There are real-world advantages for classroom teachers and standardized test developers, however, for creating scoring systems with the lowest scores possible somewhere above zero. These advantages include social and motivational benefits.) For our example, let's look at the definitions for what the 1 to 6 point options are supposed to mean for **Organization**.

1. Disorganized; little or no focus; incoherent.

2. Poorly organized; lacks focus; problems with coherence or flow of ideas.

3. Limited in organization and focus; demonstrates lapses in coherence or flow of ideas.

4. Generally organized and focused; demonstrates some coherence and attention to the flow of ideas.

5. Well organized and focused; demonstrates coherence and ideas flow well.

6. Well organized and clearly focused; clearly coherent and ideas flow seamlessly.

Notice that while there is certainly subjectivity in the phrasing used, there is also a certain level of precision and concreteness to guide the scorer's thoughts. For instance, different teachers might disagree on what it looks like when ideas flow seamlessly. This would lead to lower inter-rater *reliability* (consistency across scorers). Clarifying that the seamless flow of ideas is an indicator of quality essays, however, does likely increase the *validity* of scoring. This middle ground between objectivity and subjectivity is typical of well-designed rubrics and exemplifies the attempted balance between validity and reliability that in some ways defines modern classroom assessment.

Step 3. Design the scoring system.

The value of a rubric's scoring system depends mostly on the value in the feedback it provides to both students and teachers. Are the distinctions between each score meaningful? Is each possible score well defined in observable ways that make sense to everyone?

Rubrics play a large role in today's classroom assessment environment. They are critical not only for constructed-response items and in performance-based assessment; they also are important technologies as part of both formative assessment systems and authentic assessment approaches. Their usefulness in all those approaches is dependent on how the scoring rules are set up.

Different scoring systems are driven by the degree to which the assessment task or product is broken down into a small number of components or characteristics. If the assessment object is not subdivided in some way and scored in its entirety, this approach is similar to the traditional assignment of attaching broad categorical letter grades to assignments. We called this approach *holistic* earlier in this chapter and dismissed it as not being a particularly valid or reliable method. One can have a rubric which *is* holistic, though. It is similar to that old-fashioned global approach, but assumes a continuum of quality. A holistic rubric judges the assessment response globally, but still assigns a range of scores to a dimension of quality. It is a single dimension, however. The other approach, the *analytic* approach, has multiple scoring opportunities. A range of scores representing quality is available for many different pieces of a product (such as an essay or project) or for different characteristics (such as clarity, neatness, or creativity).

For example, Mertler (2001) provides the example of how one might assess the quality of the results of a problem-solving task. If a teacher chose a holistic scoring approach, it might look like this template he provides:

0. No response/task not attempted.

1. Demonstrates no understanding of the problem.

2. Demonstrates little understanding of the problem. Many requirements of task are missing.

3. Demonstrates partial understanding of the problem. Most requirements of task are included.

4. Demonstrates considerable understanding of the problem. All requirements of task are included.

5. Demonstrates complete understanding of the problem. All requirements of task are included in response.

This is a holistic rubric because it uses a range of scores to rate quality (which makes it a rubric), but it has a single criterion that is applied to the entire student "answer" (which makes it holistic).

If we were to create an analytic rubric to assess problem solving, it might start by identifying a few criteria of good problem solving. For example, we might decide that quality problem solving has these important characteristics, components, or dimensions:

- Organization
- Collaboration
- Use of strategies

Then each of these three criteria would be rated using relevant definitions. Collaboration, for instance, might be scored this way:

1. The student worked independently.

2. The student spoke with and listened to one or two other students, but did not check his or her work with other students.

3. The student spoke with and listened to one or two other students and checked his or her work with other students.

4. The student spoke with and listened to all the students in his or her group, but did not check his or her work with other students.

5. The student spoke with and listened to all the students in his or her group, and checked his or her work with other students.

Other scoring rules would be assigned to the other two criteria. (How might you score those criteria?) Finally, the three scores would be summed to provide a total assessment score. Different teachers might create entirely different rubrics to measure the same thing, of course. For instance, in this example, whether the problem is solved or not does not matter. You might choose to include that requirement. The final rubric for any assessment task depends on the choices teachers make in each of the three steps in rubric creation.

Rubistar

The Rubistar website, http://rubistar.4teachers.org, is a valuable open source for hundreds of authentic scoring rubrics that real classroom teachers have developed and used to score performance-based assessments. Anyone can download and use these

Technology

rubrics or share them with others; the site is the primary source for the rubrics presented in this chapter and Chapter 7. Unfortunately, it is difficult to credit the teachers who created the rubrics, because the site does not require that contributors provide their full names.

Though the site describes itself as a place to find and produce "projects-based" scoring guides, you will find every conceivable type of classroom rubric there. The searchable catalog groups rubrics into these categories: Oral Projects, Multimedia, Math, Writing, Products (Maps, Posters), Reading, Art, Work Skills (Collaboration, Self-Evaluation), Science, and Music. You also can produce your own rubrics using the starter templates provided.

The site is a creation of 4Teachers.org and supported by the Center for Research on Learning at the University of Kansas. Companion sites offer examples of, and development tools for, online quizzes, curriculum tracks for students, note taking for research papers, attitude surveys, webpage development, and a host of other teacher tasks. You can find links to these resources at http://4teachers.org/tools.

Advantages of Rubrics

As an assessment strategy, rubrics have much to offer:

- *Rubrics allow for quick scoring and quick feedback*. Rubrics can provide frequent formative feedback (see Chapter 4), so students can monitor and adjust their own learning. They also allow teachers to spend less time on scoring and grading and more time on teaching.
- *Rubrics improve teaching*. The process of rubric development requires teachers to analyze and identify their key instructional objectives. A good rubric defines characteristics of high-quality performance and supports focused and strategic teaching. It also allows teachers to more precisely evaluate their own teaching and monitor student learning.
- *Rubrics encourage the growth of student metacognitive and critical thinking skills*. Students who participate in rubric creation and application start to think about their own learning and develop the ability to judge for themselves the quality of their own work.
- *Rubrics allow for meaningful sharing of student performance data*. Teachers can show scored rubrics to students and parents. Because good rubrics break learning goals down into specific skills, components, or criteria of quality, they make it clearer where a student stands developmentally, especially compared with a holistic score or grade.

Ms. Merz Gets a Call From a Parent (Part II)

Stories From the Classroom

After the conversation with Angie's mother, it seemed that Angie might do better with an essay format. She could express the depth of her knowledge better and not feel tricked. Just as important, Ms. Merz would get a better sense of her students' understanding and learning, as well.

So she developed an essay test for the next exam. First, she thought about what kinds of information she would need to evaluate whether or not a student understood the next novel. She knew that comprehending character development would be a key instructional objective, so she wrote one question about that. As she went down the list of other objectives, she was able to draft essay questions for each. The next step was to define what a great answer looked like.

Creating questions for the test was easier than creating great, good, and not so good examples of answers. Ms. Merz began jotting down different types of answers each essay question might produce. She then decided the relative quality of those possible answers in terms of demonstrating understanding. This information would be used to create the directions for the test and the scoring rubric that she planned to use when grading their tests.

To get more ideas for her rubric, Ms. Merz went to the *Rubistar.com* website. She found dozens of example rubrics covering the novel her students would read next. Because each of her questions required students to provide different types of information, each question needed a separate scoring rubric. From the dropdown menu she selected the categories and twice added her own category. Next to the categories, Ms. Merz listed the descriptions of the different scores, 4 being the highest and 1 being the lowest score. A click on the submit button allowed her to print the rubric so her students could use this as a guide to what a good answer would look like. She knew this would help many of them read with a purpose.

Three weeks later, Ms. Merz announced, "All right, class, we are going to take the test, so please put away your books. As I told you before we started reading this novel, this test is a short-essay test, and you should have been following your rubric as we read along. The directions are given before each question, so pay attention to how many details I am looking for and how long I expect a great answer to be!"

That evening she was grading the tests and found that scoring was relatively simple with the scoring checklist she had It was not as easy to grade as a multiple-choice test; that was for sure. But with the rubric it was fairly quick, and she felt better seeing the level of understanding reflected more clearly in the students' responses. She was also gaining a great deal more insight into her students' thought processes and how they internalized the readings and conversations about the book. Some students would write the correct answers but would also struggle explaining in great detail and answer the question fully. This was a good way to gauge where the students might have gaps and how to best help them since the rubric was tied to specific objectives. She really felt that she knew the students better after reading their answers. She liked that. She also liked that she might actually look forward to the next call from Angie's mom.

THINGS TO THINK ABOUT

1. Do students prepare more for essay tests or multiple-choice tests?

2. With the enduring popularity of traditional paper-and-pencil tests and the increase in technology, some teachers are concerned about students losing their writing skills. Are you?

3. Some studies have found that females outperform males on constructed-response tests. Why might this be true?

4. What are the strengths and weaknesses of the subjective scoring required for constructed-response items?

Looking Back in This Chapter

- Constructed-response items are assessment tasks that ask students to create a complex answer. The answer can be written, like an essay or book report, or designed like a map or graph.
- Constructed-response items are likely authentic assessments because they produce behaviors that are similar to the academic things we want students to do in the real world. They also allow assessment of deep understanding.
- The most common constructed-response item type and one with a long history is the essay assignment. This chapter focuses on essays used to assess understanding, not to measure writing skill. To evaluate essays in terms of student knowledge and understanding requires a well-defined set of criteria as to what a great answer looks like.
- Scoring rubrics make teacher-chosen criteria for quality concrete and allow for more subjective (reliable) scoring. They are the assessment tool of choice for constructed-response items.

ON THE WEB

Presentations on the use of constructed-response items
http://writingfix.com/RICA/constructed_response.htm

Collection of checklists for a variety of constructed-response formats
http://www.edteck.com/dbq/basicworksheet.htm

One school district's approach to constructed-response assessments
http://www.duluth.k12.mn.us/education/components/docmgr/default.php?section detailid=15770

A generic scoring rubric for constructed-response problem-solving assessments
http://woub.org/etseo/gofigure/gfx/media/pdf/constructedresponserubrics.pdf

STUDENT STUDY SITE

Visit www.sagepub.com/frey to access additional study tools including eFlashcards, web quizzes, web resources, additional rubrics, and links to SAGE journal articles.

REFERENCES

Allen, S., & Knight, J. (2009). A method for collaboratively developing and validating a rubric. *International Journal for the Scholarship of Teaching and Learning*, 3(2), 1–17.

Battaglia, A. (2008). Challenging the essay culture. *King's Institute of Learning & Teaching*, 57.

Faiz, U. (n.d.). Retrieved from http://www.pieas.edu.pk/umarfaiz/workshop/qualitycrqs.pdf

Hannon, B. (2012). Test anxiety and performance-avoidance goals explain gender differences in SAT-V, SAT-M, and overall SAT scores. *Personality and Individual Differences*.

Jonsson, A., & Svingby, G. (2007). The use of scoring rubrics: Reliability, validity and educational consequences. *Educational Research Review*, 2(2), 130–144.

Mertler, C. A. (2001). Designing scoring rubrics for your classroom. *Practical Assessment, Research & Evaluation*, 7(25).

Oxford English Dictionary (Online). (2011). *rubric, n. and adj.* Oxford University Press.

Pope, D. G., & Sydnor, J. R. (2010). Geographic variation in the gender differences in test scores. *Journal of Economic Perspectives*, 24(2), 95–108.

Popham, W. J. (1997). What's wrong and what's right with rubrics. *Educational Leadership*, 55(2), 72–76.

Popham, W. J. (2011). *Classroom assessment: What teachers need to know*. Boston, MA: Pearson.

Reddy, Y. M., & Andrade, H. (2010). A review of rubric use in higher education. *Assessment & Evaluation in Higher Education*, 35(4), 435–448.

Reiner, C. M., Bothell, T. W., Sudweeks, R. R., & Wood, B. (2002). *Preparing effective essay questions*. Stillwater, OK: New Forums Press.

Schellscheidt, K. (2006). *How to score the SAT essay: The SAT essay rubric*. Retrieved from blog .eprep.com/2006/12/04/sat-essay-rubric/

Schmitt, V. L. (2007). *The quality of teacher-developed rubrics for assessing student performance in the classroom*. Unpublished doctoral dissertation, University of Kansas.

Shepard, L. (1991). Interview on assessment issues with Lorrie Shepard. *Educational Researcher*, 20(2), 21–27.

Smith, M. L. (1991). Put to the test: The effects of external testing on teachers. *Educational Researcher*, 20(5), 8–11.

Thaler, N., Kazemi, E., & Huscher, C. (2009). Developing a rubric to assess student learning outcomes using a class assignment. *Teaching of Psychology*, 36(2), 113–116.

Weidemann, C. C., & Morris, B. J. (1938). The essay-type test. *Review of Educational Research*, 8(5), 517–522.

Young, J. W., & Fisler, J. L. (2000). Sex differences on the SAT: An analysis of demographic and educational variables. *Research in Higher Education*, 41(3), 401–416.

Zeidner, M. (1987). Essay versus multiple-choice type classroom exams: The student's perspective. *Journal of Educational Research*, 80(6), 352–358.

CHAPTER 7

PERFORMANCE-BASED ASSESSMENT

Looking Ahead in This Chapter

Though treated as a fairly modern approach to classroom assessment, performance-based assessment actually has a long history as a commonsense way to evaluate people. It is the best format for assessing skill or ability. The most useful ways to use this approach are illustrated in this chapter. Performance-based assessment is best scored using a rubric. This chapter provides lots of examples of real-world performance-based assessments for a variety of subjects and grade levels.

Objectives

After studying this chapter, you should be able to

- Define performance-based assessment
- Identify the characteristics of performance-based assessment
- Provide examples of what performance-based assessment looks like in real classrooms
- Evaluate the quality of performance-based assessments and their scoring rubrics

Mr. Wilcken Wonders What His Students Can Do

Mr. Wilcken was excited when he received a districtwide e-mail about an upcoming exhibit at a local museum. His 8th grade students had just begun their Social Studies unit on "Manifest Destiny," and he thought about the possibilities for a partnership with the museum. He picked up the phone and called the principal to see what options were available for his class. "Well Mr. Wilcken, we don't have money to rent buses, so see whatever you can put together with the parents and the museum, transportation-wise." Mr. Wilcken knew that arranging this through parents and the museum would be pretty tough. So he thought of another way to involve the museum.

Mr. Wilcken talked with museum staff. "Would somebody from the museum be willing to be a guest speaker and bring some real artifacts for the students to see?"

"That would be something we could do. Send me an e-mail of days and times that will work best, and we will get it worked out for you."

"Thanks. I am sure this will be a great learning opportunity for my students."

It was the day of the presentation and Mr. Wilcken told the class, "We have been studying Manifest Destiny, and today we have a guest speaker coming with artifacts from that time period of Native American history. Don't be afraid to ask questions because our speaker is an expert in the field."

During the presentation, the director showed a couple of quotes from a book about Tecumseh. Students' hands went into the air to defend the European viewpoint, while some expressed an understanding of the Native perspective. This intense conversation led Mr. Wilcken to reconsider the multiple-choice test he had been planning. Thinking of an instructional objective that *students will be able to make a historical interpretation and support that perspective with evidence*, he realized he could use a different format, one which would really focus on the skill of the historian, as opposed to the knowledge of historians . . .

(To Be Continued)

When students or critics occasionally complain about traditional paper-and-pencil assessment, it sometimes is a reflection of student frustration at "being stuck in a box," unable to show what they know and can do because of the limits of the assessment format. Some students long to be given the freedom to demonstrate their abilities without being stuck in that box of traditional multiple-choice tests. A format where students demonstrate their abilities through a performance (like by giving a speech, acting, debating, dancing, or conducting an experiment) or the construction of a product (like a birdhouse, a painting, a scientific report, or a short story) can provide that freedom. With the wider-open opportunities that this type of assessment provides, however, there is a necessary structure, necessary limits. The teacher has in mind some criteria for success, standards of quality, but he or she wishes to allow some latitude, some flexibility in what students can produce. The purpose of this assessment approach is to go beyond assessing student knowledge and understanding and assess student ability and skill. The generally accepted label for this type of classroom assessment, which requires that students produce a product or deliver a performance for the purpose of evaluating skill or ability, is performance-based assessment. The art of valid and reliable performance-based assessment lies in the tension created between the wish to have fairly objective standards by which to judge quality and the wish to allow students to demonstrate the full potential of their abilities.

WHAT IS PERFORMANCE-BASED ASSESSMENT?

"Don't throw the past away, You might need it some rainy day, Dreams can come true again, When everything old is new again."

Everything Old Is New Again, 1974,
Song by Peter Allen and Carole Bayer Sager

So what exactly is the approach we are focusing on in this chapter? Madaus and O'Dwyer (1999), on whose thoughtful essay about performance-based assessment we are basing the brief history I provide in the paragraphs ahead, offer this simple definition: "performance assessment requires examinees to construct (or) supply answers, perform, or produce something for evaluation" (p. 689). Add to that the common purpose of performance-based assessment, which is to measure skill or ability, and you have a definition that nicely distinguishes performance-based assessment from traditional paper-and-pencil assessment.

The fairly recent rise in performance-based assessment is essentially a reaction to the historic reliance on paper-and-pencil multiple-choice types of testing, but the performance-based approach has actually been around much longer than what we label the "traditional" approach. China used a performance-based system for selecting civil servants for more than 2,000 years until the 20th century. One exam even required people to write compositions and poetry and analyze literature (e.g., the writings of Confucius). By 1000 CE, the exams included assessment of higher-order thinking skills such as problem solving and reasoning, but interestingly, the scoring was considered too subjective and that aspect of the testing faded away in favor of more objectively scorable constructs. As Madaus and O'Dwyer write, "Subjectivity has cast a shadow on performance assessments ever since" (p. 690).

Until the start of the industrial revolution throughout Europe in the 1800s, there was little interest in evaluating or even describing things or thoughts with numbers. Mathematics existed, of course, but the matters of the world, and certainly people, weren't measured so much with quantities, but reality was assessed using what social science researchers would later call *qualitative* methods. The population explosion, the rise of the merchant class, international trade, exploration, and engineering and scientific advances changed all that, and ideas and people began to be counted and measured. An emphasis on precision and comparison necessitated a movement toward objective assessment.

Even while educational assessment began to focus almost entirely on objectively scorable student evaluation methods, performance-based assessment remained a part of the classroom experience. Oral exams have been a staple in American education from the 1700s through today. To make this approach a bit more standardized and (presumably) less subjectively scored, the Boston Public Schools in the mid-1800s (under the guidance of Horace Mann) added an innovative written essay exam. This allowed for all students to receive the same questions at the same time under standardized conditions. (Madaus and O'Dwyer argue that this was a partly political move to allow for comparison of schools, principals, and teachers to each other. This sounds very much like the controversy today about using standardized test scores to evaluate teachers, principals, and schools.)

The development of the standardized intelligence test (1905) and multiple-choice item (1914) prompted another surge in reliance on objective paper-and-pencil assessment, and the use by teachers of written essays and similar approaches began to fade. As the 20th century came to an end, however, the "modern" approach of performance-based assessment had been rediscovered (partly as a backlash to multiple-choice testing) with the development of portfolio and other performance-based evaluation systems. Performance-based assessment today is common in real-world classrooms with about 40% of teacher-made tests including some performance-based components (Frey & Schmitt, 2010). The long history of performance-based assessment and education is summarized in Figure 7.1.

Figure 7.1 History of Classroom Assessment

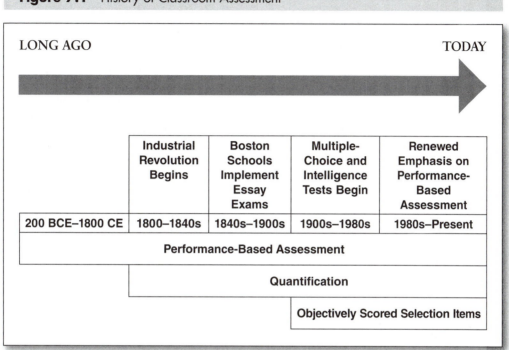

HOW AND WHEN TO USE PERFORMANCE-BASED ASSESSMENT

A recurring difficulty as we compare the different classroom assessment approaches in this book is in defining the different perspectives in ways that make useful distinctions without pretending that the variety of techniques and methods that help define the approaches can't be used together. Real-world classroom teachers use a mixed approach that borrows and applies tools from different theoretical classroom assessment perspectives for different purposes as needed. One confusion in the field about the definition of performance-based assessment is apparent when it is compared with another of our modern approaches to classroom assessment, authentic assessment. Authenticity is essentially the idea that assessment tasks should be realistic (though even that simple definition is not adequate to cover how educational researchers use the term, as is explored in Chapter 8). It is worth taking a second to reflect on this fuzziness in how the terms are used by educational practitioners, trainers, and researchers, because if one wishes to learn best practices when it comes to a

Figure 7.2   Perspectives on Performance Assessment

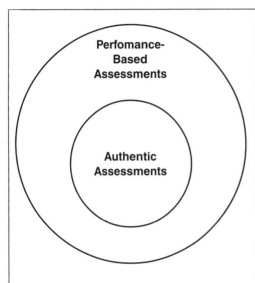

Perfomance-Based Assessments

Authentic Assessments

- Performance assessment [measures] outcomes in more authentic contexts (Kubiszyn & Borich, 2003).
- As authentic performances, [performance assessment] seems more relevant to the real world (Taylor & Bobbit-Nolen, 2005).
- [Performance assessments] may be called authentic assessments. [They] permit students to show what they can do in real situations (Airasian, 2001).
- Virtually all [performance] tasks should be authentic in nature or they lose some relevance to the students. This distinction between performance and authentic assessments becomes insignificant and unnecessary (Mueller, 2005).

- Authentic assessments are performance assessments, but the inverse is not true (Oosterhof, 2003).
- Many performance-based assessments are also classified as authentic assessments (Mertler, 2003).
- In some instances ... school-tasks rather than real-world tasks may be suitable for performance assessment (Popham, 2002).
- Performance assessment is the use of a performance criteria to measure achievement (Stiggins, 1992).

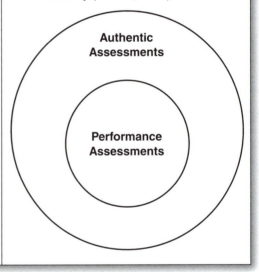

Authentic Assessments

Performance Assessments

Source: Adapted from Frey & Schmitt, 2007.

particular approach, it is useful to know the characteristics of that approach that are important. Considerable overlap in the scholarly definitions of performance-based assessment and authentic assessment exists, especially as to whether all performance-based assessment is authentic, all authentic assessment is performance-based, or neither (Frey & Schmitt, 2007). Two Venn diagrams of sorts that reflect these differing perspectives are presented in Figure 7.2.

The Format of Performance-Based Assessment

"An ounce of performance is worth pounds of promises."

Mae West, Movie Actress (1893–1980)

In Chapter 4, in our discussions about traditional paper-and-pencil assessment, it was possible to list the various formats for items (e.g., multiple-choice, matching, fill-in-the-blank) and provide a brief example. For performance-based assessment, however, there are almost an infinite number of "formats," limited only by the creativity of the teacher. Typically, though, all performance-based assessments require performance of a multistep behavior or creation of a multipart product. Scores are based on observation of the behavior or analysis of the product and are meant to reflect skill or ability. Really good performance-based assessments, however, have a few more characteristics in common:

- Performance-based assessment items are **supply items**. The student must supply the response, not select it. The response is constructed or performed.

For example, students might be asked to attempt to climb a rope using the correct form as taught by their physical education teacher.

- They have a purpose that identifies the decision to be made.

Continuing with our example, the purpose of the assessment is to evaluate students' rope-climbing ability.

- The parts or steps are directly observable.

For example, the instructor has analyzed the process of rope-climbing as including several identifiable steps that can be seen. These steps have been taught to students as the "right way" to climb a rope.

- There are predetermined scoring criteria. When well done, the criteria relate to the purpose of the assessment and the observable parts or steps. Scoring is based on ratings, quantified observations that are criterion-referenced, or rankings, ordered observations that are norm-referenced.

Following our example, the teacher will have taken the steps to rope climbing and created a scoring rubric where students receive a range of points for their attempts at each step of the process.

Figure 7.3 Which Grade Levels Use Performance-Based Assessment?

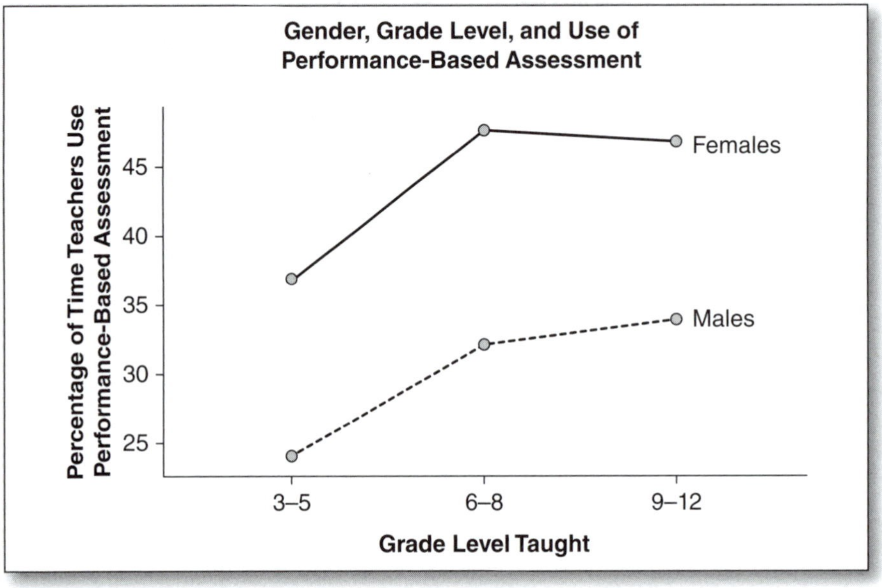

Source: Adapted from Frey & Schmitt, 2010.

Who Uses Performance-Based Assessment?

In today's school, there is substantial use of performance-based assessment across grade levels and subjects, with essays and written assignments as the single most common assessment format (Frey & Schmitt, 2010). However, traditional paper-and-pencil testing remains the predominant approach overall. Performance-based assessment is used much more frequently by language arts teachers than by those who teach other subjects and is more common at secondary levels than at the elementary level. Female teachers choose performance-based assessment more often than male teachers. Figures 7.3 and 7.4 show the relative frequency that performance-based assessment is used.

Interestingly, things have not changed too much, actually, since performance-based assessment began its comeback in the 1980s. Back then, teacher-made objectively scored traditional paper-and-pencil tests were the most common method used across all levels and subjects taught, and language arts teachers were more likely than science or social science teachers to use some performance-based methods like papers and oral reports (Gullickson, 1985). Performance-based assessment is an important part of the assessment environment of modern classrooms, but traditional multiple-choice types of formats still lead in popularity.

Figure 7.4 Which Subjects Use Performance-Based Assessment?

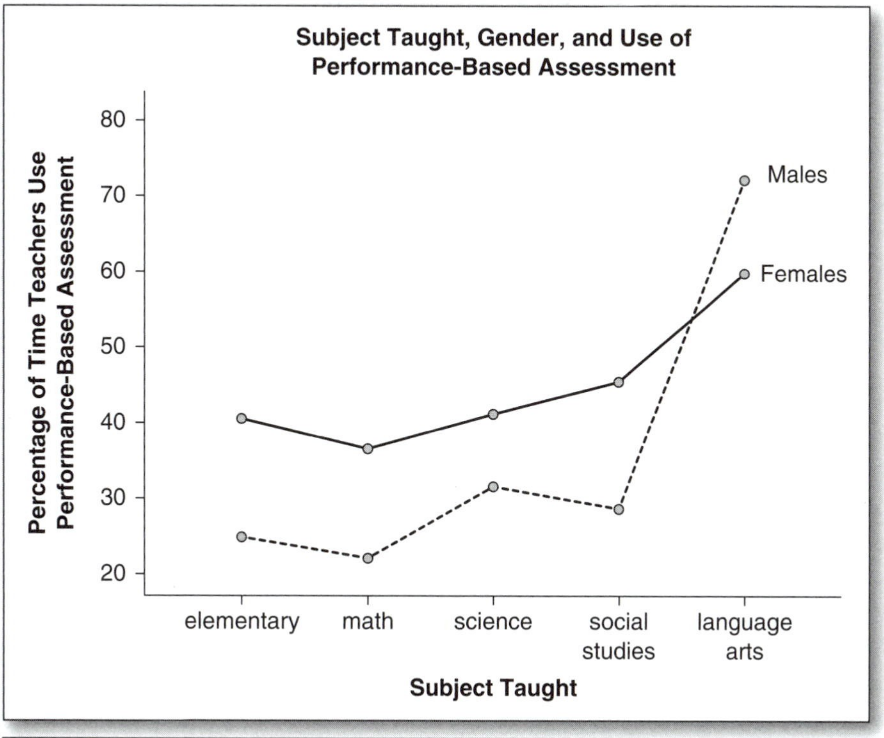

Source: Adapted from Frey & Schmitt, 2010.

Validity of Performance-Based Assessment

Claims for the validity of performance-based assessment are typically based on a line of reasoning that goes like this:

1. Objectively scored formats, such as multiple-choice, rely on recognition and recall, essentially memorization skills. It is difficult to use these formats to make a process (the act of doing something) directly observable. Any number of reasons could explain choosing the correct answer on a traditional test item, including chance, cheating, or "educated" guesses. These are examples of what measurement folks call *construct-irrelevant variance*, differences in student scores due to anything other than the construct of interest: the trait one wishes to measure.

(Continued)

A Closer Look

(Continued)

2. Ask a student to actually do something, however, and observe the performance or analyze the product he or she produces and you probably are almost directly observing the skill or ability of interest.

The relative benefits in increased validity believed to be associated with performance-based assessments are sometimes described as being part of a trade-off. Samuel Messick (1993), an educational psychologist who explored the philosophical nature of assessment validity arguments, described this trade-off as between the greater coverage of a topic that is possible with the use of many short and efficient multiple-choice items (which might be thought of as *content* validity) and the greater depth of understanding and procedural knowledge that is assessable through performance-based assessment.

PORTFOLIOS

In London in the early 1980s, three teachers, Myra Barrs, Hilary Hester, and Sue Ellis, were worried that standardized testing was not adequately measuring their students' literacy skills. As a solution, they created the *Primary Language Record,* a collection of students' writings and other products providing evidence of literacy levels. These individualized collections were seen as a more meaningful, in-depth substitute for a single test score or letter grade, and it gave parents, teachers, administrators, and students a broader understanding of what students knew and could do and how those skills changed over time (Barrs, Ellis, Hester, & Thomas, 1989). By 1991, in the United States, California implemented similar methods to track student progress, the *California Learning Record.* These "portfolios" (named after the large folders that artists carry with them to show their work to others) meant that people could see what students were actually doing, learning, and producing in class by comparing previous work to later work. Teachers could also use portfolios to assess themselves as to which assignments or lectures were presented well or which were unclear to the students. By tracking their own work, it was believed that students would gain insight by seeing their own patterns of behavior and would be inspired to work harder on skill development.

"A portfolio is a purposeful collection of student work that exhibits the student's efforts, progress, and achievements in one or more areas. The collection must include student participation in selecting contents, the criteria for selection, the criteria for judging merit, and evidence of student self-reflection." (Paulson, Paulson, & Meyer, 1991)

Portfolios can provide both formative and summative assessment information. In a sense, they do both because they are a collection of summative assessments representing different units or steps in the developmental process and provide formative feedback along the way (Afflerbach, 2007; Almasi & Fullerton, 2012; Chang & Tseng, 2008; Tubaishat, Lansari, & Al-Rawi, 2009). Portfolios provide samples of a students' ongoing work, such as tests, quizzes, journals, creative writing, and teacher and peer commentary. They can be different shapes and sizes to accommodate any amount of materials. Sometimes they are folders, binders, boxes, or, more and more common now, electronic files. Portfolios are viewed as a way of moving from the teacher being in charge of instruction into a partnership role between the teacher and the students to guide instruction over time. They reflect "a move away from normative, test score, quantitative methods of addressing student performance to more standards-based, authentic, qualitative methods" (McAlpine, 2006, p. 1). What is to be included and how the portfolio will be assessed is a discussion between both the teacher and the student. These are some common characteristics of portfolios:

- They are person-centered, qualitative, and holistic.
- They accentuate the positive (though some portfolios include examples of student work that is less accomplished).
- There is student choice over what to include.
- They provide a rich variety of products.
- They reflect student work over time.
- There are opportunities for reflective self-assessment.

Valencia and Calfee (1991) describe three functions of portfolios: (1) documentation, (2) evaluation, and (3) showcase. A documentation portfolio provides a detailed account of student work and progress over time. It includes a compilation of work, good and bad, and includes assessments of students' work as completed by the teacher or the students themselves. The evaluation portfolio is defined by the standardization of its contents and the process by which the contents are evaluated. All students turn in the same set of products, and a predetermined set of scoring criteria is used. Showcase portfolios encourage students to select and represent their best work. Whatever the purpose of the portfolio, as an assessment tool it affects student learning when students are able to reflect on their work and assess their own progress (Afflerbach, 2007; McDonald, 2012; Tochel et al., 2009).

As an assessment methodology, portfolios have the potential to be used with great validity (Chang, Tseng, Chou, & Chen, 2011; Van der Schaaf, Baartman, & Prins, 2011; Yao, Foster, & Aldrich, 2009). Some research suggests that

A portfolio is a collection of a student's work across time.

portfolios are not always used as intended, however. Sometimes students make little attempt to reflect on their own growth, cannot identify evidence that could be used to demonstrate progress, and draw few conclusions about themselves (Sahakian, 2002; Robertson, Elster, & Kruse, 2004). Regarding reliability, summarizing a portfolio of multiple work products can be difficult to do with any objectivity. A few years ago, the Vermont Department of Education restricted the reporting of portfolio scores because of low inter-rater reliability concerns. A study found that different teachers summarizing the same portfolios only had moderate agreement (Driessen, Van Der Vleuten, Schuwirth, Van Tartwijk, & Vermunt, 2006).

Though portfolios are a tremendous contribution to the tools available for performance-based assessment, they may, unfortunately, be on their way out because of the current *No Child Left Behind*–influenced environment in American schools. Students are now evaluated at the school level, and some administrators are mostly interested in the percentage of students making "adequate yearly progress" (AYP standards), so their use is currently in decline. Portfolios do not provide common standards that are easily quantifiable (Sahakian, 2002).

There is more than a little irony in the decline of this assessment method, because the creation of portfolio assessment strategies was originally a response to the 1980s movement toward standardized testing. Teachers' evaluation of student performance was losing the trust of policymakers and administrators, so teachers had to find a way to produce assessments that people had faith in and that the teachers could defend as valid. Portfolios were meant to be a solution to this growing mistrust (Hirvela & Pierson, 2000). Instead of the pendulum of public opinion swinging back toward classroom teachers, however, it has continued its trajectory toward external accountability (and, some would argue, further away from validity).

PERFORMANCE-BASED ASSESSMENT IN THE SCIENCE CLASSROOM

"First, we have to take a sampling approach to assessment construction. We view the assessments we create as exchangeable for an indefinitely large number of assessments that could be developed. Our intent is to generalize the findings from a sample of assessments to a large domain of science process performance."

Shavelson, Baxter, and Pine (1991, p. 349)

Science as a subject can be thought of as a collection of scientific facts. If so, then traditional paper-and-pencil multiple-choice types of tests are all we need to assess knowledge of the subject. Of course, for most modern classroom teachers, science is an ability or skill, not just a set of facts. Science is something that can be *done*. Performance-based assessment has become a mainstay of the science classroom environment.

To perform the activities of scientists and assess those activities in realistic, meaningful, and applied ways might be time (and cost) prohibitive in the classroom. Shavelson et al. (1991), quoted at the start of this section, present a theoretical framework of performance-based assessment tasks for science education that identifies tasks as *valid* to the extent that they closely represent real-world scientific knowledge, cognitive processes, and behaviors. They suggest a group of *benchmarks*, external tasks, or performance-based indicators that are accepted as evidence of science knowledge and skill, and what they call *surrogates*, indicators that are not the benchmarks themselves but are similar tasks or miniaturized versions of benchmarks. Benchmarks are things like standardized tests of basic science skills given in many states and hands-on investigations that scientists might conduct over the course of a long time or with the aid of large teams and expensive equipment. Surrogates include smaller scale hands-on investigations, notebooks, simulations, and constructed-response tasks.

Shavelson et al. (1991) suggest five guidelines for valid science performance assessments, which essentially require that science assessment be performance-based to be valid:

1. Assessments need to go beyond factual recall and selecting a single correct response and assess students' scientific understanding, reasoning, and problem solving. Assessments should allow for constructed and novel responses.

2. Student participation should be active and hands-on. Experimental apparatus should be used. Assessments should include manipulatives to be held, touched, and examined.

3. Computer software and websites that simulate various scientific procedures might be used as surrogates for benchmark activities, such as real-world investigations.

4. Assessments should reflect what we know about cognitive processes and the way the mind understands phenomena and natural laws. Students' understandings and misunderstandings should be assessed.

5. Scoring should be criterion-referenced, but consistent with curriculum. In this way, administrators will more easily see the alignment between classroom assessments and state testing.

WHAT PERFORMANCE-BASED ASSESSMENT LOOKS LIKE IN THE CLASSROOM

The quality of an assessment is driven by the scoring methods used. The scoring rubric, an organized set of construct-relevant components to a performance and a product with quantified scales that allow for scoring each component, is the scoring system of choice for performance-based assessment. Rubrics are discussed in great detail in Chapter 6, but as a reminder, they make assessment more valid and more reliable if they

- make public relevant criteria of quality,
- score multiple pieces or steps,

- establish performance guidelines, and
- provide detailed, formative feedback (Stevens & Levi, 2005).

Generally speaking, a good scoring rubric makes clear the purpose of a performance-based assessment, the scoring system, and rules for assigning different ratings or values. The purpose should align with clear, academic goals, and the activity should be complex cognitively and match the intended purpose. Criteria should be clear, be positively worded, cover the objectives, and be grade level appropriate. The scoring system should be precise, allow for a range or continuum of performance, and provide useful feedback. Regarding general qualities, rubrics should be organized and free of mechanical errors, and the assessment should reflect real-world expectations of performance.

For performance-based assessments, the assessment itself is made of two pieces, the performance or product that students provide and the rubric used to assess the performance or product. What follows are many real-life examples of rubrics across many common content areas where performance-based assessment is used. *Rubistar* (rubistar.4teachers.org) is a nonprofit website that offers examples of real-world scoring rubrics for dozens of subject areas and grade levels that have been constructed and used by real-life teachers. This incredible resource is described in greater detail in Chapter 6. The examples that follow are taken from the site and are in the public domain. In most cases, only a last name is given as to the creator of these rubrics, so it is hard to give proper credit, but *thank you* to these anonymous classroom teachers for sharing their work.

Writing

Table 7.1 is a rubric based on the *6 traits of writing* model. The teacher has chosen to focus on just four of the six. Table 7.2 is a rubric from another teacher that breaks the six traits down into subcategories.

Another common, and somewhat more traditional, approach to writing assessment is analytical in nature. This approach identifies different pieces of a composition and applies a score to the different pieces. Table 7.3 provides an example of how a persuasive essay might be scored using this approach. There is a goodly amount of text to make the different point objects as concrete as possible.

An example of a hybrid rubric that combines the 6-trait model with analytic scoring is shown in Table 7.4. This rubric also demonstrates how one can

(Text continues on page 180)

Table 7.1 6-Trait Model (Using Just Four Traits); Teacher: Kniep

CATEGORY	4	3	2	1
Flow & Rhythm (Sentence Fluency)	All sentences sound natural and are easy-on-the-ear when read aloud. Each sentence is clear and has an obvious emphasis.	Almost all sentences sound natural and are easy-on-the-ear when read aloud, but 1 or 2 are stiff and awkward or difficult to understand.	Most sentences sound natural and are easy-on-the-ear when read aloud, but several are stiff and awkward or are difficult to understand.	The sentences are difficult to read aloud because they sound awkward, are distractingly repetitive, or difficult to understand.
Word Choice	Writer uses vivid words and phrases that linger or draw pictures in the reader's mind, and the choice and placement of the words seems accurate, natural and not forced.	Writer uses vivid words and phrases that linger or draw pictures in the reader's mind, but occasionally the words are used inaccurately or seem overdone.	Writer uses words that communicate clearly, but the writing lacks variety, punch or flair.	Writer uses a limited vocabulary that does not communicate strongly or capture the reader's interest. Jargon or clichés may be present and detract from the meaning.
Adding Personality (Voice)	The writer seems to be writing from knowledge or experience. The author has taken the ideas and made them "his own."	The writer seems to be drawing on knowledge or experience, but there is some lack of ownership of the topic.	The writer relates some of his own knowledge or experience, but it adds nothing to the discussion of the topic.	The writer has not tried to transform the information in a personal way. The ideas and the way that are expressed seem to belong to someone else.
Focus on Topic (Content)	There is one clear, well-focused topic. Main idea stands out and is supported by detailed information.	Main idea is clear but the supporting information is general.	Main idea is somewhat clear, but there is a need for more supporting information.	The main idea is not clear. There is a seemingly random collection of information.

Table 7.2 6-Trait Model; Teacher: Ms. Duenas

CATEGORY	4	3	2	1
Sources (Content)	All sources used for quotes and facts are credible and cited correctly.	All sources used for quotes and facts are credible and most are cited correctly.	Most sources used for quotes and facts are credible and cited correctly	Many sources used for quotes and facts are less than credible (suspect) and/or are not cited correctly.
Accuracy of Facts (Content)	All supportive facts are reported accurately.	Almost all supportive facts are reported accurately.	Most supportive facts are reported accurately.	NO facts are reported OR most are inaccurately reported.
Support for Topic (Content)	Relevant, telling, quality details give the reader important information that goes beyond the obvious or predictable.	Supporting details and information are relevant, but one key issue or portion of the storyline is unsupported.	Supporting details and information are relevant, but several key issues or portions of the storyline are unsupported.	Supporting details and information are typically unclear or not related to the topic.
Focus on Topic (Content)	There is one clear, well-focused topic. Main idea stands out and is supported by detailed information.	Main idea is clear but the supporting information is general.	Main idea is somewhat clear but there is a need for more supporting information.	The main idea is not clear. There is a seemingly random collection of information.
Introduction (Organization)	The introduction is inviting, states the main topic and previews the structure of the paper.	The introduction clearly states the main topic and previews the structure of the paper, but is not particularly inviting to the reader.	The introduction states the main topic, but does not adequately preview the structure of the paper nor is it particularly inviting to the reader.	There is no clear introduction of the main topic or structure of the paper.

(Continued)

Table 7.2 (Continued)

CATEGORY	4	3	2	1
Conclusion (Organization)	The conclusion is strong and leaves the reader with a feeling that they understand what the writer is "getting at."	The conclusion is recognizable and ties up almost all the loose ends.	The conclusion is recognizable, but does not tie up several loose ends.	There is no clear conclusion, the paper just ends.
Sequencing (Organization)	Details are placed in a logical order and the way they are presented effectively keeps the interest of the reader.	Details are placed in a logical order, but the way in which they are presented/introduced sometimes makes the writing less interesting.	Some details are not in a logical or expected order, and this distracts the reader.	Many details are not in a logical or expected order. There is little sense that the writing is organized.
Transitions (Organization)	A variety of thoughtful transitions are used. They clearly show how ideas are connected.	Transitions clearly show how ideas are connected, but there is little variety.	Some transitions work well; but connections between other ideas are fuzzy.	The transitions between ideas are unclear or nonexistent.
Pacing (Organization)	The pacing is well-controlled. The writer knows when to slow down and elaborate, and when to pick up the pace and move on.	The pacing is generally well-controlled but the writer occasionally does not elaborate enough.	The pacing is generally well-controlled but the writer sometimes repeats the same point over and over, or spends too much time on details that don't matter.	The pacing often feels awkward to the reader. The writer elaborates when there is little need, and then leaves out necessary supporting information.
Word Choice	Writer uses vivid words and phrases that linger or draw pictures in the reader's mind, and the choice and placement of the words seems accurate, natural and not forced.	Writer uses vivid words and phrases that linger or draw pictures in the reader's mind, but occasionally the words are used inaccurately or seem overdone.	Writer uses words that communicate clearly, but the writing lacks variety, punch or flair.	Writer uses a limited vocabulary that does not communicate strongly or capture the reader's interest. Jargon or clichés may be present and detract from the meaning.

CATEGORY	4	3	2	1
Sentence Structure (Sentence Fluency)	All sentences are well-constructed with varied structure.	Most sentences are well-constructed with varied structure.	Most sentences are well-constructed but have a similar structure.	Sentences lack structure and appear incomplete or rambling.
Sentence Length (Sentence Fluency)	Every paragraph has sentences that vary in length.	Almost all paragraphs have sentences that vary in length.	Some sentences vary in length.	Sentences rarely vary in length.
Flow & Rhythm (Sentence Fluency)	All sentences sound natural and are easy-on-the-ear when read aloud. Each sentence is clear and has an obvious emphasis.	Almost all sentences sound natural and are easy-on-the-ear when read aloud, but 1 or 2 are stiff and awkward or difficult to understand.	Most sentences sound natural and are easy-on-the-ear when read aloud, but several are stiff and awkward or are difficult to understand.	The sentences are difficult to read aloud because they sound awkward, are distractingly repetitive, or difficult to understand.
Grammar & Spelling (Conventions)	Writer makes no errors in grammar or spelling that distract the reader from the content.	Writer makes 1–2 errors in grammar or spelling that distract the reader from the content.	Writer makes 3–4 errors in grammar or spelling that distract the reader from the content.	Writer makes more than 4 errors in grammar or spelling that distract the reader from the content.
Capitalization & Punctuation (Conventions)	Writer makes no errors in capitalization or punctuation, so the paper is exceptionally easy to read.	Writer makes 1 or 2 errors in capitalization or punctuation, but the paper is still easy to read.	Writer makes a few errors in capitalization and/or punctuation that catch the reader's attention and interrupt the flow.	Writer makes several errors in capitalization and/or punctuation that catch the reader's attention and greatly interrupt the flow.

(Continued)

Table 7.2 (Continued)

CATEGORY	4	3	2	1
Penmanship (Conventions)	Paper is neatly written or typed with no distracting corrections.	Paper is neatly written or typed with 1 or 2 distracting corrections (e.g., dark cross-outs; bumpy white-out, words written over).	The writing is generally readable, but the reader has to exert quite a bit of effort to figure out some of the words.	Many words are unreadable OR there are several distracting corrections.
Commitment (Voice)	The writer successfully uses several reasons/ appeals to try to show why the reader should care or want to know more about the topic.	The writer successfully uses one or two reasons/ appeals to try to show why the reader should care or want to know more about the topic.	The writer attempts to make the reader care about the topic, but is not really successful.	The writer made no attempt to make the reader care about the topic.
Recognition of Reader (Voice)	The reader's questions are anticipated and answered thoroughly and completely.	The reader's questions are anticipated and answered to some extent.	The reader is left with one or two questions. More information is needed to "fill in the blanks."	The reader is left with several questions.
Adding Personality (Voice)	The writer seems to be writing from knowledge or experience. The author has taken the ideas and made them "his own."	The writer seems to be drawing on knowledge or experience, but there is some lack of ownership of the topic.	The writer relates some of his own knowledge or experience, but it adds nothing to the discussion of the topic.	The writer has not tried to transform the information in a personal way. The ideas and the way they are expressed seem to belong to someone else.

Table 7.3 Analytic Scoring: Persuasive Essay; Teacher: Dr. Castberg

CATEGORY	4	3	2	1
Introduction	The introduction is inviting, provides necessary background information and states the main argument clearly and elegantly.	The introduction provides necessary background information and states the main argument clearly.	The introduction provides some background information and states the main argument but too generally or broadly.	There is no clear introduction of the topic or argument. The paper just starts with body paragraphs.
Body Paragraphs	Each paragraph includes a topic sentence, a well-chosen, persuasive embedded quote. Paragraphs are not repetitive, connect well, and demonstrate a depth of understanding about a narrowly focused issue.	Most paragraphs include a topic sentence, a persuasive embedded quote. Paragraphs are not repetitive, connect well, and demonstrate some understanding about a focused issue.	Most paragraphs are poorly organized. They may or may not include a quote; the quote may or may not be well-chosen and persuasive. Paragraphs are repetitive and demonstrate a vague or general understanding about an issue.	Paragraphs are missing many of the required elements: quotes and/or analysis and/or depth of understanding. Paragraphs are disconnected, and understanding of the issue is lacking.
Conclusion	The conclusion is strong and leaves the reader with a clear sense of what the writer is "getting at." It is not repetitive or predictable. It includes a subtle call for action.	The conclusion is recognizable and ties up almost all the loose ends. It is adequate, although general and predictable.	The conclusion is a mere repetition of the essay without any synthesis. It is predictable and uninspiring.	There is no clear conclusion, the paper just ends.

(Continued)

Table 7.3 (Continued)

CATEGORY	4	3	2	1
Focus and Support	There is one clear, well-focused topic. Main argument stands out and is expertly supported by insightful, reliable and valid sources that are properly quoted and referenced in the body of the essay.	There is one clear, well-focused topic, but may be somewhat general or broad. Main argument stands out, and is supported by reliable and valid sources that are mostly properly quoted and referenced in the body of the essay.	The topic is somewhat general and vaguely defined. Main argument is not altogether clear and is supported by some sources that may not be reliable or may be improperly cited, and/or not referenced in the body of the essay.	The main idea is not clear. There is a seemingly random collection of information with little support.
Capitalization & Punctuation	Writer makes no errors in capitalization or punctuation, so the paper is exceptionally easy to read. No spelling errors. Works cited is included and flawless.	Writer makes 1 or 2 errors in capitalization or punctuation, but the paper is still easy to read. Few spelling errors. Works Cited is included but incomplete or inaccurate in minor ways.	Writer makes enough errors in capitalization and/or punctuation to interrupt the flow of reading. Several spelling errors. Works cited is included but contains major flaws.	Writer makes numerous errors in capitalization and/or punctuation that greatly interrupt the flow. Numerous spelling errors. No Works cited.

Table 7.4 Scoring a 20-Point Essay; Teacher: Mrs. Williams

CATEGORY	4	3	2	1	0
Focus on Topic		Entire essay is focused on the assigned topic and does not stray to unrelated topics.	Most of the essay is focused on the assigned topic but some areas of the essay depart from the assigned topic.	Most of the essay is not focused on the assigned topic.	No essay was turned in.
Introduction		The introduction is clear, engaging and previews the structure of the paper.	One of the previously mentioned aspects of the introduction is lacking.	More than one of the previously mentioned aspects of the introduction is lacking.	No essay was turned in.
Organization		The paper is well organized and details are placed in a logical order. There are no awkward aspects of the paper which leave the reader trying to understand what is being said.	Some areas of the paper are not well organized or not placed in a logical order. There are awkward aspects of the paper which leave the reader trying to understand what is being said.	There are several areas within the paper which are not well organized and are not placed in a logical order. There are several awkward aspects of the paper which leave the reader trying to understand what is being said.	No essay was turned in.

(Continued)

Table 7.4 (Continued)

CATEGORY	4	3	2	1	0
Conclusion		The conclusion is strong, ties the paper together and leaves the reader feeling they understand what the writer was getting at.	One of the previously described aspects of the conclusion is lacking.	More than one of the previously mentioned aspects of the conclusion is lacking.	No essay was turned in.
Mechanics	The number of spelling, punctuation, capitalization and grammar mistakes is 0–1.	The number of spelling, punctuation, capitalization and grammar mistakes is 2–3.	The number of spelling, punctuation, capitalization and grammar mistakes is 4–5.	The number of spelling, punctuation, capitalization and grammar mistakes is 6–7.	The number of spelling, punctuation, capitalization and grammar mistakes is 8 or greater or no paper was turned in.
Presentation	Paper is double spaced using New Roman Times font, size 12, all margins are set at one inch and the paper is 3 full pages long.	One of the previously described aspects is missing.	Two of the previously described aspects are missing.	Three of the previously described aspects are missing.	All four of the previously described aspects are missing or no paper was turned in.

Table 7.5 How Professions Use Math; Teacher: Arlint

CATEGORY	4	3	2	1
Mathematical Reasoning	Uses complex and refined mathematical reasoning.	Uses effective mathematical reasoning	Some evidence of mathematical reasoning.	Little evidence of mathematical reasoning.
Mathematical Errors	90–100% of the steps and solutions have no mathematical errors.	Almost all (85–89%) of the steps and solutions have no mathematical errors.	Most (75–84%) of the steps and solutions have no mathematical errors.	More than 75% of the steps and solutions have mathematical errors.
Checking	The work has been checked by two classmates and all appropriate corrections made.	The work has been checked by one classmate and all appropriate corrections made.	Work has been checked by one classmate but some corrections were not made.	Work was not checked by classmate OR no corrections were made based on feedback.
Strategy/ Procedures	Typically, uses an efficient and effective strategy to solve the problem(s).	Typically, uses an effective strategy to solve the problem(s).	Sometimes uses an effective strategy to solve problems, but does not do it consistently.	Rarely uses an effective strategy to solve problems.
Explanation	Explanation is detailed and clear.	Explanation is clear.	Explanation is a little difficult to understand, but includes critical components.	Explanation is difficult to understand and is missing several components OR was not included.
Neatness and Organization	The work is presented in a neat, clear, organized fashion that is easy to read.	The work is presented in a neat and organized fashion that is usually easy to read.	The work is presented in an organized fashion but may be hard to read at times.	The work appears sloppy and unorganized. It is hard to know what information goes together.
Completion	All problems are completed.	All but one of the problems are completed.	All but two of the problems are completed.	Several of the problems are not completed.

179

Table 7.6   Understanding Geometry; Teacher: Mrs. Spencer

CATEGORY	2 points	1 point	0 points	Total
Definition of Boundary Equation		States correct definition	No definition or incorrect definition	
How Boundary Equation Is Used	Describes how boundary equation is used	Gives example of how boundary equation is used	No description or no example	
Definition of Half-Plane		States correct definition	No definition or incorrect definition	
How Half-Planes Are Used	Describes how half-planes are used	Gives example of how half-planes are used	No description or no example	
Series of Steps	Provides at least 4 steps used in graphing	Provides 3 steps used in graphing	Provides 2 or less steps used in graphing	
Complete Sentences		Writes in complete sentences	Does not write in complete sentences	

differentially weight different components. Notice that *Focus on the Topic* is worth 3 points, while *Mechanics* is worth 4 points.

Mathematics

As a subject, mathematics has a long history of using performance-based assessment, because math is as much about process as it is about knowledge and understanding. Two rubrics are presented here. Table 7.5 is a scoring system based on the ways mathematics is used to solve problems in the real world. (This is a great example of authentic assessment as we explore it in Chapter 8.) Table 7.6 offers a rubric for probing for depth of understanding of some math concepts. It is another example of how different components in a rubric can be weighted differently; notice that the category of "Complete Sentences" is only worth 1 point at most.

Speech

A good speech has structure, with a beginning, middle, and end, and requires good communication skills, eye contact, and appropriate posture. Table 7.7 offers a scoring rubric for a persuasive speech used by a real teacher in the real world. Most of the scorable components are directly observable; this increases the objective, reliable nature of the scoring.

Science

A rubric is presented that treats science assessment as the assessment of *higher order thinking skills*. Table 7.8 represents not only performance-based assessment, but authentic assessment, as well (see Chapter 8). It also assesses an entire group of students at one time, a common dilemma for teachers who make group assignments. Notice how the whole group is evaluated in the "Scientific Knowledge" row.

Athletics and Physical Education

Physical education is primarily about performance. Consequently, it is a field that is rife with performance-based assessment and scoring rubrics. The sample rubric presented in Table 7.9 assesses basketball skills. It uses quantitative language (e.g., rarely, usually, always) but doesn't require actual data collection.

Social Skills

Especially in the primary grades, teachers often wish to develop their students' social skills, their ability to cooperate, collaborate, make friends, and get along. The rubric offered in Table 7.10 assesses collaboration skills while working in a group. In this example, the score values of the columns have been replaced by descriptive words, but there are still scores associated with each point on the scale.

Table 7.7 Scoring a 3–4 Minute Speech; Teacher: Richert

CATEGORY	4	3	2	1
Introduction	Effective "attention getter." Main Points are clearly previewed. Topic is introduced.	Basic "attention getter." MP briefly previewed. Topic is introduced.	"Attention getter," but no MP preview, or MP preview, but no "attention getter." Topic is introduced.	No "attention getter." No MP preview. Topic only.
Body	MPs flow smoothly from one to the next. MPs are given full support.	MPs are clearly organized. MPs are given some support.	MPs need a more definite organization and support.	MPs are not organized or supported.
Conclusion	Conclusion is signaled clearly. MPs clearly summarized.	Conclusion is signaled. MPs are vaguely summarized.	Conclusion is not clearly signaled. MPs are not clearly summarized OR New information is introduced.	Conclusion is not signaled. MPs are not summarized.
Eye Contact	Makes consistently strong eye contact with audience.	Makes more eye contact than not, but in multiple short bursts.	Makes eye contact once or twice with audience for no significant length of time.	No eye contact with audience.
Citing Sources	All sources are cited while speaking.	3 sources are cited while speaking.	2 sources are cited while speaking.	1 source is cited while speaking.
Posture	Appropriate posture at all times.	Alternated between leaning on podium and appropriate posture (more appropriate).	Alternated between leaning on podium and appropriate posture (more leaning).	Leans on podium during entire speech.

Table 7.7

CATEGORY	4	3	2	1
Gestures and Facial Expressions	Appropriate gestures and facial expressions.	Rigid gestures and facial expressions.	Inappropriate gestures and facial expressions (e.g., laughing, tapping on podium).	Lack of facial expression and gestures.
Rate	Consistent rate of speaking.	Rate of speaking is too fast/slow for audience to follow. Occasional "uh/um" or "like."	Hesitant at times, frequent "uh/um" or "like."	Inconsistent rate, seemed unsure about information, frequent "uh/um," "like."
Outline & Bibliography	2 copies of correctly formatted outline, typed. 4 sources cited in correct bibliographic format.	2 copies of correctly formatted outline, typed. 3 sources cited correctly in biblio format OR 4 source not in correct biblio format.	1 copy of correctly formatted outline, typed. 2–3 sources cited correctly in biblio format OR incorrectly formatted outline and incorrectly formatted biblio (2–3sources).	1 copy of outline, incorrectly formatted. 1–2 sources, incorrectly formatted biblio.
Time	3 min – 4 min	Between 2 min 30 sec and 2 min 59 sec OR 4 min 1 sec– 4 min 30 sec	Between 2 min and 2 min 29 sec OR 4 min 31 sec – 5 min	2 min. and less OR over 5 min

Table 7.8 Building a Structure; Teacher: Mr. Youngblood

CATEGORY	4	3	2	1
Modification/ Testing	Clear evidence of troubleshooting, testing, and refinements based on data or scientific principles.	Clear evidence of troubleshooting, testing and refinements.	Some evidence of troubleshooting, testing and refinements.	Little evidence of troubleshooting, testing or refinement.
Function	Structure functions extraordinarily well, holding up under atypical stresses.	Structure functions well, holding up under typical stresses.	Structure functions pretty well, but deteriorates under typical stresses.	Fatal flaws in function with complete failure under typical stresses.
Data Collection	Data taken several times in a careful, reliable manner.	Data taken twice in a careful, reliable manner.	Data taken once in a careful, reliable manner.	Data not taken carefully OR not taken in a reliable manner.
Information Gathering	Accurate information taken from several sources in a systematic manner.	Accurate information taken from a couple of sources in a systematic manner.	Accurate information taken from a couple of sources but not systematically.	Information taken from only one source and/or information not accurate.
Scientific Knowledge	Explanations by all group members indicate a clear and accurate understanding of scientific principles underlying the construction and modifications.	Explanations by all group members indicate a relatively accurate understanding of scientific principles underlying the construction and modifications.	Explanations by most group members indicate relatively accurate understanding of scientific principles underlying the construction and modifications.	Explanations by several members of the group do not illustrate much understanding of scientific principles underlying the construction and modifications.

Table 7.9 Basic Basketball Skills; Teacher: Mr. Langridge

CATEGORY	1	2	3	4
Dribbling	-steady pushing motion, rarely -eyes never up unable to dribble for extended periods of time with either hand	-steady pushing motion sometimes -eyes up rarely -unable to dribble with both hands for extended periods of time	-steady pushing motion almost always eyes up most of the time -able to do this with at least one hand	-steady pushing motion, always -eyes up always -able to do this with both hands
Passing	-almost never hits target -passes are always too fast or slow -not able to catch passes	-rarely hits target -passes are either too fast or too slow most of the time -rarely catches passes	-hits target most of the time -not too fast or hard most of time -able to catch most passes	-always hits target -not too fast or hard not too slow or soft -able to catch passes always
Shooting	-almost never shoots with shooting arm bent and straight -almost never shoots with other hand to side, forming T	-rarely shoots with shooting arm bent and straight -rarely shoots with other hand to side, forming T	-usually shoots with shooting arm bent and straight -usually shoots with other hand to side, forming T	-always shoots with shooting arm bent and straight -always shoots with other arm to side, forming T

185

Table 7.10 3rd Grade Group Behavior Skills; Teacher: Ms. Knisely

CATEGORY	Excellent	Great	Good	Decent	Poor
Stay in Your Own Space	Stays in seat the entire time. (5 points)	Stays in seat most of the time. (4 points)	Stays in seat at least half the time. (3 points)	Stays in seat less than half the time. (2 points)	Out of seat most of the time. (0–1 point)
Participate	Responds on cue all the time. (5 points).	Responds on cue most of the time. (4 points)	Responds on cue at least half the time. (3 points)	Responds on cue less than half the time. (2 points)	Does not respond on cue. (0–1 point)
Take Turns Speaking	Takes turns speaking the entire time. (5 points)	Takes turns speaking most of the time. (4 points)	Takes turns speaking at least half the time. (3 points)	Takes turns speaking less than half the time. (2 points)	Does not let other students respond, interrupts them or answers first. (0–1 point)
Speak in a Nice Voice/ Expression	When talking the student's tone of voice match their words the entire time. (5 points)	When talking the student's tone of voice match their words most of the time. (4 points)	When talking the student's tone of voice match their words at least half the time. (3 points)	When talking the student's tone of voice match their words less than half the time. (2 points)	When the student talks their tone of voice does not match what they are saying the entire time. (0–1 point)
Body Posture	The student sits up in chair, head up, hands to themselves, and feet on the floor the entire time. (5 points)	The student sits up in chair, head up, hands to themselves, and feet on the floor most of the time. (4 points)	The student sits up in chair, head up, hands to themselves, and feet on the floor at least half the time. (3 points)	The student sits up in chair, head up, hands to themselves, and feet on the floor less than half the time. (2 points)	The student does not sit up in their chair, puts head in hands or table, touches other students/ teacher or their things the entire time. (0–1 point)

Table 7.10

Face Front	The student faces forward the entire time. (5 points)	The student faces forward most of the time. (4 points)	The student faces forward at least half the time. (3 points)	The student faces forward less than half the time. (2 points)	The student does not face forward during the lesson. (0–1 point)
Eye Contact	The student looks at the teacher and/or book the entire time. (5 points)	The student looks at the teacher and/or book most of the time. (4 points)	The student looks at the teacher and/or book at least half the time. (3 points)	The student looks at the teacher and/or book less than half the time. (2 points)	The student does not look at the teacher and/or book during the lesson. (0–1 point)
Use Appropriate Voice	Student uses appropriate volume so as not to disturb students not in group the entire time. (5 points)	Student uses appropriate volume so as not to disturb students not in group most of the time. (4 points)	Student uses appropriate volume so as not to disturb students not in group at least half the time. (3 points)	Student uses appropriate volume so as not to disturb students not in group less than half the time. (2 points)	Student does not use appropriate volume and disturbs students not in group. (0–1 point)

Assessing Social Skills

Teachers may wish to assess the social life of their students. How popular are they? Who has the most friends? Who is lonely? A clever, but simple assessment technique called *sociometry* allows teachers to map the friendship patterns in their classroom. By asking questions about students' friends, a picture can be drawn that identifies the popular students, and also highlights possible *isolates,* those students who do not have close friends at school. These pictures are *sociograms.*

There are four steps for creating a sociogram.

1. Ask all the students in your class to answer a question like this: *Who would you like to have at a birthday party?* If they are old enough (say, 4th grade or higher), ask them to rank order the three names regarding who is their first choice, and so on. Sometimes, teachers also ask who students do *not* want at a party.

2. Record all the responses in a table that has each student's name and their three choices. A sample of this table might look like this:

Respondent	1st Choice	2nd Choice	3rd Choice
George	Martha	John	Louis
Martha	George	John	Frank
John	George	Class Hamster	Leroy
Abigail	Margie	John	Throckmorton

3. Use the data from Step 2 to make a matrix of all students in the class. The rows are each student who responded and the columns are each student. For each row, place a + or an X for each of the students they chose. Part of a matrix using the data in our example would look like this:

Students	George	Martha	John	Abigail
George		+	+	
Martha	+		+	
John	+			
Abigail			+	

4. Columns with many plus signs indicate students who are popular or have many friends. Columns with few or no plus signs may be social isolates who have few friends at school. A simple chart can be made that shows students' friendships in a space made up of circles (friends) and arrows (friendships). Arrows with two points mean the students nominated each other; one-way arrows mean that a choice was not reciprocated. In this sociogram, Abigail appears to have the fewest social connections and John seems to be a social leader.

Figure 7.6   Sociogram

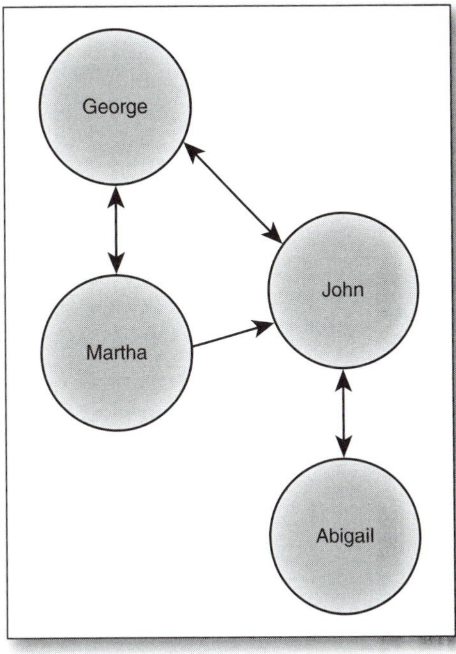

There are many variations on the methods described here. Sometimes, especially with younger children, photos of students are used instead of asking them to list names. Another method avoids asking students to nominate friends and, instead, describes someone (using positive phrases, such as *good friend*, *nice*, or *fun*) and asks students to guess who is being described.

Performing Arts

Two good examples of scoring rubrics for the performing arts are presented here. Table 7.11 suggests a rubric for evaluating actors. Not only can you assess various aspects of acting with this scoring guide, but the clever design allows for the evaluation of more than one student working in the scene together at the same time. Musical ability, as exemplified by drumming, in this case, is assessable through the rubric presented in Table 7.12.

ASSESSING THE ASSESSMENT

Schmitt (2007) created a meta-rubric, a rubric for "scoring" rubrics. It is provided here as a way for you to assess your own rubrics or to develop your own

(Text continues on page 195)

Table 7.11 Acting Class; Teacher: Mr. Schwartz

CATEGORY	Excellent 20–25	Good 14–19	Fair 7–13	Poor 0–6	Actor 1	Actor 2	Actor 3	Actor 4	Actor 5
Full and Thorough Memorization	complete and confident memorization through the whole scene	memorization is good thru most of the scene	memorization has several problems	memorization is a problem thru the whole scene					
Spontaneity	spontaneous performance through the whole scene	spontaneous performance through most of the scene	spontaneous at times	performance is rarely or never spontaneous					
Organic Movement	movement and gesture are totally organic	movement and gesture are often organic	movement and gesture are sometimes organic	movement and gesture are rarely or never organic					
Full Commitment to Character	actor is fully committed	actor is often committed	actor is sometimes committed	actor is rarely or never committed					
Strong Connection With Partner(s)	connection with partner is strong thru the whole scene	connection with partner is strong thru most of the scene	connection with partner is good thru some of the scene	there is little or no connection with partner					

Table 7.12 Percussion; Teacher: Mr. Critchlow

CATEGORY	4	3	2	1
Rhythm	The beat is secure and the rhythms are accurate for the style of music being played.	The beat is secure and the rhythms are mostly accurate. There are a few duration errors, but these do not detract from the overall performance.	The beat is somewhat erratic. Some rhythms are accurate. Frequent or repeated duration errors. Rhythm problems occasionally detract from the overall performance.	The beat is usually erratic and rhythms are seldom accurate, detracting significantly from the overall performance.
Sticking Patterns	Correct sticking. Markings (staccato, sticking patterns, etc.) are executed accurately as directed by the score and/or the conductor.	Sticking patterns are usually correct, though there might be an isolated error. Markings are executed accurately as directed by the score and/or the conductor.	Sticking patterns are rarely secure, but markings are often executed accurately as directed by the score and/or the conductor.	Few secure stickings. Markings are typically not executed accurately.
Technique	Correct technique is used. Palms are down. Fingers are used to control the level of bounce. Hits the instrument with only enough force to make a pleasing, clear sound.	Correct technique is usually used. Hits instrument with a little too much force but incorrect technique does not distract from the quality of the performance.	Correct technique is sometimes used. Incorrect technique distracts from the quality of the performance, but usually does not strike with excessive force.	Correct technique is rarely used. Incorrect technique distracts greatly from the quality of the performance.

Table 7.13 Meta-Rubric for Assessing Rubrics

Purpose				
Criterion	3	2	1	0
Purpose/ Objective (Why)	The purpose/ objective of the assessment is clearly stated and is separate from the performance task.	The purpose/ objective of the assessment is stated as a part of the performance task.	The purpose/ objective of the assessment is *only implied in* the rubric.	Unable to infer the purpose/ objective from the task or the rubric.
Academic Performance & Knowledge Standards (What)	The assessment includes clearly stated *academic performance/ knowledge* standards to which the task is aligned.	The *academic performance/ knowledge* standards can be inferred from the stated objective.	The *academic performance/ knowledge* standards can only be inferred from the performance task or rubric.	Unable to determine the assessment's alignment with *academic performance/ knowledge* standards
Method (How)	The performance event matches the purpose of the assessment providing an accurate measure of students' performance.	The assessment may measure student performance on the learning objective but other information may also be assessed.	While the assessment may provide information about student learning, performance on the objective may be unknown.	The assessment may measure student performance in some area; however, the information provided is *completely* irrelevant to the objective(s).
Cognitive Complexity	The assessment requires students to utilize higher order thinking at the synthesis level or higher.	The assessment requires students to utilize higher order thinking at the analysis level.	The assessment requires students to utilize higher order thinking at the application level.	The assessment requires students to utilize only knowledge/ comprehension level thinking.

Source: From Schmitt, 2007.

Table 7.13 (Continued)

	Criteria			
Criterion	3	2	1	0
Clarity/Detail	Performance criteria are clearly stated and each degree of performance is specifically detailed.	Performance criteria are stated or implied and each degree of performance is outlined with some detail.	Performance criteria are stated or implied but only one degree of performance is detailed.	Performance criteria may be stated or implied but the degrees of performance are absent.
Wording (Positive/ Negative)	All criteria/degrees of performance are stated using positive vocabulary designed to motivate students.	The majority of criteria /degrees of performance are stated using positive vocabulary to motivate students.	At least one of the criteria/degree of performance is stated using positive vocabulary.	All criteria/degrees of performance are stated using negative vocabulary.
Content Coverage	All criteria/degrees of performance reflect quality performance for the specified/implied objective(s).	The majority of criteria /degrees of performance reflect quality performance for the specified/implied objective(s).	At least one criterion/ degree of performance reflects quality performance for the specified/implied objective(s).	Criteria/degrees of performance fail to reflect quality performance for the specified/implied objective(s).
Grade Level Expectation (GLE)	All criteria/degrees of performance are appropriate for the grade assessed.	The majority of criteria /degrees of performance are appropriate for the grade assessed.	At least one criterion/ degree of performance is appropriate for the grade assessed.	Criteria/degrees of performances fail to reflect appropriately for the grade assessed.

(Continued)

Table 7.13 (Continued)

	General Qualities			
Criterion	3	2	1	0
Authenticity	The setting allows students to thoroughly complete the performance criteria though use of a "real-world" task.	The setting allows students to complete the performance criteria though use of a simulated "real-world" task.	While the setting may allow students to complete the performance criteria, the task is less "authentic" in nature.	The setting hinders students' ability to complete performance task.
Organization	The organizational structure of the documents allows for the criteria, degrees of performance, and scale to be clearly identified.	The organizational structure of the documents makes it difficult to clearly identify one of the following: criteria, degrees of performance, or scale.	The organizational structure of the documents makes it difficult to clearly identify two of the following: criteria, degrees of performance, or scale.	The organizational structure of the documents makes it difficult to clearly identify all of the following: criteria, degrees of performance, or scale.
Spelling/ Grammar	The document is free of errors associated with the standard conventions of writing (eg. spelling, grammar, etc.).	1–3 Minor errors associated with the standard conventions of writing (eg. spelling, grammar, etc.) are present but do not interfere with meaning or readability.	4–6 Errors associated with the standard conventions of writing (eg. spelling, grammar, etc.) are present making readability difficult.	7+ errors associated with the standard conventions of writing (eg. spelling, grammar, etc.) are present making the document difficult to read and understand.

assessments. Practice applying it to the sample rubrics presented in this chapter. How well do they perform?

Mr. Wilcken Wonders What His Students Can Do (Part II)

The next day, Mr. Wilcken told his students, "The 'test' for this unit will be a debate that will take place on Wednesday." This was the first time that his students had participated in a debate. Lizzy raised her hand first with questions. "How will we be graded, and will this this be a group activity?"

"Lizzy, great questions. This will be a group activity, but you will receive an individual grade on your presentation of information. I have a scoring rubric that I will use to score your presentation that I am handing out now. What questions does anyone have over this rubric? Anthony."

"Why are there two sections?"

"You will be graded on both the accuracy of the information you present and whether it supports your position. If you look next to the title it tells you the point value of each category. I am most interested in the information you know, and I have assigned more points to that category, but at the same time I want you to explain why you believe what you do. I want you to know the information well enough that you can carry on a conversation with your fellow classmates in the debate and also be able to argue for your side. The rubric also asks you to turn your notes in to me, so please do not think that I just want you to wing it. I want you to prepare solid arguments."

Alec asked, "You have put on here that we have to cite our sources. Can we use anything or just the textbook?"

"You can use sources on my website but nothing outside of that. When you give a statistic or information that the other side or I question, you will need to provide the source of that quote. The rubric says that to get all the points, you need to have six citations in your notes *and* present at least three of them in you presentation. Please do not forget that during your presentations. Are you guys ready to choose sides?"

When Debate Day came around, Mr. Wilcken actually scored the presenters during the presentations. He had a great time watching the students express themselves and engage in a meaningful analysis of American history. He had always been confident in the past that his tests told him what his students *knew*, but he was surprised to see what his students could *do*.

THINGS TO THINK ABOUT

1. How do you know performance-based assessment "when you see it"?

2. What is easy and what is hard about designing an assessment with the most important performance-based characteristics?

3. What is it about those subjects that invite performance-based assessment approaches as compared with those areas for which traditional paper-and-pencil assessment seems best?

4. What tips would you give a colleague for designing a high-quality scoring rubric?

Looking Back in This Chapter

Performance-based assessment is a valid and reliable approach when well designed for the evaluation of a skill or ability. Descriptions and examples of real-world performance-based assessments for writing, math, speech, science, physical education, social skills, and the performing arts are provided. The chapter ends with a "meta-rubric" to evaluate the quality of performance-based assessment rubrics.

ON THE WEB

Source for hundreds of teacher-made rubrics for scoring performance-based assessments rubistar.4teachers.org

Generic scoring-guide maker for performance-based assessments
http://www.mcasmentor.com/interactiverub ric.pdf

A variety of free sociogram utilities for assessing student social skills
http://free.windows9download.net/download/sociogram-template.html

The process one county's schools use to develop performance-based assessment tasks
http://www.pgcps.pg.k12.md.us/~elc/design steps.html

STUDENT STUDY SITE

Visit **www.sagepub.com/frey** to access additional study tools including eFlashcards, web quizzes, web resources, additional rubrics, and links to SAGE journal articles.

REFERENCES

Afflerbach, P. (2007). *Understanding and using reading assessment, K–12.* International Reading Association.

Airasian, P. W. (2001). *Classroom assessment: Concepts and applications.* New York, NY: McGraw-Hill.

Almasi, J. F., & Fullerton, S. K. (2012). *Teaching strategic processes in reading.* New York, NY: Guilford Press.

Barrs, M., Ellis, S., Hester, H., & Thomas, A. (1989). *The primary language record handbook for teachers.* United Kingdom: Inner London Education Authority.

Chang, C. C., & Tseng, K. H. (2008). Use and performances of web-based portfolio assessment. *British Journal of Educational Technology, 40*(2), 358–370.

Chang, C. C., Tseng, K. H., Chou, P. N., & Chen, Y. H. (2011). Reliability and validity of web-based portfolio peer assessment: A case study for a senior high school's students taking computer course. *Computers & Education, 57*(1), 1306–1316.

Driessen, E., Van Der Vleuten, C., Schuwirth, L., Van Tartwijk, J., & Vermunt, J. (2006). The use of qualitative research criteria for portfolio assessment as an alternative to reliability evaluation: A case study. *Medical Education, 39,* 214–220.

Frey, B. B., & Schmitt, V. L. (2007). Coming to terms with classroom assessment. *Journal of Advanced Academics, 18*(3), 402–423.

Frey, B. B., & Schmitt, V. L. (2010). Teachers' classroom assessment practices. *Middle Grades Research Journal, 5*(3), 107–117.

Gullickson, A. R. (1985). Student evaluation techniques and their relationship to grade and curriculum. *Journal of Educational Research, 79*(2), 96–100.

Hirvela, A., & Pierson, H. (2000). Portfolios: Vehicles for authentic self-assessment. In G. Ekbatani & H. Pierson (Eds.), *Learner-directed assessment in ESL* (pp. 105–126). Mahwah, NJ: Lawrence Erlbaum.

Kubiszyn, T., & Borich, G. (2003). *Educational testing and measurement: Classroom application and practice* (7th ed.). Hoboken, NJ: Wiley.

Madaus, G. F., & O'Dwyer, L. M. (1999, May). A short history of performance assessment: Lessons learned. *Phi Delta Kappan,* 688–695.

McAlpine, D. (2006). *Portfolio assessment: G & T related reading on school policies and programmes.* Retrieved from http://www.tki.org.nz/gifted/reading/assessment/portfolio

McDonald, B. (2012). Portfolio assessment: Direct from the classroom. *Assessment & Evaluation in Higher Education, 37*(3), 335–347.

Mertler, C. A. (2003). *Classroom assessment: A practical guide for educators.* Los Angeles, CA: Pyrczak.

Messick, S. (1993). Trait equivalence as construct validity of score interpretation across multiple methods of measurement. In R. E. Bennett & W. C. Ward (Eds.), *Construction versus choice in cognitive measurement.* Hillsdale, NJ: Lawrence Erlbaum.

Mueller, J. (2005). *Authentic assessment toolbox.* Retrieved from http://jonathan.mueller.faculty.noctrl.edu/toolbox/

Oosterhof, A. (2003). *Developing and using classroom assessments.* Englewood Cliffs, NJ: Prentice Hall.

Paulson, F. L., Paulson, P. R., & Meyer, C. A. (1991). What makes a portfolio a portfolio? *Educational Leadership, 48*(5), 60–63.

Popham, W. J. (1997). What's wrong and what's right with rubrics. *Educational Leadership, 55*(2), 72–76.

Robertson, J. F., Elster, S., & Kruse, G. (2004). Portfolio outcome assessment: Lessons learned. *Nurse Educator, 29*(2), 52–53.

Sahakian, P. (2002). The birth and death of portfolio assessment. *Quarterly, 24*(1).

Schmitt, V. L. (2007). *The quality of teacher-developed rubrics for assessing student performance in the classroom.* Unpublished doctoral dissertation, University of Kansas.

Shavelson, R. J., Baxter, G. P., & Pine, J. (1991). Performance assessment in science. *Applied Measurement in Education, 4*(4), 347–362.

Stevens, D. D., & Levi, A. J. (2005). *Introduction to rubrics: An assessment tool to save grading time, convey effective feedback, and promote student learning.* Sterling, VA: Stylus.

Stiggins, R. J. (1991). Assessment literacy. *Phi Delta Kappan, 72*(7), 534–539.

Taylor, C. S., & Nolen, S. B. (2005). *Classroom assessment: Supporting teaching and learning in real classrooms.* Upper Saddle River, NJ: Pearson.

Tochel, C., Haig, A., Hesketh, A., Cadzow, A., Beggs, K., Colthart, I., & Peacock, H. (2009). The effectiveness of portfolios for post-graduate assessment and education: BEME Guide No 12. *Medical Teacher, 31*(4), 299–318.

Tubaishat, A., Lansari, A., & Al-Rawi, A. (2009). E-portfolio assessment system for an outcome-based information technology curriculum. *Journal of Information Technology Education, 8*, 43–53.

Valencia, S. W., & Calfee, R. (1991). The development and use of literacy portfolios for students, classes, and teachers. *Applied Measurement in Education, 4*(4), 333–345.

Van der Schaaf, M., Baartman, L., & Prins, F. (2012). Exploring the role of assessment criteria during teachers' collaborative judgment processes of students' portfolios. *Assessment & Evaluation in Higher Education, 37*(7), 847–860.

Yao, Y., Foster, K., & Aldrich, J. (2009). Interrater reliability of a team-scored electronic portfolio. *Journal of Technology and Teacher Education, 17*(2), 253–275.

CHAPTER 8
AUTHENTIC ASSESSMENT

Looking Ahead in This Chapter

A modern wrinkle in classroom assessment is the movement toward "authentic" assessment. Defining what makes assessment *authentic* is not a simple matter, though. Methods for ensuring that assessment is authentic and scored reliably are presented. This chapter also shares many real-world examples of authentic assessment across many subjects and grade levels. A research-based scoring rubric that can be used to assess the authenticity of an assessment is included at the end of the chapter.

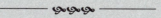

Objectives

After studying this chapter, you should be able to

- Identify the characteristics of assessment that make it authentic
- Explain the reasons today's teachers wish to make their assessments authentic
- Design authentic assessments that can be scored fairly and objectively
- Identify authentic assessment tasks for different populations and subject areas
- Describe what a schoolwide approach to authentic assessment might look like

Mr. Hernandez Gets Real

"All right, it is time to start math, so please get your homework from yesterday with a red pen to grade," Mr. Hernandez said.

Riel started complaining and was slowing pulling out his math book from his desk. He took forever finding a red pen to grade the homework. Mr. Hernandez asked students to open to Chapter 14 over the measures of central tendency— mean, median, mode. "Riel, face the front please. Open your book please."

Now Riel began complaining about how stupid math is. Mr. Hernandez continued with the lesson, working a few examples on the board, having students work a few, and then assigning another worksheet for additional practice. Riel got the worksheet, put it in his folder without working on it, and then started making faces.

"Have you completed your assignment?"

"Almost. I can do the rest at home though."

"Let me see it, please." Looking at a blank assignment, Mr. Hernandez said, "Let me watch you do a few to make sure you understand what we are doing."

"I know *how* to do it; I don't know why we *have* to do it. When am I ever going to have to calculate the mode of anything in my life? I have never heard my mom or dad use the word *mode*, so why do I have to learn it?"

That was a good question. Mr. Hernandez had thought about this before, of course. He had heard the "why do we need to know this?" question before. It was a dilemma he had faced when it came to assessment, as well. Usually the way he tested for a topic or a skill wasn't very much like the way the real world would expect that knowledge or ability to be used. It was a problem he had always struggled with for much of what he taught. This time, though, he began to think of a more permanent solution to the problem . . .

(To Be Continued)

For decades, one of the criticisms leveled at education by some is that students aren't being equipped with the right tools to do well in the real world (e.g., on the job, in college, in a democracy, in an information-driven economy), and schools are constantly evaluating and modifying curricula to meet the needs of "the marketplace." It makes sense, then, that a parallel concern in classroom assessment would arise, and a growingly accepted principle in the modern world of classroom assessment is that it is best if assessments are "realistic," whatever that means.

Of course, there is something intrinsically artificial about testing situations, and it may create a paradox to attempt to test reality. A classroom teacher may find it difficult (and perhaps it is theoretically impossible) to observe student classroom performance in ways that reflect how students would perform outside the classroom. Nevertheless, it is reasonable on its face that assessment tasks that somehow match real-world tasks and expectations should provide a more valid picture of the student skills that matter most, those skills and knowledge sets that prepare students for success in whatever comes next for them in the world. For example, it is clear that in the real world students do not answer multiple-choice questions very often, so any multiple-choice test is bound to be more artificial than, for example, asking students to write a persuasive letter or e-mail.

Performance Assessment and Authentic Assessment

Good Question!

Q: Is authentic assessment the same as performance-based assessment?

A: A simple question with an almost simple answer. And an important enough question that it was asked before in Chapter 1. Let's start with definitions of those terms. We have been defining performance-based assessment as *assessment that requires examinees to perform or produce something for evaluation that is intended to assess skill or ability.* Let's use the simplest definition of authentic assessment (though this chapter explores the usefulness of more complex definitions): *Assessment that aligns with real-world tasks and expectations.* So the two approaches to assessment are not the same. Certainly, some performance-based assessments are authentic. The performance-based format, because it usually includes an intrinsically meaningful task and assesses generalizable skills, lends itself to authenticity. But one could easily design a performance-based assessment that is not authentic. It is the way one assesses that determines whether it is authentic, not simply whether one is assessing skill or basic knowledge.

IN SEARCH OF "AUTHENTIC" ASSESSMENT

The development of standardized testing procedures and the statistical methods of analyzing items and test scores, beginning early in the 20th century, brought the tools of *science* to the *art* of education and classroom assessment. As the emphasis on standardized test administration and performance grew to eclipse the perceived value of other assessment approaches, however, criticisms of the artificially low level of task complexity and lack of teacher control in large-scale objectively scored testing resulted in a movement to return classroom assessment to a more realistic, student-centered approach that measured more complex and deeper student thinking. This approach has been labeled as **authentic assessment**.

A frequent piece of advice given to teachers designing their own assessments is that the *best* classroom assessments are *authentic* (Archbald & Newmann, 1988; Burke, 2009; Gronlund, 2003; Swaffield, 2011; Wiggins, 1989; Wilson & Schwier, 2012), which in most textbooks and in teacher training materials is usually defined as some version of "realistic" or "mirroring the real world." However, while most agree that "authentic" assessment is best practice, there are a variety of definitions of authenticity presented in the research literature and the teachings of experts in classroom assessment.

The earliest reference to *authentic* tests is likely that made in a book critical of standardized testing by Archbald and Newmann in 1988. Newmann argued that assessment is authentic if it assesses tasks that "have meaning or value beyond success in school" (Newmann, Brandt, & Wiggins, 1998, p. 19). The other early advocate, and the most cited, is Grant Wiggins. "'Authentic' refers to the situational or contextual realism of the proposed tasks," he tells us (Newmann et al., 1998, p. 20). However, while many others also speak of authentic in the context of application outside the classroom, some don't, and some emphasize other aspects of assessments as "authentic." For example, Wiggins and early advocates of authenticity emphasized the importance of taking a mastery approach in the assessment process (i.e., using a criterion-referenced philosophy with a goal of moving all students toward the same teacher-determined level of mastery), although most others who wrote later pay little attention to that component.

If the field recommends that teachers should do a particular "thing," it is important to know what that thing is. What criteria should be used in determining whether any specific teacher-made assessment is authentic and, therefore, produces the benefits presumably associated with authenticity? A recent study reviewed hundreds of journal articles, presentations, books, and dissertations to identify concrete criteria for evaluating the authenticity of an assessment (Frey, Schmitt, & Allen, 2009). Surprisingly, beyond the simple requirement that assessments should be realistic (whatever that means), nine different components or dimensions were identified in the literature as characteristics of authentic assessment.

These different dimensions that define authenticity amount to a nice list of qualities to which all classroom assessment, regardless of format, can aspire. Authentic assessment is defined in a wide variety of ways, usually including one or more of these nine characteristics, which can be grouped into three broad categories:

- The context of the assessment
  - Realistic activity or context.
  - The task is performance-based.
  - The task is cognitively complex.
- The role of the student
  - A defense of the answer or product is required.
  - The assessment is formative.
  - Students collaborate with each other or with the teacher.
- The scoring
  - The scoring criteria are known or student developed.
  - Multiple indicators or portfolios are used for scoring.
  - The performance expectation is *mastery*.

Notice that two components of authenticity are two of our broad approaches to modern classroom assessment; authentic assessment should be *performance-based* and *formative*. This illustrates the overlapping understanding in the field as to what *authenticity* means as a distinct assessment philosophy. Table 8.1 presents a small sampling of the different definitions of authentic assessment one finds across textbooks and research articles. Some experts emphasize the realism aspect, some stress the importance of student participation or collaboration in the assessment process, and some place importance on the scoring criteria or the portfolio nature (multiple indicators or samples of work) of the assessment.

Defining Authentic Assessment

Q: I understand that different researchers define authentic assessment differently, but this is a textbook, right? Can't you just provide a simple definition, if we promise to remember that it is a complicated issue?

A: Fair enough. Assessment is authentic when the tasks, content, expectations, and evaluation methods of the assessment are similar to the meaningful tasks, content, expectations, and evaluation methods outside the classroom in the real world. The real world for students depends on their age; it could be playing and socializing with others, engaging in higher education, or performing on the job, now or in the future.

Good Question!

Table 8.1 Varying Definitions of Authentic Assessment

	Context			Student Role			Scoring		
	realistic activity or context	performance-based	cognitively complex	defense required	formative assessment	collaborative	known or student developed criteria	multiple indicators or portfolios	mastery expectation
Abernethie, 2006	■	■				■	■		
Archbald, 1991	■	■							■
Darling-Hammond, Ancess, & Falk, 1995	■		■						
Dez, Moon, & Meyer, 1992	■				■				
Dutt-Doner & Maddox, 1998					■			■	
Engel, Pulley, & Rybinski, 2003	■								
French, 2003	■		■						
Green, 1998	■						■		
Herrington & Oliver, 2000	■		■			■			
Jolly & Kettler, 2000	■		■			■			
Kellaghan & Madaus, 1993		■							
Lawton, 2000							■		
Maden & Taylor, 2001	■						■	■	
Meisels, 1996		■					■		
Meyer, 1992	■	■							
Moorcroft, Desmarais, Hogan, & Bekowitz, 2000	■	■							
Mueller, 2005			■						
Newmann, Brandt, & Wiggins, 1998			■						
Paris & Ayres, 1994					■				
Ratcliff, 2001	■								
Schnitzer, 1993							■		
Spinelli, 1998	■				■	■			
Stripling, 1993		■							
Suen, 1997			■						
Torrance, 1993		■							
Wiggins, 1989	■			■					■

Source: Adapted from Frey, Schmitt, & Allen, 2009.

Note: Shaded areas indicate presence of the component.

WHAT WE KNOW ABOUT AUTHENTIC ASSESSMENT

Advocates for authentic assessment suggest that assessment systems that focus on higher-order thinking skills, problem solving, investigation, and analysis (some of the key real-world skills) can drive improved teaching and curriculum coverage (Torrance, 2009). These perceived strengths of authentic assessment are difficult to evaluate in the current political and policy environment that now treats assessment as a critical step in the school improvement process (and, of late, critical data in evaluating teachers).

Scores on tests are no longer treated as indicators of learning, but more and more often they have *become* the outcome of interest. Learning is not the goal; high test scores are the goal. Of course, the tests in this perspective are typically large-scale standardized tests, not teacher-made classroom assessments, but, nevertheless, the national discussions about education tend to merge summative tests with curriculum and classroom objectives as if they are all the same thing. The assessment *is* the objective. Consequently, this sort of risky thinking can be fueled by any suggestion that an assessment approach can improve teaching. The point as it applies to authentic assessment, though, is reasonable. Assessment that involves students collaboratively in identifying criteria for quality of performance, choosing tasks or questions that require thinking at the high levels of Bloom's Taxonomy (for instance), and developing realistic problems or complex creative activities to evaluate requires instruction, teaching examples, and modeling that supports development of the necessary cognitive skills and knowledge base. Once outcomes are authentic, teaching should ultimately become integrated with assessment.

A Closer Look

Knowledge and Context

A theory about conceptual knowledge and the difficulty that students have transferring that knowledge to other situations suggests that abstract learning generalizes better when it occurs in multiple settings with students playing multiple roles. If true, then authentic assessment would seem to be the best approach to support generalization and transfer.

Brown, Collins, and Duguid's (1989) *Theory of Situated Cognition* is based on research that found, contrary to classic beliefs by educators for centuries, that conceptual knowledge cannot easily be transferred out of a specific context and applied to a new problem. Instead, the theory goes, knowledge is situated and is part of the activity, context, and even culture in which it is developed and learned. An

(Continued)

(Continued)

instruction and assessment strategy that the authors call **cognitive apprenticeship** is suggested as an alternative to traditional practice.

Cognitive apprenticeship is a collaborative approach that emphasizes group learning. Key components of the instructional and (performance) assessment tasks include these:

Collective problem solving. Groups act as more than just separate insights that are combined and cataloged. They often produce results that are more than just the sum of parts.

Displaying multiple roles. Students need to understand different parts of the process, different pieces of the product. Opportunities are created for students to play different roles in the activity, and by adding a reflective component, the task becomes more authentic.

Confronting ineffective strategies and misconceptions. Authentic assessment includes identifying what does not work or what is wrong. The discussions and observations available in group interactions allow for presenting misunderstandings.

Assessing collaborative work skills. The real world of work requires working together. Collaborative tasks allow for assessment of collaborative skills as students work and learn as a group.

It turns out that using authentic assessment well can be tough. After reviewing a series of studies of implementation of authentic assessment systems in schools a few years ago across the United Kingdom, Torrance (1995) concluded that teachers "had enormous difficulty in interpreting, conducting and assessing the tasks—precisely because they were 'authentic', they were too complicated to communicate easily . . . and too demanding for teachers to conduct under ordinary classroom conditions" (p. 55). He suggests that teachers' willingness and ability to adopt new assessment approaches is influenced by their long-standing notions of what assessment is and what its purpose is. Authentic assessment might be adopted more easily if it is viewed as a framework for assessment, as opposed to a particular distinctive approach. In other words, performance-based assessment, formative assessment, and even traditional assessment might benefit, in terms of validity, from the layering on of authentic elements to the established components of these other more accepted approaches.

THE CASE FOR AUTHENTIC ASSESSMENT

Let's assume that, whatever the precise definition of authentic assessment is (or should be), it includes the dimensions of realism, student involvement, and multiple components for scoring. Those basic aspects have strong support across most experts. What, then, makes that approach a best practice? What is the theoretical mechanism by which the approach should work? What makes authentic assessment valid?

Judith T. M. Gulikers (2006), a Dutch researcher, suggests several reasons for embracing authentic assessment. Though writing primarily about college students and others training for specific jobs, her conclusions also make sense regarding elementary and secondary school. First, contextualizing assessment in interesting, real-life tasks is a "crucial element" of competency-based assessment that is consistent with modern approaches to education. Second, authenticity should increase validity. This could happen in several ways. Construct validity (i.e., the assessment measures the trait of interest) should be increased when tasks "represent the real-life problems of the knowledge domain assessed and that the thinking process that experts use to solve the problem in real life are also required by the assessment task" (p. 21). Further, the common assessment concern of underrepresenting the construct can be countered by providing a richly detailed context, which is frequently seen in authentic assessment and in real life. Another potential validity benefit suggested by Gulikers has to do with the process by which assessment tends to eventually drive instruction. By focusing the assessment on real-world skills and expectations, the curriculum remains likewise focused, as does instruction.

Gulikers suggests two mechanisms by which authentic assessment might influence student learning. This would place authentic assessment in the same rarified air as formative assessment—a classroom assessment approach that can actually increase learning. First, it may stimulate a "deep study" approach leading to greater understanding and skill development. Second, authentic assessment may increase student motivation to learn when tasks are seen as relevant and useful.

Theories of Learning

There is a classic theory of how student learning happens based on the behavior of students, and there is a modern theory of learning, which focuses on how the mind works. As one might expect, the modern theory is more supportive of modern classroom assessment approaches like authentic assessment.

ABC Model

The traditional theory explains learning by describing the classroom as a series of (A)ntecedents, the environmental context that leads to some behavior; the

(Continued)

A Closer Look

(Continued)

(B)ehavior of interest; and the (C)onsequences, which are whatever happens to the student after the behavior. For example, the teacher lectures (Antecedent), the student takes notes (Behavior), and then the student receives a high score on the test (Consequence).

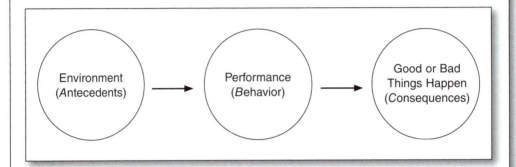

Cognitive Model

A recent theory of learning (starting to appear about 40 years ago, which is just yesterday in terms of human civilization) understands student learning as a cognitive process. The teacher and student bring certain elements to the process—the student has particular characteristics (intelligence, skills, experience,

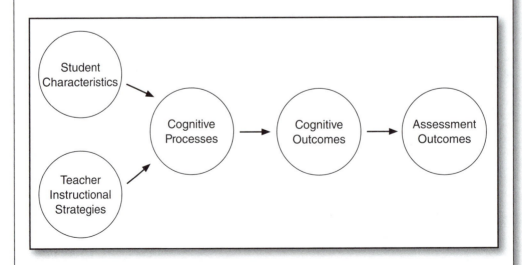

motivation) and the teacher provides some instruction. This results in some thinking inside the head of the student, learning occurs, and assessment makes that learning observable.

Tombari and Borich (1999), in a nice guide on applying authentic assessment in the classroom, point out that the behavioral ABC model envisions that the goal of a classroom environment is to produce correct answers on tests. The cognitive model assumes the goal of good teaching is to promote good thinking, the smart, cognitive processes that result in those correct answers (Borich & Tombari, 2004). This is clearly consistent with one goal of authentic assessment, to produce what Wiggins (1989) and others call healthy "habits of mind."

Reality as a Construct

Teachers might disagree with students and students might disagree with each other about whether a particular assignment or assessment task is realistic and meaningful. It depends on one's individualized experiences and perceptions (Gulikers, 2006). Teachers must choose tasks they consider realistic. This is easier said than done. What is reality, after all?

This big question about the nature of reality is, of course, one of the major philosophical questions of modern civilization. A famous story, Plato's *Allegory of the Cave*, provides a metaphor for both understanding reality and, usefully for us, interpreting test scores as mere shadowy indications of student ability and knowledge. Plato writes of an imagined conversation between a teacher, Socrates, and a student, Glaucon.

Socrates: And now, let me show in a figure how far our nature is enlightened or unenlightened: – Behold! human beings living in an underground cave, which has a mouth open towards the light and reaching all along the cave; here they have been from their childhood, and have their legs and necks chained so that they cannot move, and can only see before them, being prevented by the chains from turning round their heads. Above and behind them a fire is blazing at a distance, and between the fire and the prisoners there is a raised way; and you will see, if you look,

(Continued)

(Continued)

	a low wall built along the way, like the screen which marionette players have in front of them, over which they show the puppets
Glaucon:	I see.
Socrates:	And do you see, men passing along the wall carrying all sorts of vessels, and statues and figures of animals made of wood and stone and various materials, which appear over the wall? Some of them are talking, others silent.
Glaucon:	You have shown me a strange image, and they are strange prisoners.
Socrates:	Like ourselves, and they see only their own shadows, or the shadows of one another, which the fire throws on the opposite wall of the cave?
Glaucon:	True, how could they see anything but the shadows if they were never allowed to move their heads?
Socrates:	And of the objects which are being carried in like manner they would only see the shadows?
Glaucon:	Yes.
Socrates:	And if they were able to converse with one another, would they not suppose that they were naming what was actually before them?
Glaucon:	Very true.
Socrates:	To them, the truth would be literally nothing but the shadows of the images.

The Republic, Plato (Lindsay, 1991)

The choices teachers make when they use authentic assessment are twofold: Determine what is authentic and then determine a way of producing scores that represent reality. Whatever that is.

SCORING AUTHENTIC ASSESSMENTS

If one applies the nine key dimensions of authenticity, some characteristics hinder reliability, while others should increase reliability. The dimensions of authenticity overlap substantially with performance-based assessment; consequently, authentic assessment shares some of the same reliability issues.

Chapter 7 discusses the scoring concerns with performance assessments in general.

Subjective assessment leads to subjective scoring, so inter-rater reliability might be a problem for the authentic assessment format. On the other hand, if the scoring criteria themselves are created collaboratively with students, this suggests that both the teacher and the students may share a fairly precise understanding of how the criteria should be applied. A solid scoring rubric developed with input from all members of the learning community may provide enough concrete guidance that the subjective nature of rubric scoring is lessened. Gipps (1995) examined a series of authentic assessments put into place across Great Britain and did indeed find that the subjective nature of scoring authentic assessment tasks resulted in poor inter-rater reliability both between teachers and within individual teachers (scoring the same products differently on different occasions). The British assessments, however, were national, standardized (or intended to be) tests and developed administratively. These were not individual classroom assessments developed collaboratively with student involvement.

One of the characteristics of authentic assessment that are commonly emphasized among scholarly publications is that scoring for authentic assessment should be based on multiple indicators, at a minimum, and based on a portfolio of work products at best. As Chapter 2 explained, internal reliability, the consistency of scores across the pieces, tasks, and items within an assessment, often increases as the number of those items increases. Simply put, scores based on a large number of subscores tend to be more reliable. This aspect of authentic assessment, then, could help with reliability, perhaps protecting against the chance element of subjective scoring.

WHAT AUTHENTIC ASSESSMENT LOOKS LIKE IN THE CLASSROOM

"I can't claim to be an authority on anything, but I can honestly say that certain matters absolutely fascinate me, and that I write about them all the time. The two basic topics which fascinate me are 'What is reality?' and 'What constitutes the authentic human being?' . . . I consider that the matter of defining what is real—that is a serious topic, even a vital topic. And in there somewhere is the other topic, the definition of the authentic human. Because the bombardment of pseudo-realities begins to produce inauthentic humans very quickly, spurious humans—as fake as the data pressing at them from all sides."

Philip K. Dick, Science Fiction Author (1928–1982)

A recurring theme in this book is that there is often a gap between the theoretical classroom assessment approach that one wishes to apply and what that approach looks like when it is actually put into practice in some form. There are realities and logistics (e.g., time in the day, energy and motivation, policies, pressures, training) that often prevent valid application of assessment principles relevant to the chosen approach. This is very much the case with authentic assessment because, as the title of one book on authentic assessment proclaims, "authenticity is in the eye of the beholder" (Gulikers, 2006). As the quotation that opens this section suggests, agreeing on reality is perhaps the toughest step in designing authentic assessments, but it is only the first step. The rest of this chapter describes the ways that real-life classroom teachers and school districts can and have translated the principles of authentic assessment into day-to-day assessment practices. For authentic assessment, perhaps more than any other approach, though, it is the thoughtful teachers who can best evaluate what skills and knowledge base are most relevant for the real-world problems, challenges, and tasks facing their students.

Broad Strategies for Developing Authentic Assessments

Baron and Boschee (1995) and others (Burke, 2009; Meyers & Nulty, 2009) provide specific suggestions for developing assessments of a wide variety of authentic tasks. They begin by offering three points to keep in mind when planning for assessments with authenticity:

1. Not all assessments have to be authentic. Traditional paper-and-pencil tests are still very useful tools for assessing important basic knowledge and many skills. If the majority of your own classroom assessments are made up of matching and multiple-choice questions, that might be perfectly appropriate.

2. Regardless of the specific tasks or content involved, authentic assessment should be considered. Consider the extent to which each instructional objective reflects valued skills outside the classroom. This advice is consistent with the logic of backward assessment described in Chapter 3.

3. Not all authentic tasks need be assessed; they may be formative or act as instruction. Authenticity is likely to improve the quality of any type of assessment.

The most difficult part of authentic assessment is the creativity and thoughtfulness necessary to think of and identify authentic tasks that have value. Start by identifying several critical or clearly relevant issues (within the domain of interest) and then listing one or two learner outcomes for each of those issues. Next, identify the criteria for success in each of those outcomes. Pick several criteria, but don't worry if you haven't covered them all. The tasks are likely authentic if they involve complex thought (e.g., problem solving, analysis, investigation), are interesting, and seem relevant and engaging to students.

Baron and Boschee also suggest a simple multistep process for producing scoring rules for authentic assessment:

1. Design a scoring rubric for each criterion. It should evaluate the degree to which students have incorporated all the important components of the thinking process involved.

2. Verify that the task will provide all the information necessary to produce a valid score.

3. Consider modifying the task to increase interest or the amount of information produced.

4. For your records, include on the rubric the task, learner outcome (objective), and complex thinking skill required.

5. Consider assigning different weights to each criterion if they differ in importance.

6. Share the criteria with students and your reasoning in selecting the criteria. (Consider student involvement in criteria selection.)

7. Of course, share results with students, emphasizing what they have mastered or learned.

Fischer and King (1995) published a concise guide to implementation of authentic assessment. They suggest that a portfolio assessment approach is best and provide a list of eight authentic characteristics that are found in real-world classroom assessments. This style of assessment will contain several of these components:

1. Represents realistic tasks in a variety of contexts done for a variety of purposes

2. Ongoing, formative assessment

3. Samples a wide range of cognitive strategies

4. Designed for different developmental levels

5. Individualized

6. Provides for collaborative reflection between students and teachers

7. Assessment guides instruction

8. Emphasizes what students know and can do

Dozens of concrete examples of what authentic assessment looks like in elementary classrooms are provided by Montgomery (2001). She points to many authentic activities already seen in most contemporary schools, such as map-making, writing plays, producing videos, writing computer programs, and making up stories. She argues that authentic assessment tasks simulate important real-world challenges and require high levels of complex thinking. These sorts of assessable tasks are becoming more and more common in modern classrooms. She suggests many authentic assignments for real-world teachers to try (pp. 36–37), including the following:

1. Keep a five-day record of precipitation and temperature for any five cities in the United States. Graph the results.

Table 8.2 Assessing Skills With Authentic Tasks

Skill	Definition	Assessable Tasks
Procedural knowledge	Knowledge of how to perform, how to do something	• Thinking aloud • Using a computer • Safety procedures • Driving a car • Conducting an experiment • Showing work while solving a math problem
Problem solving	Use of critical-thinking and decision-making skills to find a solution	• Testing a hypothesis • Writing a research paper • Making value judgments • Solving mathematical "story problems" • Judging the credibility of evidence • Deductive reasoning (e.g., geometry problems) • Concept mapping to identify variables of a problem
Collaboration	Working with others toward a shared goal	• Listening (e.g., eye contact, asking questions, reflective responses) • Cooperation (e.g., turn-taking, sharing, being polite) • Produce a product as a group • Present as a group
Motivation	Level of desire or willingness to do something	• Setting goals • Creating a plan to reach a goal • Self-assessing success • Demonstrating persistence

2. Read a rabbit care guidebook that contains information about real rabbits. Pretend that your class will be getting a rabbit to take care of as a class pet. Prepare a shopping list of things you will need to take care of the rabbit. Design and "build" paper airplanes, experimenting with different designs and use of weights (paper clips). Fly the planes with the goal of distance or time aloft.

3. Using a restaurant menu, pick out six meals for you and your friends. Calculate the cost and keep within a budget.

Authentic Assessment of Specific Skills

Common skills for which authentic assessment is especially suited include procedural knowledge, problem solving, collaboration, and motivation (Borich & Tombari, 2004). Table 8.2 provides examples of tasks that allow for observation of these skills. What makes these examples authentic is that they are part of a teaching and assessment plan with the goal of increasing generalizable skills, as opposed to a goal of high test performance. They focus on complex abilities, not low-level knowledge.

Technology

Computers and Authentic Assessment

It's likely no coincidence that the 20-some-year movement toward assessment designed to promote and measure complex thinking skills has grown parallel to the rise of computer-based educational technology. Computers and the web provide great opportunities for authentic assessment (Chang & Tseng, 2008) through, among other avenues, web-based collaboration (Chiu, Yang, Liang, & Chen, 2010; Donnan, McCormack, Battye, & Hart, 2008; Hron & Friedrich, 2003), computer-based (or supported) assessment (Laurier, 2000), and the use of multimedia (Neo, Neo, & Tan, 2011).

Web-Based Collaboration

Collaborative learning is "a joint construction of meaning through interaction with others" (Hron & Friedrich, 2003, p. 71). Authentic skills that can be assessed through collaborative educational activities include deduction, induction, synthesis, investigation, and a variety of social skills. Structured online interactions, whether local or outside the classroom, can allow for assessment through the role of moderator—monitoring the social exchange, providing predetermined discussion topics, providing formative feedback, and strategically controlling participation.

(Continued)

(Continued)

Computer-Based Assessment

Standardized testing is now substantially administered and scored online or on computer. The authentic assessment movement is alive and well in large-scale standardized assessment, as well, but it is still an open question how well the principles of authenticity can translate to standardized tests. Some powerful elements of authentic assessment (e.g., local, student involvement in development, public defense, collaboration) might be impossible (or, at best, very difficult) for large scale assessment. The computer, though, can be a useful tool in authentic assessment. Computers can be used for assessment of those tasks that in the real world occur on computers (e.g., literacy tasks, such as chatting or discussions and writing), for efficiency (if computers allow for quicker assessment, then a greater number of assessments can be administered and included in portfolio-type systems) and, of course, to test computer skills themselves, which are often objectives in the modern classroom (Laurier, 2000).

Multimedia Authentic Assessment

Though computer-based testing and authenticity have yet to fully embrace each other, computer technology is great at providing interactive multimedia assessment environments. Videos, sound, animations, games, graphs, journals, and simulated documents can all be integrated into a coordinated environment of learning, exploration, and problem-solving tasks. This supports authentic assessment, especially in terms of providing a multidimensional, complex context, student participation and motivation, multiple indicators of performance, and fairly unstructured challenges (Herrington & Herrington, 1998).

Authentic Assessment of Literacy

The teaching and assessment of reading, writing, listening, and speaking is foremost among the goals of modern education. Though there are standardized tests to assess these skills, they do not assess the high levels of literacy needed to fully engage in today's world (Koda, 2005; Ratcliff, 2002). Consequently, authentic assessment of reading and other literacy skills is a hot topic that has received a great deal of notice in teacher education. The analysis of important aspects of authenticity discussed at the start of this chapter found that among language arts researchers (e.g., Hirvela & Pierson, 2000; Laurier, 2000), the important components of assessment were a match between language tasks, such as reading, and the way these skills are applied outside the classroom and the use of multiple indicators of skill, such as portfolios (Chang & Tseng, 2008).

Figure 8.3 Authentic Literacy Assessment Process

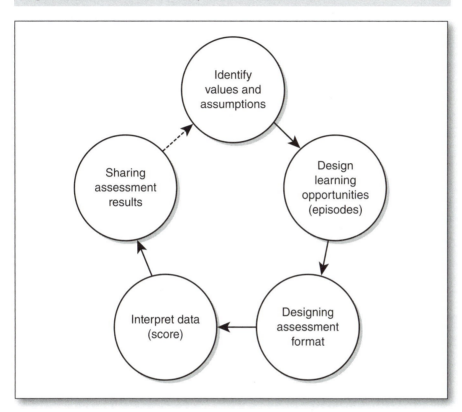

Hancock, Turbill, and Cambourne (1994), a team of Australian literacy researchers, developed authentic classroom assessment activities while observing real-world teachers. They described their work some years ago, but their insights and suggestions are modern. The authors suggest a process by which authentic assessment can be developed, evaluated, and shared. As shown in Figure 8.3, the assessment process begins with identifying one's beliefs and assumptions about the skills to assess (e.g., *what is literacy? how is it learned?*) and ends with the sharing of assessment results with students and parents.

Among the educators observed was an experienced 6th grade teacher who provided an example of how he filled the 2-hour "literacy block" in his classroom with authentic assessment. Literacy blocks are very common today in U.S. schools, and his approach is a good model for the multifaceted structure

Table 8.3 Authentic Assessment as Part of a 2-Hour Literacy Block in a 6th Grade Classroom

Segment	Time	Purpose	Assessment
Teacher reading	15 mins	Shows reading is fun Demonstrates fluent reading Encourages students to ask questions	Observation Learner logs
Sustained silent reading	20 mins	Shows reading is rewarding Students responsible for choices Uninterrupted period to connect to text	Observation Reading logs
Modeling	10 mins	Demonstrates assigned tasks Models strategies	Conferences Interviews Surveys
"Workshop" tasks	60 mins	Working in groups Opportunity to listen Opportunity to clarify ideas Using language to communicate ideas	Observations Retellings
Discussion and sharing	15 mins	Identifies what learning has occurred Identifies common difficulties in learning Guides students to respect others	Learning logs

Source: Adapted from Hancock, Turbill, & Cambourne, 1994.

of authentic assessment and what an authentic literacy assessment environment might look like in the modern classroom. The different "episodes" (segments) in a typical literacy block in his classroom are presented in Table 8.3.

Authentic Assessment in Mathematics

It is more difficult to identify authentic tasks in math than it is in many other school subject areas because there seems to be a disconnect between the common mathematics activities in classrooms and the tasks that real-world mathematicians (or other professionals who use math in their work) engage in (Goos, Stillman, & Vale, 2012; Lajoie, 1995). Inside the classroom, solving a "math problem" is often a solitary activity with an emphasis on mental calculation; outside the classroom, tools and technology are often available and the process may take place in a collaborative group setting. (See Chapter 7 for a scoring rubric based on behaviors of real-world mathematicians.) Consequently, some math education researchers suggest that *authenticity* be defined a bit differently for this subject matter. Instead of focusing on how math is practiced in the real world, those mathematical skills that are *valued* in the outside world might be a more reasonable focus.

Worthwhile mathematical tasks, those that are valued outside the classroom, include the following:

- **Problem-solving.** Challenging cognitive processes include gathering and discovering knowledge and analyzing numbers. Authenticity can be increased by using real data and assigning interesting problems.
- **Communication.** Reading about, writing about, and discussing mathematical ideas. Activities that encourage reflection, synthesis, collaboration, and a "public" defense support authenticity.
- **Reasoning.** Understanding the structure and assumptions of a math problem and applying deductive and inductive thought to reach a solution. Authenticity is strengthened when problems are complex and ill-defined and are experienced across a variety of contexts.
- **Making Connections.** A curriculum that incorporates math tasks and assessment across topics encourages students to generalize and transfer their skills instead of treating each task or application in isolation. An authentic assessment environment incorporates assessment of all these math skills together throughout the entire mathematics curriculum (Lajoie, 1995).

Because mathematical skill assessments that are meant to be authentic do not always match the way mathematical tasks are completed outside the classroom, some argue that a balance can be found between opportunities to simulate workplace practices (the realistic aspect) and opportunities for students "to act like children learning mathematics" (Moschkovich, 1998, p. 16).

Authentic Assessment in Visual Arts

"Artwork created by students are objects of meaning that reflect artistic valuing and aesthetic intents that provide sensory perception and appreciation because they involve elements of human motivation and interactions between the student and his or her environment. . . . (They) contribute to the enrichment of conscious life experiences through providing meaning on a symbolic level and affectively through feelings that contribute to the enrichment of sensory competence and cognitive enrichment."

Dorn, Madeja, and Sabol (2004, p. 1)

In the current budget-focused climate, art educators often face pressure to justify their content area as representing a set of authentic and necessary real-world skills. As the quotation that opened this section demonstrates, however, visual arts assessment has the potential to be authentic and realistic because it reflects authentic human experience.

Dorn et al. (2004) were involved in large-scale attempts to develop art instruction and authentic assessment in schools in Florida, Indiana, and Illinois. When developing authentic tasks for use in the projects' assessment, they followed a set of guidelines (p. 100) for maintaining the validity of the process:

1. Identify both the procedural and focal knowledge of the students needed for them to know how and be able to do various learning activities in the arts.

2. Identify the core performance roles or situations that all pre-K–12 students should encounter and be expected to master.

3. Choose the most salient discriminators that can be used in evaluating performance.

4. Design tasks with sufficient depth and breadth to assess competence.

5. Train evaluators to (among other things) reach high levels of inter-rater reliability.

6. Apply a clear understanding of the intended audience.

In their description of scoring rubrics for the authentic assessment of art assignments, they emphasize several points, all consistent with the criteria for quality rubrics presented in Chapters 6 and 7. The rubric should be written in ordinary language and be based on directly observable characteristics of the product or performance, and the criteria should be based on the critical demands of performance.

Posters

An authentic assessment format that can be used for any content area, not just art, is the poster. Teachers sometimes choose the "poster" as an assessment format for a variety of contexts. MacAndrew and Edwards (2002) describe the characteristics of a poster as an assessment, compare it to the more traditional *essay*, and provide suggestions for a valid scoring rubric. Posters for this purpose are similar to those one sees at professional conferences (present a question, describe the methods of research, and share and interpret results). In format, poster sessions have much in common with the traditional science fair (an example of authentic assessment that has been around long before modern approaches to assessment). The posters are displayed at a "conference" gathering of students and teachers and, often, parents and staff. Students stand in front of the poster and answer questions about it and the work they have done.

To score the posters, a rubric should include assessment criteria developed collaboratively by students and teachers, but reasonable criteria include

- Title
- Clear goals
- Well organized
- Easy to read
- Effective use of graphics
- Research quality (appropriate sources cited, evidence of reading in the field, methodology is sound, interpretation of results is correct)

Students and other stakeholders (parents, administrators) tend to be comfortable with essays because they are used to them. It is important to train students as to the nature of a research poster and the characteristics of quality before expecting high levels of performance.

AUTHENTIC ASSESSMENT FOR ENGLISH LANGUAGE LEARNERS

There has been quite a bit of study and scholarly reflection on authentic assessment of English language learners (ELL) and students who use English as a second language (ESL). Wise suggestions for developing authentic assessments for this population can be found in books by Ekbatani and Pierson (2000), who are interested in the self-assessment and formative aspects of authenticity, and O'Malley and Pierce (1996), whose work focuses on practical advice for authentic classroom assessment. The suggestions that follow are found in these books and the work of others (Ekbatani, 2008; Shibliyev & Gilanlıoğlu, 2009; Toscano, 2009) and are meant for evaluating English language learning.

One approach is to turn the classroom into a writing environment, not a grading environment (Gearhart, 2009; Hirvela & Pierson, 2000), and to establish portfolio assessment that is maintained and self-assessed by students. To allow for a developmental picture to form, the portfolios should be sequential, produced over a defined period of time, with assignments focused on a particular context or purpose. A key in owning one's own learning is to make the decisions about what to include in the portfolio; the greater the role played by the student in designing the portfolio, the more realistic the assessment becomes. North (2000) provides a template for a generic scoring scale developed by the educational advisory group *Council of Europe*, which could be used for authentic assessment rubrics for ELL or ESL students. The descriptions of the score points make use of many of the concepts that we have come to associate with authentic assessment, such as *complex, encountered in work, relevance*, and *demanding*. A condensed version of that scale, with point values added, is below.

0. Breakthrough

   Can understand and use familiar everyday expressions and very basic phrases. Can interact in a simple way.

1. Waystage

   Can understand sentences and frequently used expressions related to the areas of most immediate relevance.

2. Threshold

   Can understand the main points of clear standard input on familiar matters regularly encountered in work, school, and leisure.

3. Vantage

   Can understand the main ideas of complex text on both concrete and abstract topics, including technical discussions within domains of interest.

4. Effective Operational Proficiency

   Can understand a wide range of demanding, longer texts, and recognize implicit meaning.

5. Mastery

   Can understand with ease virtually everything heard or read.

O'Malley and Pierce (1996) present detailed descriptions of many authentic assessable classroom tasks. They observed teachers' real-life efforts at applying

Table 8.4 Examples of ESL Authentic Assessments

Level	Subject	Task	Description
Elementary	Language Arts	Responding to Reading	Student reads to whole class and students give feedback.
Elementary	Language Arts	Anecdotal Records	Teacher takes notes while observing individual reading.
Elementary	Language Arts	Book Talks	Students present personal responses to readings and answer other students' questions.
Middle	Mathematics	Geoboard	Geometric concepts are assessed.
Middle	Science	Magnet Experiment	Students are observed while comparing magnets to each other.
Secondary	Language Arts	Talk Show	Students simulate a TV talk show and interview each other as if they are famous.
Secondary	ESL	Interpreting Portfolios	Two teachers examine portfolios and discuss their evaluations.

Source: Based on O'Malley & Pierce, 1996.

authentic assessment with ELL and ESL students and interviewed many others about their techniques. Among the authentic elements of the tasks they describe are organized use of multiple indicators (such as portfolios) and student relevance (students' individual reactions to text or communication activities are central). Table 8.4 (based on a figure in their book) gives examples. Some examples are for teaching language; others are for teaching and assessing other subjects for ESL students.

Simulation Computer Games

Technology

There are several useful websites that provide free and simple games that simulate real-life problem-solving situations for children. Similar games are very popular on Facebook and other social networking sites. Though not entirely realistic, performance on these games could be used as part of authentic assessment strategies or provide ideas for in-class simulations. Of course, screen these games thoroughly to make sure they meet

(Continued)

(Continued)

your standards regarding age appropriateness, Internet use, and commercialization. (All these sites have advertising and hope to sell things.) Some games can be downloaded so they could be used on classroom computers without being connected to the web. http://www.youdagames.com/

Youda Games. Several fun and somewhat complex simulation games are available here. Some good possibilities are *Virtual Farm, Goodgame Farmer, Virtual City, Hotel Mogul*, and *Roads of Rome*. http://www.123-games.net/

123 Games. Some richly detailed business simulation games at this site include *Cookie Tycoon, Shop Empire*, and *Corporation, Inc.* and a variety of "lemonade stand" type games such as *Hot Dog Stand* and *Pizza King*. Many of these games emphasize money decisions to a much lesser degree than the "move quickly and make that taco" aspect, but there are still good possibilities here. dan-ball.jp/en/

Dan-ball. Science and physics-based simulations are available here. Fun and educational games include *Planet Simulation*, where you must design solar systems; *Earth Editor*, where you develop the planet; and *Elemental Box*, where various objects react to each other using real physics. These are "sandbox" games where students can explore and try things just to see what happens.

AUTHENTIC ASSESSMENT AND YOUNG CHILDREN

Thinking of authentic assessment as a strategy to increase job-related skills or develop the abilities that employers are looking for doesn't have much meaning when one is assessing a 3-year-old. It is useful to view authenticity somewhat differently when teaching preschool children or students in the early elementary grades. Here the emphasis should be on the developmental skills supportive of future learning. One can think of a young child's "job" as growing, learning, and being a student.

Puckett and Black (2008), in their book on assessing young children, define authentic assessment for this population as obtaining information that "truly reflects how a child pursues knowledge and skills and the outcomes of the child's efforts. [Assessment should be] teacher-mediated, child-centered . . . and based on multiple theories and knowledge about child growth and development" (p. 75). While one concern that teachers may have is that young children cannot meaningfully take part in the collaborative aspect of authentic assessment, they argue that empathic interactions are possible with the teacher encouraging children's natural eagerness to learn and prove how "smart" they are. Ways to increase the authenticity of assessments with young children include the following:

- The teacher assumes the role of mentor, with the child as novice.
- Student and teacher share experiences from outside the classroom.
- The teacher incorporates children's interests into classroom activities and assessments.
- Learning is understood as being partly social and emotional.

AUTHENTICITY AT THE SCHOOL LEVEL

"Do we want to evaluate student problem-posing and problem-solving in mathematics? Experimental research in science? Speaking, listening, and facilitating a discussion? Doing document-based historical inquiry? Thoroughly revising a piece of imaginative writing until it 'works' for the reader? Then let our assessment be built out of such exemplary intellectual challenges."

Grant Wiggins (1990, p. 1)

Darling-Hammond, Ancess, and Falk (1995; Darling-Hammond, 2012) studied real-life examples of schools that had implemented systems of authentic assessment. For their analysis, they used a framework of Wiggins's (1989) and applied four observable characteristics that distinguish authentic assessment in practice from other approaches:

1. Assessment tasks are representative of the "field." Students actually write and conduct experiments rather than taking spelling tests and recalling science facts.

2. Carefully designed standards of performance evaluate the essential qualities of performance. These aren't secret, they are shared with students and guide instruction.

3. Students play a role in evaluating their own work. Real-world contexts require that people self-assess and self-motivate to be successful, and authentic assessment aims to develop those skills.

4. Students frequently present their work "publicly." This requires that they reflect on their work and what they know and share it in an understandable way.

Three case studies of New York schools presented by the authors, in particular, provide useful models for what various aspects of authentic assessment—portfolios, projects, and collaboration with students—look like at the school level.

Central Park East Secondary School structured student performance expectations around a portfolio approach. The portfolios contain work samples—writings, math papers, and, principally, projects—which are meant to demonstrate independent reasoning and action and "habits of mind" (a concept that is emphasized across many perspectives of authentic assessment) which encourage the weighing of evidence, awareness of different viewpoints, seeing connections, speculating on possibilities, and assessing value. Portions of the portfolios are presented and "defended" by students to a committee of faculty.

Hodgson Vocational Technical High School responded to their district's drive for higher expectations for vocational students in the areas of mathematics, literacy, and science. As a first step toward the goal of a diploma based on performance, a three-part Senior Project was instituted. The three parts are

1. A research paper. This paper is "shop"-based; students at this school are training to be carpenters and such.

2. A shop project. This is to be a large, complex project that students design and build themselves. Their research paper is meant to support the production of the project.

3. A public, formal oral presentation. Teachers, parents, and other students attend.

At the time that Darling-Hammond and colleagues visited Hodgson, the evaluations of the project's pieces were conducted separately by the different departments (e.g., the English faculty evaluated the research paper and the presentation). An interdisciplinary approach, however, would have been more consistent with authentic assessment principles.

Another case study described concerns International High School, which emphasized collaborative learning. International High School in New York City is exclusively for recent immigrants with a relatively low English proficiency. A community learning and assessment environment was established supported by a core belief that students learn from each other's different experiences and knowledge. Authentic assessment is operationalized as a three-pronged approach—self-assessment, peer assessment, and teacher assessment. These three sources of assessment apply to an ongoing series of formative, performance-based assessments designed to provide meaningful feedback, summative assessments that are multidimensional, and collaborative broad evaluations from multiple perspectives. Group work and working in pairs is common, and much of the assessment occurs in these contexts.

Figure 8.4 Authenticity of Assessment Scoring Rubric

	High				Low
Context of the Assessment					
Realistic activity or context The task and methods of evaluation are similar to what would be required or expected in the real world, outside of an artificial classroom environment.	20	15	10	5	0
Cognitively complex Successful performance of the task requires high levels of understanding or critical thinking.	10	8	5	2	0
Performance-based Skill or ability (as opposed to knowledge) is assessed through a performance or creation of a product.	5	4	3	2	0
Role of the Student					
Formative assessment The assessment is designed to provide feedback to students to control their own learning. Scores do not affect grades.	10	8	5	2	0
Collaborative Students work with each other or with the teacher during the task, to evaluate their performance and, perhaps, to create the assessment.	10	8	5	2	0
Defense is required Students defend their "answers" or performance. This might be a formal, oral defense in front of students and adults or a written defense as part of the assessment.	5	4	3	2	0
Scoring Procedures					
Multiple indicators or portfolio The "score" on the assessment is a composite of multiple scores reflecting the quality of multiple components or a portfolio of products and student work.	20	15	10	5	0
Criteria known by students Scoring rules are well understood by students or they participated in their creation. Teachers may have used these criteria as part of their instruction.	15	12	8	4	0
Mastery expectation The task and scoring are designed to provide feedback on whether the student has mastered a skill or ability (as opposed to comparing the student with other students).	5	4	3	2	0
Total					

From Frey, B. B., Schmitt, V. L., & Allen, J. P. (2009, November). *Assessing authentic assessment.* Presented at the Annual Meeting of the American Evaluation Association, Orlando, FL.

ASSESSING THE ASSESSMENT

The different definitional dimensions of authenticity discussed in this chapter can be organized into a scoring rubric to evaluate the degree of authenticity within a teacher-made assessment (Frey et al., 2009). To find out "how authentic is it?" with your own assessments or others', apply this set of scoring guidelines based on those nine components. The different point values are rough approximations of the relative frequency that these components were offered as critically necessary for assessments to be authentic. For the publications dealing with authenticity for school-aged students, the relative frequencies of the dimensions required as part of the definition of authentic assessment were *assessment task mirrors reality outside of the classroom*, 60%; *multiple indicators or portfolios for scoring*, 54%; *known or student developed criteria*, 47%; *formative assessment*, 31%; *cognitively complex*, 30%; *performance-based*, 23%; *collaborative*, 20%; *a required defense*, 15%; and *mastery expectation*, 13%.

Mr. Hernandez Gets Real (Part II)

Stories From the Classroom

Mr. Hernandez took an Elementary Statistics course during college and had covered a bit in his classroom assessment course, too. He actually used data analysis in his everyday teaching and knew of multiple applications of mean, median, mode, and range and other ways of understanding data. He wanted to show his students a real-world application of the data analysis tools that would engage them more fully. He planned a lesson around the data analysis he used as part of his job and created a formative quiz. The quiz wouldn't affect students' grades, but it would create some real-world data that he could use in his teaching.

When the students had completed the test (after Mr. Hernandeze assured them that this was just to create some data to play with and they wouldn't need their names on it), he mixed them up and had the students score them as he read out the correct answers. The students then converted the raw score to a percent correct score. Mr. Hernandez went to the board and had the students tell them all the percent scores. He listed them all on the board.

"What does this information tell me?" asked Mr. Hernandez. Shiloh raised her hand. "That we do not know very much?" After the laughter, Mr. Hernandez asked, "How did the class do overall? If I needed one score to tell me, which should I use?"

Shiloh responded, "Mean?"

"Okay class, find the mean, median, mode, and range of our data set and then tell me what decision I should make based on that information." After a few minutes of computation, Hunter raised his hand and said, "I don't think that in real life you should use your normal grading rules for this sort of quiz."

"Interesting—why not?"

"The mean score is 68, so most of the class would get, like, a D!" The class agreed. Mr. Hernandez asked, "Are the median and mode higher, the same, or lower than the mean?" The class agreed it was much lower. "Why, and what does that tell me about the test?"

The class agreed that it was because one test score was really high and made the mean higher. Mr. Hernandez explained that many decisions in the real world, many real-world jobs, used descriptive statistics like these to make decisions all the time. That included teachers. He then asked the students what other types of jobs might also use statistics to make decisions and how those jobs might use them. There were a lot of good suggestions, which led perfectly into the final assessment.

"For our end of unit assessment I am going to have you gather, organize, analyze, and display some data. You will need to come up with two data collection questions, one that counts frequencies in terms of a few categories and one that uses scores on some measure like our quiz. Think of questions that different occupations might really want to know the answers to."

Sergio wanted to know if he could do favorite pizza toppings for his categorical question. "Who would want to know this information?" asked Mr. Hernandez. "Pizza Hut or maybe the lunch lady," Sergio said.

On the day the project was due, Mr. Hernandez got enough butcher paper for all the students to hang their completed projects. Students were allowed to discuss their results with other classes that came by to see the project. Even Riel said he enjoyed the assignment. Mr. Hernandez knew that it made a difference to Riel that the work he did was the kind of work real people did in the real world. And that made a difference. Really.

THINGS TO THINK ABOUT

1. Think about the word "realistic." What would a *realistic* classroom assessment actually be like?

2. When would it be important to design authentic assessments in the classroom? When would it not be as important?

3. How does *authenticity* in assessment change as the context changes?

4. Which aspects of authenticity (those nine dimensions) seem to you to be most important?

5. What would a school dedicated to authentic assessment principles look like?

Looking Back in This Chapter

Applying authentic assessment procedures in the real classroom can be challenging. Though the community of classroom assessment scholars agrees that authentic assessments are potentially a powerful, transformative tool, there is not yet agreement on which aspects of authenticity are most important. Nine different dimensions of authenticity were presented, with the realistic nature of the assessment being emphasized. The overlap between the modern assessment approaches of authentic, formative, and performance-based was discussed. Validity and reliability issues of authentic assessment include determining what is authentic and the necessarily subjective nature of the scoring. General strategies for operationalizing authenticity and illustrations of authentic assessment tasks and scoring methods were provided for literacy and reading, mathematics, visual arts, and other content areas and purposes. A scoring rubric for determining *how authentic a particular assessment is* was provided.

ON THE WEB

Selection of authentic task suggestions across many areas
http://jfmueller.faculty.noctrl.edu/toolbox/examples/authentictaskexamples.htm

Authentic assessment resources for classroom teachers
http://www.uwstout.edu/soe/profdev/assess.cfm

Overview of authentic assessment with linked supports
http://www.teachervision.fen.com/teaching-methods-and-management/educational-testing/4911.html

Authentic assessment and multiple intelligences
http://teachersnetwork.org/teachnet-lab/mbhs/scragg/multiple.html

STUDENT STUDY SITE

Visit **www.sagepub.com/frey** to access additional study tools including eFlashcards, web quizzes, web resources, additional rubrics, and links to SAGE journal articles.

REFERENCES

Abernethie, L. (2006). Authentic assessment as a neo-liberal technology of government. *Teaching and Learning Forum*, 1–9.

Archbald, D. A. (1991). Authentic assessment: Principles, practices, and issues. *School Psychology Quarterly*, 6(4), 279–293.

Archbald, D. A., & Newmann, F. M. (1988). *Beyond standardized testing: Assessing authentic academic achievement in the secondary school*. Reston, VA: National Association of Secondary School Principals.

Baron, M. A., & Boschee, F. (1995). *Authentic assessment: The key to unlocking student success*. Lancaster, PA: Technomic.

Borich, G. D., & Tombari, M. L. (2004). *Educational assessment for the elementary and middle school classroom*. Englewood Cliffs, NJ: Prentice Hall.

Brown, J. S., Collins, A., & Duguid, P. (1989). Situated cognition and the culture of learning. *Educational Researcher*, 18, 1, 32–42.

Burke, K. (2009). *How to assess authentic learning*. Thousand Oaks, CA: Corwin.

Chang, C. C., & Tseng, K. H. (2008). Use and performances of web-based portfolio assessment. *British Journal of Educational Technology*, 40(2), 358–370.

Chiu, C. H., Yang, H. Y., Liang, T. H., & Chen, H. P. (2010). Elementary students' participation style in synchronous online communication and collaboration. *Behaviour & Information Technology*, 29(6), 571–586.

Darling-Hammond, L. (2012). *Powerful teacher education: Lessons from exemplary programs*. San Francisco, CA: Jossey-Bass.

Darling-Hammond, L., Ancess, J. A., & Falk, B. (1995). *Authentic assessment in action: Studies of schools and students at work*. New York, NY: Teachers College Press.

Dez, M., Moon, J., & Meyer, C. (1992). What do we want students to know? . . . and other important questions. *Educational Leadership*, 49(8), 38–42.

Donnan, P., McCormack, C., Battye, G., & Hart, I. (2008, July). *Doing group assessment: A web-based resource of good practice case-studies*. Paper presented at the meeting of the 31st Annual HERDSA Conference, Rotorua, New Zealand.

Dorn, C. M., Madeja, S. S., & Sabol, F. R. (2004). *Assessing expressive learning*. Mahwah, NJ: Lawrence Erlbaum.

Dutt-Doner, K., & Maddox, R. (1998). Implementing authentic assessment. *Kappa Delta Pi Record*, 34(4), 135–137.

Ekbatani, G. (2008). *Measurement and evaluation in post-secondary ESL*. New York, NY: Routledge.

Ekbatani, G., & Pierson, H. (Eds.). (2000). *Learner-directed assessment in ESL*. Mahwah, NJ: Lawrence Erlbaum.

Engel, M., Pulley, R., & Rybinski, A. (2003). *Authentic assessment: It really works* (Master's thesis). Available from ERIC database. (ERIC ED479959)

Fischer, C., & King, R. M. (1995). *Authentic assessment: A guide to implementation*. Thousand Oaks, CA: Corwin.

French, D. (2003). A new vision of authentic assessment to overcome the flaws in high stakes testing. *Middle School Journal*, 35(1), 14–23.

Frey, B. B., Schmitt, V. L., & Allen, J. P. (2009, November). *Assessing authentic assessment*. Presented at the annual Meeting of the American Evaluation Association, Orlando, FL.

Gearhart, M. (2009). Classroom portfolio assessment for writing. In G. A. Troia (Ed.), *Instruction and assessment for struggling writers: Evidence-based practices* (pp. 311–336). New York, NY: Guilford Press.

Gipps, C. (1995). Reliability, validity, and manageability in large-scale performance assessment. In H. Torrance (Ed.), *Evaluating authentic assessment*. Buckingham, England: Open University Press.

Goos, M., Stillman, G., & Vale, C. (2012). *Teaching secondary school mathematics: Research and practice for the 21st century*. Crows Nest NSW, Australia: Allen & Unwin.

Green, J. (1998). Authentic assessment: Constructing the way forward for all students. *Education Canada, 38*(3), 8–12.

Gronlund, G. (2003). *Focused early learning: A planning framework for teaching young children*. St. Paul, MN: Redleaf Press.

Gulikers, J. T. M. (2006). *Authenticity is in the eye of the beholder: Beliefs and perceptions of authentic assessment and the impact on student learning*. Maastricht, The Netherlands: Datawyse.

Hancock, J., Turbill, J., & Cambourne, B. (1994). Assessment and evaluation of literacy learning. *Authentic Reading Assessment: Practices and Possibilities*, 46–62.

Herrington, J., & Herrington, A. (1998). Authentic assessment and multimedia: How university students respond to a model of authentic assessment. *Higher Education Research and Development, 17*(3), 305–322.

Herrington, J., & Oliver, R. (2000). An instructional design framework for authentic learning environments. *Educational Technology Research and Development, 48*(3), 23–48.

Hirvela, A., & Pierson, H. (2000). Portfolios: Vehicles for authentic self-assessment. In G. Ekbatani & H. Pierson (Eds.), *Learner-directed assessment in ESL* (pp. 105–126). Mahwah, NJ: Lawrence Erlbaum.

Hron, A., & Friedrich, H. F. (2003). A review of web-based collaborative learning: Factors beyond technology. *Journal of Computer Assisted Learning, 19*(1), 70–79.

Jolly, J., & Kettler, T. (2000). Authentic assessment of leadership in problem-solving groups. *Gifted Child Today, 27*(1), 32–39.

Kellaghan, T., & Madaus, G. F. (1993). The British experience with "authentic" testing. *Phi Delta Kappan, 74*(6), 458–466.

Koda, K. (2005). *Insights into second language reading: A cross-linguistic approach*. United Kingdom: Cambridge University Press.

Lajoie, S. P. (1995). A framework for authentic assessment in mathematics. In T. A. Romberg (Ed.), *Reform in school mathematics and authentic assessment*. Albany: State University of New York Press.

Laurier, M. (2000). Can computerized testing by authentic? *ReCALL, 12*(1), 93–104.

Lawton, D. (2000). Authentic assessment in South Brunswick schools. *Knowledge Quest, 29*(2), 30–38.

Lindsay, A. D. (1991). *The Republic: The complete and unabridged Jowett translation*. New York, NY: Vintage Books.

MacAndrew, S. B., & Edwards, K. (2002). Essays are not the only way: A case report on the benefits of authentic assessment. *Psychology Learning & Teaching, 2*(2), 134–139.

Maden, J., & Taylor, M. (2001, February 27–March 3). *Developing and implementing authentic oral assessment instruments*. Paper presented at the Annual Meeting of Teachers of English to Speakers of Other Languages, St. Louis, MO.

Meisels, S. (1996). Using work sampling in authentic assessment. *Educational Leadership*, 60–64.

Meyer, C. (1992). What's the difference between authentic and performance assessment? *Educational Leadership, 49*(8), 39–40.

Meyers, N. M., & Nulty, D. D. (2009). How to use (five) curriculum design principles to align authentic learning environments, assessment, students' approaches to thinking and learning outcomes. *Assessment & Evaluation in Higher Education, 34*(5), 565–577.

Montgomery, K. (2001). *Authentic assessment: A guide for elementary teachers.* New York, NY: Longman.

Moorcroft, T., Desmarais, K., Hogan, K., & Bekowitz, A. (2000). Authentic assessment in the informal setting: How it can work for you. *Journal of Environmental Education, 31*(3), 20–24.

Moschkovich, J. N. (1998). Rethinking authentic assessments of student mathematical activity. *Focus on Learning Problems in Mathematics, 20(4)* 1–18.

Mueller, J. (2005). Authentic assessment in the classroom and the library media center. *Library Media Connection, 23*(7), 14–18.

Neo, M., Neo, K. T. K., & Tan, H. Y. J. (2011, June). Content restructuring with authentic learning strategies in a multimedia learning environment (MMLE). In T. Bastiaens & M. Ebner (Eds.), *Proceedings of World Conference on Educational Multimedia, Hypermedia and Telecommunications 2011* (pp. 2233–2242). Chesapeake, VA: AACE.

Newmann, F., Brandt, R., & Wiggins, G. (1998). An exchange of views on semantics, psychometrics, and assessment reform: A close look at "authentic" assessments. *Educational Researcher, 27*(6), 19–22.

North, B. (2000). Defining a flexible common measurement scale: Descriptors for self and teacher assessment. In G. Ekbatani & H. Pierson (Eds.), *Learner directed assessment in ESL*. Mahwah, NJ: Lawrence Erlbaum.

O'Malley, J. M., & Pierce, L. V. (1996). *Authentic assessment for English language learners.* Saddle River, NJ: Pearson Education.

Paris, S. G., & Ayres, L. R. (1994). *Becoming reflective students and teachers with portfolios and authentic assessment.* ERIC Reproductive Services No. 378166.

Puckett, M. B., & Black, J. K. (2008). *Meaningful assessments of the young child* (3rd ed.). Saddle River, NJ: Pearson Education.

Ratcliff, N. J. (2002). Using authentic assessment to document the emerging literacy skills of young children. *Childhood Education, 78*(2), 66–69.

Schnitzer, S. (1993). Designing an authentic assessment. *Educational Leadership, 50*(7), 32–35.

Shibliyev, J., & Gilanhoğlu, İ. (2009). Language testing and assessment: An advanced resource book. *ELT Journal, 63*(2), 181–183.

Spinelli, C. G. (1998). *Teacher education reform: Promoting interactive teaching strategies and authentic assessment for instructing an increasing diverse population of students.* West Long Branch, NJ: 120 Opinion Papers.

Stripling, B. (1993). Practicing authentic assessment in the school library. *School Library Media Annual (SLMA), 11*, 40–57.

Suen, H. K., Sonak, B., Zimmaro, D., & Roberts, D. (1997). Concept map as scaffolding for authentic assessment. *Psychological Reports, 83*, 734.

Swaffield, S. (2011). Getting to the heart of authentic assessment for learning. *Assessment in Education: Principles, Policy & Practice, 18*(4), 433–449.

Tombari, M., & Borich, G. (1999). *Authentic assessment in the classroom: Applications and practice.* Upper Saddle River, NJ: Prentice Hall.

Torrance, H. (1993). Combining measurement-driven instruction with authentic assessment: Some initial observations of national assessment in England and Wales. *Educational Evaluation and Policy Analysis, 15*(1), 81–90.

Torrance, H. (1995). Teacher involvement in new approaches to assessment. In H. Torrance (Ed.), *Evaluating authentic assessment.* Buckingham, England: Open University Press.

Torrance, H. (2009). 4.2 Using assessment in education reform. In H. Daniels, H. Lauder, & J. Porter (Eds.), *Knowledge, values and educational policy: A critical perspective* (pp. 218–236). New York, NY: Routledge.

Toscano, L. M. (2009). ELL authentic assessment defined. *Assessment.* Retrieved from http://www .ibrarian.org/assesstask1.pdf

Wiggins, G. (1989). Teaching to the (authentic test). *Educational Leadership, 46*(7), 41–47.

Wiggins, G. (1990). The case for authentic assessment. ERIC Digest. ERIC Document Reproduction Service No. ED, 328 611.

Wilson, J., & Schwier, R. (2012, March). A model of authentic learning processes in instructional design. In P. Resta (Ed.), *Proceedings of Society for Information Technology & Teacher Education International Conference 2012* (pp. 1285–1289). Chesapeake, VA: AACE.

CHAPTER 9
UNIVERSAL TEST DESIGN

Looking Ahead in This Chapter

The modern classroom assessment approach of universal test design is presented. Universal design of assessment is based on the principle that all classroom assessment should be equally valid and accessible to every student. Validity and reliability issues relevant to universal test design are explored. Examples and guidelines for applying universal design in a real-life classroom are presented.

Objectives

After studying this chapter, you should be able to

- Define *universal design* and *universal test design*
- Summarize the principles of *universal design* and *universal test design*
- Provide examples of how universal design principles are applied in real classrooms
- Evaluate the extent to which universal design principles have been applied in a given classroom assessment

Ms. Clark Believes Variety Is the Spice of Life

Ms. Clark always appreciated a little variety in her life. After being in the same school for 5 years, Ms. Clark was excited to make the change to a new location, new students, and something a little different. She loved her old school and the students she got to work with there, but the new school was a little closer to home and would provide the opportunity to work with friends she has had in the district. Ms. Clark had also worked with the assistant principal in the past, training new teachers on the district plan to integrate Social Studies and English Language Arts, so she knew she would love the administration, too.

The diversity of the student population was not a surprise. Ms. Clark lived close to the school and knew the community well. There were even a few students who she saw regularly at the park near her house. She knew the material she was using at her old school would work just as well for the students in her new school. After all, it was the same district curriculum. There wouldn't be much new prep at all because she already had a bunch of assessments she had made and those had been perfected over the years.

At the end of every school year, teachers are asked to fill out a form with notes on each individual student. Teachers who will be getting the student the following year can then look at these files and plan accordingly. Ms. Clark was a little surprised when she noticed three intermediate level English Language Learners along with three additional students with minor disabilities who required instructional modifications. She thought she would need to teach a little differently to make sure everyone in the class had the opportunity to learn the material.

Two weeks had passed and Ms. Clark was happy with how the teaching had been going. It was time for the chapter test to really see how well those instructional changes had helped students learn the material. This took her a little off guard when some of her students appeared to have a really hard time taking the test. Looking over the completed tests, Ms. Clark decided that maybe her tests needed a little adjustment as well. Ms. Clark realized that maybe her assessments didn't work well for every student in her class. She remembered something from college about ways to ensure that tests worked equally well for every student, regardless of their characteristics. Maybe she still had some of her textbooks (though she had sold most of them back to the bookstore). When she got home, she started searching . . .

(To Be Continued)

"Universal design is . . . an enduring design approach that assumes that the range of human ability is ordinary, not special; . . . the experience of imaginative designers around the world reveals the range of applications that delight the senses and lift the human spirit when universal design is integral to the overall concept."

Elaine Ostroff, *Universal Design Handbook*
(Preiser & Ostroff, 2001)

The opening quotation in this chapter describes a general design process that is wide-open and creative and that results in products useful to the fullest variety of people. The concept of **universal design** began as an architectural and engineering philosophy, but it has lately been embraced by teachers and other assessment designers. The idea, popularized by architect Ron Mace, who developed the nation's first state building accessibility code in North Carolina in the *1970s*, was to produce buildings and other physical environments so that they were accessible to all, including those who use wheelchairs or have other physical disabilities (Bowe, 2000, 2005). The underlying assumption of universal design is that all aspects of our world can be planned from the beginning to allow access and use by everyone.

Let's start with a concrete definition of what we are talking about:

Universal design the design of products and environments to be useable in a meaningful and similar way by all people.

The approach has spread to include other populations besides those with physical disabilities, such as the elderly, those with cognitive disabilities, and those whose primary language is not English, and to other areas, such as computer and website use, and education (Mcguire, Scott, & Shaw, 2006; Thompson, Johnstone, & Thurlow, 2002; Thompson, Johnstone, Anderson, & Miller, 2005). Those standards, which initially described a physical environment, have been applied to processes that include some physical aspects, but include experiential aspects as well. This chapter explores how this very modern concept of universal design can be applied to the very modern world of classroom assessment.

THE CASE FOR UNIVERSAL TEST DESIGN

Many of today's classrooms work very differently from the ones your parents remember, especially when it comes to assessment. It wouldn't necessarily be clear, though, how different today's teacher-made tests might be because if you saw a quiz sitting on a teacher's desk, it would look at first glance like a "normal" everyday classroom test. It's more and more likely, however, that that multiple-choice quiz has been designed from the start to be meaningful, valid, and reliable for *all* students. It began with the teacher's choice of what to measure. He or she probably carefully defined the assessment objectives to match important instructional objectives and did not assign points for irrelevant knowledge or skills. Then, the teacher likely paid careful attention to the test instructions. He or she worded the directions simply, not assuming that students would remember or completely understand the rules from previous tests. Many modern teachers also do something on their assessments that few teachers did in the past. They give an example of an item and show how to respond correctly. The items themselves are written in clear language, and unless there is a reason for doing it otherwise, the vocabulary level is no more advanced than necessary. These choices remove some of the language obstacles that can affect performance for some of their students. Another concern that many of today's teachers have is the actual printed formatting regarding font size, the use of lots of "white" space (the space on the test that is blank), the use of capitals, and so on. This makes things easier for students who may have vision or perceptual difficulties related to learning disabilities. These strategies, along with other simple choices many teachers make, help produce assessments that are consistent with the principles of universal design.

Universal design of assessment is part of the accessibility movement in the United States, and the common acceptance of the approach is the result of several political and legislative developments over the last half century. An outline of the brief history of universal testing highlights these developments:

- 1950s. Disabled veterans and advocates for people with disabilities demanded opportunities in education, employment, and housing. *Barrier-free Movement* began.
- 1960s. American Standards Association (ANSI) published building accessibility standards. By the end of the decade, most states had adopted ANSI standards. *Architectural Barriers Act of 1968* required that all federally funded buildings be made accessible.
- 1970s. Architect Ron Mace popularized *universal design* concept. *Section 504, Rehabilitation Act of 1973*, outlaws discrimination on the basis of disability. *Education for Handicapped Children Act of 1975* (IDEA) guarantees a free and appropriate education for all children with disabilities.

- 1980s. *Fair Housing Amendments Act of 1988* required that most housing be accessible to those with disabilities.
- 1990s. *Americans with Disabilities Act* (ADA) banned discrimination in employment and required full access to, and use of, virtually all places and services. Center for Universal Design suggested seven *Universal Design Principles*.
- 2000s Educators began to develop classroom assessment methods that apply the principles to assessment.

Universal test design, or *universal design of assessment*, is the most modern of the approaches presented in this book. As a coherent philosophy and set of guidelines, universal assessment is less than 20 years old and is even now developing. Both classroom teachers and standardized test developers have begun to explore design of assessments that work equally well for all students regardless of their characteristics. Those who use the jargon of measurement would say, more specifically, that assessments should work equally well for all students regardless of their *construct-irrelevant characteristics*. They should be valid for all.

Principles of Universal Design

There are seven broad, established standards for universal design (Center for Universal Design, 1997):

1. Equitable Use

2. Flexibility in Use

3. Simple and Intuitive Use

4. Perceptible Information

5. Tolerance for Error

6. Low Physical Effort

7. Size and Space for Approach and Use

Each of these general standards has been interpreted in a more specific assessment context. The goal of universal design in assessment would be to "allow participation of the widest range of students, and to (produce) valid inferences about performance for all students who participate in the assessment"

Universal design advocates believe that your teaching and your assessment should be open to everyone.

(Thompson et al., 2002, p. 7). Though no assessment will be completely accessible or valid for all, the objective is to be as inclusive as possible. Some of these interpretations match directly to the broad seven standards, and some do not:

1. Inclusive assessment population

2. Precisely defined constructs

3. Accessible, nonbiased items

4. Amenable to accommodations

5. Simple, clear, and intuitive instructions and procedures

6. Maximum readability and comprehensibility

7. Maximum legibility

So what do these standards look like when they are applied to classroom assessments? A teacher-developed classroom assessment built under the philosophy of universal design may on its face look somewhat similar to an assessment from 20 years ago, though there will likely be some technical differences (e.g., larger fonts, more white space) that could be noticed, and the wording of directions and questions may be simplified. The bigger differences, however, are likely to be in the choice of tasks, questions, and administrative procedures, as well as in the planning.

Table 9.1 presents the broad universal design standards and the much more specific universal test design standards and indicates how the latter standards are faithful to the former standards. It also describes in detail what the observable characteristics of a classroom assessment are that have been developed under this philosophy. Because there is an emphasis on precisely defined assessment targets, it is a goal of universal design that performance should not be based on anything other than those assessment targets (AERA, APA, & NCME, 1999) and that points are awarded for knowledge or performance, not other abilities (e.g., speed, handwriting, perhaps spelling and grammar). There also is a focus on eliminating cultural bias. In this context, items are considered biased if groups of equal ability have different probabilities of answering them correctly. A third goal for development of these universally accessible assessments is that if accommodations are necessary (if a different form or format of the assessment must be used because of a student's disability), adapting the assessment into a more accessible format is as easily accomplished as possible. Although it is the ultimate principle of universal test design that the same test can be used by all (in the same way that the same entrance to a courthouse can be used by all), accommodations will occasionally still be necessary. Universal design plans for that up front. This means, for example, that graphical material should be easily describable to a blind student or, perhaps, graphical material should not be used at all unless it is vital to the question or assessment task. The remaining applications of universal design for assessment describe various physical and formatting aspects of a test.

Table 9.1 Applying Universal Test Design Principles

Universal Design Principles							Universal Test Design Principles	Observable Characteristics
Equitable Use	Flexibility in Use	Simple and Intuitive Use	Perceptible Information	Tolerance for Error	Low Physical Effort	Size and Space for Approach and Use		
X	X						**1. Inclusive assessment population** Opportunity for participation for all members of the target population regardless of physical characteristics, culture, linguistic background, or cognitive abilities.	This information is difficult to "observe," but most teacher-developed assessments are consistent with this principle.
X				X			**2. Precisely defined constructs** Performance should not be affected by construct-irrelevant variance, processes that are extraneous to the intended construct (AERA et al., 1999).	Points awarded for knowledge or performance, not construct-irrelevant tasks (e.g., speed, handwriting, perhaps spelling and grammar). Wording for math problems should be simple and clear.
X	X						**3. Accessible, nonbiased items** Items are biased if groups of equal ability have different probabilities of answering correctly. Items also should be free of culturally offensive content.	Words, phrases, and concepts are commonly used across cultures and languages. No pop culture references (e.g., TV, music). No stereotypes or offensive terms.

Equitable Use	Flexibility in Use	Simple and Intuitive Use	Perceptible Information	Tolerance for Error	Low Physical Effort	Size and Space for Approach and Use	Universal Test Design Principles	Observable Characteristics
							Universal Design Principles	
X	X		X			X	4. **Amenable to accommodations** The way in which a test is presented can easily be changed to remove unintended disadvantages for English language learners or for those with disabilities.	Horizontal text. No construct-irrelevant graphs or pictures. Graphics are simple and clear. Keys and legends at top or right of item. No time limits. Subsections of tests are independent of each other.
X		X	X				5. **Simple, clear, and intuitive instructions and procedures** "Assessment instructions and procedures need to be easy to understand, regardless of a student's experience, knowledge (or) language skills . . ." (Thompson et al., 2002, p. 14)	Consistent instructions (e.g., circling correct answer). Directions allow students to work independently without questions. Practice or sample items are provided. Numbered items.

A Closer Look

Great Minds Think Differently

Universal test design is partly derived from a broader educational approach, *Universal Design for Learning*, which was developed to embrace the differences in students, including the different ways that people think, organize their thoughts, and learn new information and skills (Dolan & Hall, 2001). Because of modern brain imaging technology, we can now almost literally see thinking take place, and we know quite a bit about how different parts of the brain oversee different activities. It turns out that there are large differences from person to person in the nature of these different brain areas, how directions are understood, and how the brain is networked to complete simple and complex tasks. Each student brings a unique mix of strengths, challenges, and preferences to the learning environment, and it is less common these days for teachers to think of there being a few types of students or learning styles. Essentially, brain regions can be grouped into three types of networks that control learning:

- **Recognition**. This network specializes in receiving and analyzing information. It processes the content, identifies what is new, what is already known, and what is similar to current knowledge and skills, and it begins to organize the information.
- **Expression.** This type of processing plans and executes actions. If learning is the result of behaviors, it is this network that regulates those behaviors. Similarly, when taking a test or engaging in assessment tasks, it is the expression network that makes the decisions on following instructions.
- **Engagement.** This network is the affective, motivational, and attitudinal specialist. This system sets priorities and controls the energies allotted to engaging in learning or trying one's best on an assessment.

The tools, strategies, and technologies that support universal design of assessment are meant to flexibly meet the needs of all students, regardless of the ins and outs of how they individually happen to process information, engage in learning, and behave when assessed.

Technology

Universal Design Technology

New computer technologies that support universal test design allow for multiple modes of representation (Rose, Hall, & Murray, 2008; Salend, 2009) for taking in information and directions and responding with a test answer or assessment performance. For example, computers can give students control over font, size, and color of a traditional test (which we can no longer correctly label as paper-and-pencil). Instructions, tasks, items, and assignments can be presented orally or in braille. Technology exists to turn text into speech and speech into text, and text and pictures can become touchable (Dolan & Hall, 2001).

The National Center on Universal Design for Learning manages a website that gives detailed examples of technological supports for universal design of classroom assessments. Many of these tools are computer-based, some are traditional hardware solutions, and some are guidelines for teachers designing their own tests.

Technology for increasing the number of ways that information can be represented is described here:

http://www.udlcenter.org/aboutudl/udlguidelines/principle1

Tools for allowing for multiple means of expressing what students have learned are here:

http://www.udlcenter.org/aboutudl/udlguidelines/principle2

Ways of engaging all students in assessment regardless of their individual characteristics are discussed here:

http://www.udlcenter.org/aboutudl/udlguidelines/principle3

Designers of computer-based assessments have given much thought to the application of universal design principles.

WHAT WE KNOW ABOUT UNIVERSAL TEST DESIGN

There is very little real research on the effect of universal design for teacher-made classroom assessments. Recommendations for the approach are driven primarily by theory and philosophy. That doesn't mean that universal design won't increase the usefulness of classroom assessments and allow for fair access to tests by more populations; it only means that it hasn't been studied much and we do not yet know for sure whether it makes a difference regarding assessment and learning. There are a few studies of universal design principles and their effect on *standardized* test performance, however. Much of the research effort in universal design of assessment has focused on these formats because of the federal mandate to include all populations in statewide testing. Presumably, if application of universal design guidelines positively affects performance on standardized tests, the same applications should also increase performance on *classroom* assessments.

A second line of research related to universal design is the willingness of teachers to buy into the philosophy and apply its principles. Lombardi and Murray (2011) conducted a large survey of college faculty at one university about their attitudes toward the principles and instructional behaviors and expectations consistent with universal design. College teachers make many of the same decisions about their teaching as elementary and secondary teachers do, and their beliefs and understanding of this approach likely mirror those of K–12 instructors. The researchers found that teachers who were female, were newer on the job, or had been trained to teach students with disabilities felt much more positively toward minimizing barriers, adjusting assignments and requirements, providing easier access to course materials, and other universal design characteristics.

DOING A GOOD JOB OF ASSESSING ALL STUDENTS

A fairly modern validity concern with teacher-made or standardized tests is the validity of inferences made from such tests for students whose first language is not English. A second somewhat more traditional concern is the validity of these assessments for students with disabilities. Universal design is meant to respond to those validity concerns by producing assessments that not only fairly assess those students, but fairly assess all students regardless of their irrelevant characteristics. Beyond these concerns, though, there is a modern concept of validity that is frequently cited by supporters of the universal design approach. This aspect of validity is known as social consequences validity or *consequential validity*. The usefulness of an assessment is not only whether the test score accurately represents a particular domain of knowledge or skill, but includes whether the use of an assessment is *fair* and *just* in a social sense. The underlying argument for the need for universal design considerations is that traditional assessment scores may represent something a bit different for each student. If some of the variability in scoring is our old friend, *construct-irrelevant variance*, then the validity of those scores is questionable. If assessments are designed from the beginning so that all items are free from cultural bias, all students understand directions, all students can read and comprehend all items, and all students are capable of performing all assessment tasks, then construct- irrelevant variance is minimized.

Deciding the Purpose of a Test

Modern classroom teachers sometimes choose to view the validity of assessments as something a bit more than simply whether they measure what they are supposed to measure. They think of the social effect of their assessments on students. Samuel Messick (1993), a measurement philosopher, first suggested this idea of *consequential validity*. He pointed out that an assumption underlying the broad concept of validity is that tests should serve the purposes for which they are intended. If a teacher, school system, or state believes that the use of an assessment will ultimately help those involved by improving instruction, for example, or by increasing student learning, that intent becomes part of the validity requirement for the assessment. "Judging validity in terms of whether a test does the job it is employed to do—that is whether it serves its intended function or purpose—requires evaluation of the intended or unintended social consequences of test interpretation and use," he argued (Messick, 1993, p. 84). The educational and psychological measurement field incorporated Messick's arguments into a modern definition of validity which now "officially" stands as *the degree to which evidence and theory support the interpretations of test scores entailed by proposed uses of tests* (AERA et al., 1999, p. 9). Teachers with this view of validity are often concerned with the instructional time taken up by assessments, the effects of labeling on students, whether tests are biased, and other issues regarding the consequences on students from assessment.

A Changing Definition of Validity?

Q: So you just dedicated about eight chapters to the importance of validity defined as "whether the test measures what it is supposed to" and divided validity into three types: content, criterion, and construct. Now, you casually mention in a **Real-World Choices** box that validity means something else? What's up?

A: Yes, measurement folks now understand validity as defined by the phrasing in the *Standards* produced by the key relevant scientific professional organizations and quoted in this chapter. It is consistent with the modern perspective that validity refers to both the score of a test and the purpose of a test and that validity is a single thing (without three different "types"). For classroom teachers, or anyone making decisions when developing or evaluating an assessment, however, it is still very useful to separate the various types of validity evidence and validity arguments into the three moderately distinct categories: content, criterion, and construct. Strategically focusing on each of the three categories of evidence as relevant to particular validity concerns is a useful way to clarify one's own convictions, philosophies, and understanding of teacher-designed tests.

Because universal test design is an approach, a concept, that can be applied to either traditional paper-and-pencil assessment or performance assessment, there are no particular special issues of reliability. One benefit of universal design, though, should to some extent have relevance to inter-rater reliability concerns. The level of subjectivity in any scoring system affects inter-rater reliability, and one source of subjectivity is bias. Evaluating unexpected responses or dealing with task performance that does not seem to meet assessment instructions or requirements is difficult. Responses will be more uniform when directions and tasks are described using text that is easily understood by all students. The range of performances should more closely match the rubric categories and expectations when the assessment is planned from the start following universal design guidelines. So one might expect less subjectivity in scoring when this modern approach is followed.

WHAT UNIVERSAL TEST DESIGN LOOKS LIKE IN THE CLASSROOM

"I'm not sure it's possible to create anything that's universally usable. It's not that there's a weakness in the term. We use that term because it's the most descriptive of what the goal is."

Ron Mace, Architect (1947–1998)

Let's begin figuring out how to apply the universal test design principles to classroom assessment by examining them in greater detail. Table 9.2 provides the goals principles with some useful "sub-principles" from the Center for Universal Design (1997) that help provide a transition from a theoretical approach to actual teacher choices and strategies. With this table we can begin

Table 9.2   Application Guidelines for Universal Test Design

Principles	Guidelines (Sub-principles)
1. **Equitable Use** The design is useful and marketable to people with diverse abilities.	Provide the same means of use for all users: identical whenever possible; equivalent when not. Avoid segregating or stigmatizing any users. Provisions for privacy, security, and safety should be equally available to all users. Make the design appealing to all users.
2. **Flexibility in Use** The design accommodates a wide range of individual preferences and abilities.	Provide choice in methods of use. Accommodate right- or left-handed access and use. Facilitate the user's accuracy and precision. Provide adaptability to the user's pace.
3. **Simple and Intuitive Use** Use of the design is easy to understand, regardless of the user's experience, knowledge, language skills, or current concentration level.	Eliminate unnecessary complexity. Be consistent with user expectations and intuition. Accommodate a wide range of literacy and language skills. Arrange information consistent with its importance. Provide effective prompting and feedback during and after task completion.
4. **Perceptible Information** The design communicates necessary information effectively to the user, regardless of ambient conditions or the user's sensory abilities.	Use different modes (pictorial, verbal, tactile) for redundant presentation of essential information. Provide adequate contrast between essential information and its surroundings. Maximize "legibility" of essential information. Differentiate elements in ways that can be described (i.e., make it easy to give instructions or directions). Provide compatibility with a variety of techniques or devices used by people with sensory limitations.
5. **Tolerance for Error** The design minimizes hazards and the adverse consequences of accidental or unintended actions.	Arrange elements to minimize hazards and errors: most used elements are the most accessible. Hazardous elements eliminated, isolated, or shielded. Provide warnings of hazards and common errors. Provide fail-safe features. Discourage unconscious action in tasks that require vigilance.
6. **Low Physical Effort** The design can be used efficiently and comfortably and with a minimum of fatigue.	Allow user to maintain a neutral body position. Use reasonable operating forces. Minimize repetitive actions. Minimize sustained physical effort.
7. **Size and Space for Approach and Use** Appropriate size and space is provided for approach, reach, manipulation, and use regardless of user's body size, posture, or mobility.	Provide a clear line of sight to important elements for any seated or standing user. Make reach to all components comfortable for any seated or standing user. Accommodate variations in hand and grip size. Provide adequate space for the use of assistive devices or personal assistance.

Source: Adapted from Center for Universal Design, 1997.

to picture what the somewhat abstract principles look like when applied to classroom assessment. What does *Flexibility in Use* mean in classroom assessment terms? Among other things, it means designing the layout of a pencil-and-paper test so that it is easily used by both right-handers and left-handers. What does *Tolerance for Error* look like? As the table tells us, one way it might manifest itself in classroom assessment is when test instructions include "warnings" to avoid common mistakes. The sub-principles are kind of like instructional behavioral objectives; they are more concrete ways to operationalize conceptual goals.

Layout and Format of Universally Designed Tests

While the sub-principles provide a good starting point, more is needed for a teacher who wishes to develop an assessment from scratch that meets the universal design guidelines. For an evidence-based list of assessment construction decisions that are effective and consistent with universal design principles, the summary of dozens of research studies compiled by Thompson et al. (2002) is indispensable. Highlights of their cataloging of research findings are presented here, but serious universal design test-makers should get their hands on a copy of the full "manual." (There is a free online copy at www2.lexcs.org/osep/pdf/Universal_Design_LSA.pdf and many other locations.) The specific technical suggestions and construction guidelines that follow are from their review and supported by empirical research.

Text Formatting. For Western-style readers, text that is flush to the left margin is easiest to read. "Fully justified" text (which is spaced so that both the left and right margins are flush or straight) is difficult for even expert readers to handle. Students recall text better when it is left justified and "ragged" (unjustified) on the right.

Type Size. Certain types (what we nonprinting experts call *fonts*) are universally better than others: 14-point type is better than 12 or 10 and has been shown to actually increase tests scores for all students. Students with moderate visual impairment require at least an 18-point size type.

Use at least 12-point for titles, footnotes, and such on graphics and tables. Fixed-space fonts are more legible than proportional-spaced fonts and those that are serif (have the tiny perpendicular lines at the end of each stroke, e.g., Times New Roman or Courier) may work better than sans serif fonts (types without those little lines, e.g., Arial or Helvetica).

Formatting Text. It is generally best to use standard typeface with the correct use of upper- and lowercase. This is generally more readable for all students than all uppercase or italicized texts. To emphasize some text, bolding works well. It works better than switching to all caps.

Text Line Length. The distance between the left and right margin of text makes a difference for some students. One study suggested that 4 inches is the "best" length for a line on a test form. Another suggested that about 12 words is a good maximum length. Whatever the length, if the lines are longer in inches, the font should be larger.

White Space. A large amount of space on a page that is blank without text or pictures can increase legibility and aid in directing focus to the text. (A better term for *white space* is *blank space* because paper and computer screen backgrounds are often not white.) A traditional rule of thumb for test construction is that half the page should be blank. Younger students appreciate even more white space. If this sounds like a lot of white space, examine the page in this book you are reading right now. Notice the blank space in the margins and between the lines of text and so on. The ratio of text and graphics compared with blank space is probably about 50/50 and it doesn't look odd.

Leading. The amount of space between lines matters. A lead space that is too short makes reading difficult for those with low vision or certain learning disabilities. Here are some rough guidelines:

- 12-point type, 2 to 4 points of leading
  - This is 12-point type with 2 points of leading.
- 14-point type, 3 to 6 points of leading
  - This is 14-point type with 3 points of leading.
- 16-point type, 4 to 6 points of leading
  - This is 16-point type with 4 points of leading.
- 18-point type, 5 to 6 points of leading
  - This is 18-point type with 5 points of leading.

Contrast. Some research has been done on legibility as it relates to the contrast between the text and the background. Use off-white or light pastel, non-glossy paper to prevent glare. Type should be black.

Bubble Answer Options. There are several points of consideration when the answer format for a traditional paper-and-pencil test requires that students fill in bubbles. Tests with small bubbles are difficult for students with low vision or trouble with fine motor skills. Students with learning disabilities may also benefit from larger text and answer marking options. There are mixed results in the literature as to negative consequences of having the answer sheet separate from the test (it may vary with student developmental level), but fewer errors are made when one can respond on the test itself.

Graphs and Tables. While black and white is generally the best color scheme for graphs and tables, symbols need to be particularly clear and distinct when color is not used. Use labels directly on graphs and maps, instead of using a separate legend or key elsewhere. Avoid using varying degrees of grey scale in tables and figures if perceiving the differences is meant to provide information.

Illustrations. For some students, illustrations cause a problem in visual discrimination or competition for attention between picture and text. Black-and-white drawings will be clearest to all. Illustrations may be in color to attract appropriate attention, but avoid green and red combinations because some students may have color blindness. Graphics should be right next to the relevant question or text. Some illustrations are merely decorative or entertaining (e.g., a Ziggy cartoon about how tough tests are), whereas others are integral to the assessment task or question. Consider using only those illustrations that are necessary to the assessment, because some students are better than others at knowing what to ignore and what is important.

Writing Universally Designed Tests

The science of universal test design has to do with the physical characteristics of a test that follow the key principles. The art of universal test design comes into play in the actual writing of an assessment. It is word choice in items, directions, and the terms used on an assessment that may lead to the dreaded *construct-irrelevant variance* in the scores for some students. Fortunately, researchers have suggested guidelines to follow when composing items and assessment tasks and when formulating directions.

General guidelines for knowing whether the content of an assessment follows universal design principles and allows "access" to all students are provided by Rakow and Gee (1987).

1. All students would likely have the experiences and prior knowledge necessary to understand the question.

2. The vocabulary, sentence complexity, and required reasoning ability are appropriate for all students' developmental levels.

3. Definitions and examples are clear and understandable.

4. Relationships are clear and precise.

5. Item content is well organized.

6. The questions are clearly framed.

7. The content of items is of interest to all students.

The wording used in assessments can make a difference. Brown (1999) suggests a variety of ways to ensure that assessments are written in "plain language." First, shorten the length of sentences wherever possible. Reduce needless wordiness and irrelevant text; break complex sentences into several shorter sentences. Second, unless it is important to use the jargon of a field, replace unusual words with more common synonyms. Brown gives as an example to say *use* instead of *utilize*. Avoid ambiguous words. Use proper nouns only when necessary. Third, be consistent across assessments and within each assessment. This means use the consistent graphic, table, and mapping conventions. Use the same font and layout every time. Use the same word for an important concept each time you use it. Finally, number or identify in some way each question. When asking related questions or questions with many parts, clearly mark each part with a bullet, letter, or number. Brown found that when students actually know the answers or have the assessed skill, they perform higher on plain language tests, but that performance was not affected for those who did not have the knowledge or skill. This is a good indication that the use of plain language tests affects only the construct-irrelevant variance in performance and increases validity. It increases fairness without disadvantaging any students.

Gaster and Clark (1995) have a list of guidelines for increasing readability, which are similar to Brown's. Among their somewhat more specific recommendations are these:

- When technical terms must be used, define them carefully and clearly.
- When breaking up compound sentences, state the most important idea first.
- Introduce one idea at a time, and develop more complex ideas logically.

- Make it clear to whom or what a pronoun refers.
- If time or setting are important, place them at the start of the sentence.
- Sequence steps in the exact order in which they should occur or be done.

Steps for Assessment Design

A detailed example of procedures for developing classroom assessments that follows the principles of universal design is provided by Ketterlin-Geller (2005). Though her example is specifically for designing a computer-enhanced assessment, the principles and applications generalize well to traditional paper-and-pencil tests. The assessment that is described is a 3rd grade math test. As the author points out, many of the procedures and development strategies used in this test are similar to those for other classroom assessment approaches. The difference is the "conscious and deliberate consideration of individual needs" along the way (p. 11).

Step 1. **Identify and define the construct.** What skill, ability, attitude, or knowledge domain is meant to be assessed? In Ketterlin-Geller's example, the construct was mathematical ability. More specifically, the construct was the knowledge and skills identified as standards for the 3rd grade in the state in which the assessment was developed. These were measurement concepts, geometry, probability, statistics, algebra concepts, calculation skill, and estimation skill.

Step 2. **Identify and define the population.** In this example, the population was all 3rd graders. This population included students with a wide variety of disabilities, linguistically diverse students and students, with a wide variety of cultural characteristics and cognitive abilities.

Step 3. **Choose the testing "platform."** Will it be traditional paper-and-pencil, performance assessment, computer-based, or some other assessment environment? At this step, the designers decided that they wanted flexibility in the level of support (e.g., practice items, navigation options, concentration aids, text-to-speech capability) and chose a computer environment.

Step 4. **Choose the item format.** Ketterlin-Geller and colleagues wished to use a traditional multiple-choice format. To increase reliability, they used five answer options instead of four (this reduces the likelihood of randomly guessing the correct answer). A left-to-right layout was chosen (question on left; answer options on right). Answer options were vertical, one beneath the other, which is consistent with universal design guidelines. Because the answer options would be indicated on a computer screen, they did not need to be labeled with A's, B's, C's, and so on. Because some students might have physical disabilities, more than one way of indicating the correct answer was available (using a mouse or the keyboard). So that difficulties with attention and concentration were less likely to affect performance, the interface was designed so students could select an answer and review it as long as they wished before submitting it.

Step 5. **Compose and sequence the test.** This computerized, 3rd grade math test was written so that directions, prompts, and questions were simplified (the text is easy, not the difficulty level). In an example item provided (p. 15), a two-color graphic is shown of 11 circles. Each circle either is striped or has a crossed-lines pattern (crosshatch). Four of the circles are striped. The question is worded in a straightforward manner without superfluous text: "What is the probability of picking a striped ball?" Because the question is designed to assess understanding of probability concepts, and not geometry terms or anything else, the simpler word *ball* can be used instead of circle. The word *probability* should be used instead of a simpler word, though, because it is terminology central to the targeted skill. Answer options are succinct and only provide information necessary to answer the question: for example, "4 out of 11."

Step 6. **Finalize accommodation options.** This example had built-in accommodation options, such as text-to-speech options, which were available by clicking on a "speaker" icon. Students could listen to a question or directions as often as they wished. An alternative form was available with the same math questions in an even more simplified format. Access to the alternative form was automatic based on a brief pretest screening of sorts that assessed reading ability.

The author emphasizes that though this particular case example used computers for administration, the principles applied here can also be applied to traditional paper-and-pencil teacher-made classroom assessment. This is true, of course, as most universal design "rules" apply to wording of items, the layout of test components, and the up-front careful definition of the intended construct for assessment.

Examples of Universally Designed Directions and Items

The Kansas State Department of Education (2010) produces *Kansas Computerized Assessment* (KCA) tests for reading, math, and other subjects administered to Grades 3 through 11. They were developed following universal design guidelines. The publicly available test manuals include item examples, accommodation rules, and the exact directions meant to be read aloud to all students. The tests are administered on computer and include online tools for crossing off answer options and erasing those marks. The directions and examples shown here are taken from the 2010–2011 Kansas Assessment Examiner's Manual (Kansas Department of Education, 2010). The sample items are taken from free, publicly available software that allows for student practice and can be found at http://www.cete.us/kap/downloads/downloads_kca_windows.htm.

Directions (to be read to students aloud)

"Try to answer all questions, even if you have to guess. If you are not sure about the correct answer . . . cross out any answers that you think are not correct. Choose the answer that you think is best. It is important to answer all questions. Does anyone need scratch paper?

"The questions in this test are multiple-choice. There is one correct or best answer to each question. Carefully read the question. Work the problem. You may use scratch paper . . . Decide which answer is correct or clearly better than the other choices.

"You are to complete the questions in each part as directed. When you have answered the last question, raise your hand, and I will verify that all of the questions have been answered. You may use [a] calculator on this part of the test."

Items

7th grade science item

1. Roberta wants to measure the mass of a ball of foil she has made from aluminum wrappers. It is about the size of an orange. What instrument would she use to measure its mass?
   - A spring scale
   - A graduated cylinder
   - A meter stick
   - A balance

11th grade social studies

4. Due to the Miranda decision, which right are police required to inform citizens they possess?
   - Right to trial by jury
   - Right to notify family
   - Right to an attorney
   - Right to confront witnesses

4th grade mathematics

1. A company made 3000 cards for a game. Ed has collected 2,419 cards so far. How many cards must Ed collect to have all 3,000?

   (Hint: You can use the calculator.)

   - 5,419 trading cards
   - 1,419 trading cards
   - 691 trading cards
   - 581 trading cards

Item Writing and Universal Test Design

The universal test design approach provides general guidelines for producing items that are fair for all students. This is much more of an art, of course, than a science. As an illustration, let's examine the items presented as examples in this chapter of questions, which are consistent with universal design principles. These are the sample items supplied by the State of Kansas for students who wish to practice for the state assessments. Kansas produced their item pool following universal design principles. Overall, these items are very consistent with the approach, of course. Wording is simple without superfluous text. There is plenty of "white space." Online tools and accommodations are built into the assessment. But, if one got picky, one could suggest ways that even these items might work better (at least using universal design as the criterion for "work better").

In the first item, the 7th grade science question, the term "foil" is used in one part of the question, while the term "aluminum" is used later. Universal design guidelines suggest using consistent terminology throughout a test (and, certainly, an item). In the next item, the 11th grade social studies question, the stem asks about which rights police are required to inform citizens they "possess." The simpler word "have" means the same thing and is at a lower level of vocabulary. (Recall the suggestion earlier that *utilize* means *use*, so one should just say *use*.) The final example provided in this chapter, the 4th grade math item, uses an applied math example involving a game involving cards (e.g., *Magic*, *Pokémon*, and other "trading card" games). It is likely that boys have more experience with this sort of real-world problem than girls do, so from a universal design perspective, girls have less "access" to this item.

Real-World Choices Teachers Make

Figure 9.3 Universal Test Design Assessment Instrument

Universal Design Elements	Score		
Accessible, nonbiased items	**0**	**1**	**2**
Items are biased if groups of equal ability have different probabilities of answering correctly. Items also should be free of culturally offensive content. • Words, phrases, and concepts are commonly used across cultures and languages. • No pop culture references (e.g., TV, music, movies), idioms, colloquialisms. • No stereotypes or offensive terms.	More than 1 violation	1 violation	No violations
Amenable to accommodations	**0**	**1**	**2**
The way in which a test is presented can easily be changed to remove unintended disadvantages for English language learners or for those with disabilities. • Horizontal text. • No construct-irrelevant graphs or pictures; graphics are simple and clear. • Keys and legends at top or right of item. • No time limits.	More than 1 violation	1 violation	No violations
Simple, clear, and intuitive instructions and procedures	**0**	**1**	**2**
• Consistent instructions (e.g., circling correct answer). • Directions allow students to work independently without questions. • Practice or sample items are provided. • Numbered items.	More than 1 violation	1 violation	No violations
Maximum readability and comprehensibility	**0**	**1**	**2**
Plain language and well-constructed sentences should be used for items and directions. Questions should be clearly framed. Verbal and organizational complexity should be minimized. • Simple, clear, common words; no unnecessary words. Technical terms clearly defined. • No typos or spelling errors. • Short sentences. No compound sentences. Noun-pronoun link clear. • Sequenced instructions.	More than 2 violations	1 or 2 violations	No violations
Maximum legibility	**0**	**1**	**2**
Items and instructions should be easily deciphered. This applies to tables, figures, and graphics, as well. Legible tests have high contrast, large font size, and much "white space." • Off-white paper. Black type. At least 50% "white space." • Font is at least 10 point. Graphic text has at least 12-point font. • Standard typeface. Purposeful bolding is ok; otherwise text should generally not be in bold. Unjustified text. • Standard use of upper- and lowercase.	More than 2 violations	1 or 2 violations	No violations

Source: Adapted from Frey & Allen, 2010.

Precisely defined constructs Performance should not be affected by "construct-irrelevant variance." • Points awarded for knowledge or performance, not irrelevant tasks (e.g., speed, handwriting, perhaps spelling, and grammar). • Wording for math problems should be simple and clear.	**0**	**1**	**2**
	Score appears unrelated to construct	Score appears moderately related to construct	Score appears strongly related to construct
Total Score:			

ASSESSING THE ASSESSMENT

Six of the seven standards for universal test design can be observed directly (sort of) by just looking at a test. A scoring rubric that can be used to assess the extent to which any classroom assessment reflects universal design principles has been developed based on those standards (Frey & Allen, 2010). The rubric is presented as Figure 9.3. You can use this to evaluate how well any assessment (your own or others') follows the guidelines of universal design.

Ms. Clark Believes Variety Is the Spice of Life (Part II)

Stories From the Classroom

Ms. Clark knew she needed to be reminded of all the details of designing a universally "accessible" test, so she turned to her textbook (which she did still have), some old handouts, and some links to online resources from her college days. As she looked over the broad seven standards of universal design, she began asking herself questions to identify things she could do better on her test. Fortunately, it seemed she would not have to make major changes to most of her favorite questions.

She looked through her questions to make sure that irrelevant knowledge or skills were not required. This was fairly easy, because she had been careful in the past to define her assessment objectives to match her important instructional objectives.

The first adjustments she needed were to make sure that her test was technically sound. These were minor changes that she knew could make a big difference for some of her students. She wanted maximum legibility, so the font size was adjusted to 12 point, and the spacing between the questions was also adjusted to ensure more white space on each page. There were also a few questions that required purposeful bolding to make sure the students saw the key parts of the sentence.

After she was satisfied that the test was maximally legible, Ms. Clark focused on the readability of her test. Because her class contained both English Language Learners (ELL) and students with learning disabilities, she verified that her sentences were concise with simple, clear, and common words. Ms. Clark then read through the directions portion to make sure that those were just as readable. She added sample items at the front of her tests to demonstrate what was expected. Finally, Ms. Clark altered the directions slightly, making sure they were consistent throughout the test.

Another issue that Ms. Clark noticed was that one of her charts contained information about cartoon television shows that some of the students may not know. She worried this would confuse or worry some students and affect comprehension. So she removed those pop culture references and also went through the test to make sure words and phrases that are not commonly used across different cultures were changed. Really getting into it now, Ms. Clark asked a translator who worked in the school office to look it over and provide additional suggestions. After that was done, Ms. Clark felt more confident about having nonbiased items.

With the testing completed, Ms. Clark looked over the test scores to see if the results had changed since the first test of the year. Many of the students who Ms. Clark was concerned with had performed better. Even better, the class as a whole performed higher, and very few students had questions during the test. Now her tests would be ready for whatever or whoever came next. And Ms. Clark always enjoyed a little variety in her life.

THINGS TO THINK ABOUT

1. Can a standardized test follow all the principles of universal design? What about a classroom assessment?

2. What elements of universal design would you include in a test meant for a student whose first language is not English?

3. Do you think there is such a thing as a test that is fair for everyone?

4. What are some populations of students to whom classroom assessments are sometimes not fair that have not been mentioned in this chapter?

Looking Back in This Chapter

- Universal test design is derived from a philosophy originally developed in architecture and engineering.
- Teachers often struggle with designing assessments that measure the intended constructs (e.g., knowledge or skill) without scores being affected by construct-irrelevant student characteristics, such as culture, disability, or primary language.
- Assessments can be made more fair, valid, and meaningful by following guidelines for universal design in their development and administration.

ON THE WEB

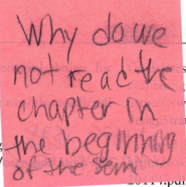

Three principles of u   s for teaching linked to rubric for
learning in general   ; classroom assessments
http://www.udlcenter   w.cte.ku.edu/preparing/design/
guidelines   tegies.shtml

Universal design of larg   esign and collaborative classrooms
http://www2.lexcs.org/   w.sst11.org/Files/PDFs/Hines%
Design_LSA.pdf   .pdf

STUDENT STUDY SITE

Visit **www.sagepub.com/frey** to access additional study tools including eFlashcards, web quizzes, web resources, additional rubrics, and links to SAGE journal articles.

REFERENCES

AERA, APA, & NCME. (1999). *Standards for educational and psychological testing*. Washington, DC: American Educational Research Association, American Psychological Association, & National Council on Measurement in Education.

Bowe, F. G. (2000). *Universal design in education*. Westport, CT: Bergin and Garvey.

Bowe, F. (2005). *Making inclusion work*. Englewood Cliffs, NJ: Prentice Hall.

Brown, P. J. (1999). *Findings of the 1999 plain language field test: Inclusive comprehensive assessment system*. Newark, DE: Delaware Education Research and Development Center, University of Delaware.

Center for Universal Design. (1997). *The principles of universal design*. Raleigh: North Carolina State University.

Dolan, R. P., & Hall, T. E. (2001). Universal design for learning: Implications for large-scale assessment. *IDA Perspectives, 27*(4), 22–25.

Frey, B. B., & Allen, J. P. (2010, May). *Assessing universal design for classroom testing*. Presented at the Annual Meeting of the American Educational Research Association, Denver, CO.

Gaster, L., & Clark, C. (1995). *A guide to providing alternate formats*. West Columbia, SC: Center for Rehabilitation Technology Services. (ERIC Document No. ED 405689)

Kansas Department of Education. (2010). *Kansas assessment examiner's manual*. Lawrence, KS: Center for Educational Testing and Evaluation.

Ketterlin-Geller, L. R. (2005). Knowing what all students know: Procedures for developing universal design for assessment. *Journal of Technology, Learning, and Assessment, 4*, 2. Retrieved from http://www.jtla.org

Lombardi, A. R., & Murray, C. (2011). Measuring university faculty attitudes toward disability: Willingness to accommodate and adopt universal design principles. *Journal of Vocational Rehabilitation, 34*(1), 43–56.

Mcguire, J. M., Scott, S. S., & Shaw, S. F. (2006). Universal design and its applications in educational environments. *Remedial and Special Education, 27*(3), 166–175.

Messick, S. (1993). Validity. In R. L. Linn (Ed.), *Educational measurement* (3rd ed.). Washington, DC: American Council on Education.

Preiser, W. F. E., & Ostroff, E. (Eds.). (2001). *Universal design handbook*. New York, NY: McGraw-Hill.

Rakow, S. J., & Gee, T. C. (1987). Test science, not reading. *Science Teacher, 54*(2), 28–31.

Rose, D. H., Hall, T. E., & Murray, E. (2008). Accurate for all: Universal design for learning and the assessment of students with learning disabilities. *Perspectives on Language and Literacy, 34*(4), 23–28.

Salend, S. (2009). Using technology to create and administer accessible tests. *Teaching Exceptional Children, 41*(3), 40–51.

Thompson, S. J., Johnstone, C. J., Anderson, M. E., & Miller, N. A. (2005). *Considerations for the development and review of universally designed assessments*. Minneapolis, MN: University of Minnesota, National Center on Educational Outcomes.

Thompson, S. J., Johnstone, C. J., & Thurlow, M. L. (2002). *Universal design applied to large-scale assessments* (Synthesis Report 44). Minneapolis, MN: National Center on Educational Outcomes.

CHAPTER 10
TEST ACCOMMODATIONS

Looking Ahead in This Chapter

Though the philosophy of universal design supports a goal of the same test form for all, there are times where the more valid approach, the fairer approach, is to allow for accommodations, small changes in how a test is administered. This chapter explores the legal, ethical, and practical issues of giving some students a changed or completely different version of a test. Many examples of common real-world accommodations are presented.

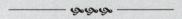

Objectives

After studying this chapter, you should be able to

- Identify the legal and ethical issues of accommodations
- Explain the reasoning behind accommodations
- Summarize the research on the use of accommodations
- List some common guidelines for when to provide accommodations
- Provide examples of how accommodations are used in the real world

Mr. West Wants to Help

Ms. Bartels walked into Mr. West's room during his planning time to talk about Grace. Grace had exited out of English as a Second Language (ESL) last year but was still seeing Ms. Bartels, the reading specialist, three times a week. Ms. Bartels was concerned that Grace would do poorly on the upcoming state test, even though she was no longer officially classified as an ESL student. Since it had been only a year, Grace was still being monitored by Mr. West, and he would decide what, if any, accommodation would be appropriate.

"Ms. Bartels, what can I do for you?" asked Mr. West.

"I just wanted to talk about Grace. How do you think she is doing?"

"She is making tremendous progress especially in reading. She is almost on grade level by most measures. When we read one-on-one, her fluency and comprehension are getting much better than at the beginning of the year."

"I have seen a great deal of improvement as well. I am concerned though that maybe she is still at a level where an accommodation for the upcoming test will be necessary. What do you think?" asked Ms. Bartels.

"I have thought about the reading test and what might help her. But, of course, the use of a dictionary wouldn't work because some of the questions directly ask about what words mean. For the math portion, it might be okay to have a dictionary though. I haven't let her use a dictionary in my own class for math tests because I think it is important to know the terminology. I do let her ask questions, though, during the test, and I pay attention to the words she struggles with."

"What about extending her time limits?" asked Ms. Bartels.

"I have noticed she is one of the last to finish, but she's rarely the absolute last, and I don't think any of those students will have that accommodation on the state test. They do get a long period of time, though. I suppose I could start letting her have a long time on my classroom tests, if that would help train her up. Let me think about whether these are appropriate or necessary and get back to you later this week," said Mr. West. "You know I always want to help!"

(To Be Continued)

"Life's unfairness is not irrevocable; we can help balance the scales for others, if not always for ourselves."

Hubert Humphrey, Vice-President of the United States (1911–1978)

In the modern age of education, federal legislation mandates that students with disabilities be included in valid ways in classroom assessment. Ethically and legally, though, it is appropriate to (borrowing from the opening quotation) "balance the scales" in select ways. The laws have focused on state mandated standardized testing, but all the reasoning and philosophy behind accommodations applies equally well to classroom assessment.

The *Individuals with Disabilities Act (IDEA) Amendments of 1997* required that large-scale statewide assessment programs involve all students, including children with disabilities, even if this requires the use of accommodations and modifications in administration (Dolan & Hall, 2001; Fuchs & Fuchs, 2001; IDEA Partnerships and CEC, 2000). The United States Department of Education in 2001 clarified that "assessment accommodations should be chosen on the basis of the individual students' needs and should generally be consistent with the accommodations provided during instruction" (Dolan & Hall, 2001, p. 4). Under the No Child Left Behind Act (NCLB) of 2001, which now mandated the reporting of standardized test results as a method of evaluating student progress, it was required that all students with disabilities be included in the state and districtwide assessments to ensure that schools are accountable for their students' knowledge and achievements. According to NCLB, these students with disabilities must be provided with accommodations necessary for them to participate in these assessments (Conderman & Pedersen, 2010; Cortiella, 2005; Salend, 2008).

The principles of including all students in assessment and developing testing that allows equal access for all are consistent with the philosophy of universal test design as discussed in great detail in Chapter 9. Changing the test in small ways because of the characteristics of some students and creating a testing environment unique to them, though, is not truly consistent with the goals of universal design. The primary universal design principle might be phrased as "one assessment experience for all," and having different procedures and environments for an assessment is not quite the same experience for all. There are times, though, when for the sake of fairness and validity, accommodations are necessary. Accommodations are "tools and procedures that provide equal access to instruction and assessment for students with disabilities" (Cortiella, 2005).

Accommodations vs. Modifications

Q: Are accommodations the same as modifications?

A: Technically, *accommodations* are different than *modifications*. In its most proper use, *accommodations* refers to physical and procedural changes in

Good Question!

testing conditions, such as a separate room, lighting changes, more time, and so on. Accommodations are something added to the testing experience. Modifications, formally, are changes; they are changes in the version used, how instructions are delivered, the use of translators or interpreters, and so on. To complicate things a bit, the term *modification* also is sometimes used in educational assessment to describe a change or reduction in a student's learning *expectations*, not to changes in the testing procedure. For the sake of simplicity, allow us to use the word *accommodations* to mean both additions to the testing procedures and changes to the testing procedures. An accommodation is, however, different from an *alternate assessment*, a different test version, which following official definitions, is a *modification*.

Generally, there are two types of accommodations, standard and nonstandard. A standard accommodation is an accommodation that is allowed for both testing and instruction that presumably does not change the construct being taught or assessed. A nonstandard accommodation is one that may change the nature of the target skill.

Accommodations can be grouped into four categories (Cortiella, 2005):

1. **Presentation.** Allows students to access information in ways that do not require them to visually read standard print, e.g., repeating directions, reading aloud, large print.

2. **Response.** Allows students to complete activities in different ways to solve or organize problems using some type of assistive device, e.g., reference aids, mark answers in the book, use a computer.

3. **Timing/Scheduling.** Increases the allowable time to complete a task, e.g., extended test time, frequent breaks.

4. **Setting.** Changing the location in which the task is given or the conditions of the setting, e.g., special lighting, separate room, a private study carrel.

Providing assistance while a student is taking a test is a common type of accommodation.

Aligning Alternate Assessments

State tests that are carefully aligned to state standards regarding content and "cut scores" have been chosen, which indicate different accepted levels of achievement. Relatively few students take alternate assessments, so there is less known about expected performance. To validly include scores from alternate test forms, which likely have vastly different testing procedures and may have important different content, in the data that are aggregated and reported at school, district, and state levels is difficult.

There are three common methods that states use to align these tests so that it is reasonable to assume the same constructs are being measured by both the standard form and the alternate form:

1. **Webb Alignment Method**. Curriculum experts (teachers mostly) review state standards and determine the appropriate depth of learning expected for students for each standard. They then review the items on the alternate assessment and categorize them in terms of the related standard and the depth of understanding apparently assessed. Commonly used goals are a minimum of six items for each standard with 50% of items clearly covering a standard and 50% of items at or above the identified cognitive level.
2. **Achieve Approach.** Begin with the Table of Specifications, the test blueprint of what is meant to be assessed. Then, the coverage of the test regarding standards is evaluated, but in much broader ways than the Webb alignment method and with less specificity. A level of cognitive demand from 1 to 4 is assigned to each item and the overall "challenge" of the test is considered.
3. **Surveys of Enacted Curriculum.** Data are collected from teachers across the state about what is actually taught. A mismatch between this "enacted curriculum" and a test form can be identified. There are no agreed-on statistical criteria for what is acceptable. These sort of data are also used to note a mismatch between classroom practice and state standards. Politically, as one might expect, the solution is most commonly to try to change teaching practice, not the tests or the standards.

These same alignment methods are used for the standard state tests, of course, but there are special difficulties when applying them to alternate forms. Alternate tests have been developed to match the characteristics of students with a variety of significant disabilities, which results in many different formats and forms. The other big problem is that assumptions about whether the student has received instruction on state standards are not as safely made, as can be done with students without disabilities. The instructional objectives for these students may, appropriately, have less emphasis on the state content standards.

The most common testing accommodation is altering the testing setting, followed by reading test questions aloud to students (Dolan & Hall, 2001). One criticism or concern with reading the instructions aloud is that a child is unlikely to ask for repeats due to embarrassment. Other common supports include test magnification, using a keyboard to respond, and allowing the use of bilingual dictionaries.

Most states have an official list of allowable accommodations available to provide guidance to special education teachers, regular classroom teachers, and anyone interested in increasing the validity of their own assessments and standardized tests. Teachers who believe that a student might need accommodations should check with what their state has available and follow these guiding principles (IDEA Partnerships and CEC, 2000):

1. Do not assume that every student with disabilities or with a primary language other than English needs assessment accommodations.

2. Base accommodations on student need, not on the category of the student's disability or official ESL designation.

3. Be respectful of the student's cultural and ethnic background.

4. Discuss the plan with parents.

5. Integrate assessment accommodations into classroom instruction. Students need ample time prior to the assessment to become familiar with the accommodation, and the intent of federal mandates is that assessment accommodations should be the same as those used during instruction.

6. Know whether your state or district has an approved list of accommodations.

7. Include the student in decision making; make sure the student is not embarrassed to use the accommodation.

8. Choose accommodations that do not interfere with the intent of the test (this is the validity concern).

9. Determine if the selected accommodation requires another accommodation (e.g., reading aloud may cause a distraction for other students, so the student may require a separate room).

10. Remember that accommodations won't necessarily eliminate frustration for the student or increase student scores (though they often do). They are intended to attempt to make things fairer and minimize construct-irrelevant variance.

Real-World Choices Teachers Make

Making Choices About Accommodations

There are many sets of guidelines a teacher can turn to when choosing whether to provide an accommodation and which type of accommodation is best. Several different pieces of federal legislation speak to what is required and allowed regarding test accommodations:

- Individuals with Disabilities Education Act (IDEA) including the Individuals with Disabilities Education Improvement Act of 2004;
- Parts 100 and 300 of the Code of Federal Regulations;
- Elementary and Secondary Education Act (ESEA), Title I (No Child Left Behind [NCLB]);
- Section 504 of the Rehabilitation Act of 1973; and
- Americans with Disabilities Act (ADA) of 1990.

In this web of rules and regulations, it is easy to get lost in terms of what accommodations are supposed to do and, perhaps more important, *not* supposed to do. New York's statewide website at www.p12.nysed.gov provides a great reminder of the goal of test accommodations:

> The purpose of testing accommodations is to enable students with disabilities to participate in assessment programs on an equal basis with their nondisabled peers. Testing accommodations provide an opportunity for students with disabilities to demonstrate mastery of skills and attainment of knowledge without being limited or unfairly restricted due to the effects of a disability. Testing accommodations promote the access of students with disabilities to assessment programs as well as to more challenging courses and programs. Testing accommodations should not be excessive and should alter the standard administration of the test to the least extent possible.
>
> Testing accommodations are *neither intended nor permitted to:*
>
> - alter the construct of the test being measured or invalidate the results.
> - provide a\n unfair advantage for students with disabilities over students taking tests under standardized conditions.
> - substitute for knowledge or abilities that the student has not attained.

WHAT WE KNOW ABOUT ACCOMMODATIONS

In many situations, accommodations have been found to be effective. *Effectiveness* is defined in most studies as students getting higher scores when accommodations were in place. (This is not the same, of course, as evidence of greater *validity*, but it tends to be treated as such.) A literature review examined accommodations from 1999 to 2001 and summarized 46 studies. Overall three accommodations showed a positive effect on student test scores: computer administration, oral presentation, and extended time. Follow-up studies have failed to quantify or find consistency in the benefits found, however. Generally, studies of accommodations and changes in testing conditions do find that scores increase compared with no accommodations (Thompson, Johnstone, & Morse, 2002).

While research generally supports the use of accommodations, results are not always straightforward and easy to interpret. As an example of the sorts of benefits found, consider a study by Dolan, Hall, Banerjee, Chun, and Strangman in 2005. They examined the effects of "text-to-speech" technology (a computer voice reading test items or directions aloud) on standardized test performance for students with learning disabilities. Using the *National Assessment of Educational Progress* U.S. history test, they recruited a small sample of students who had been identified as having a learning disability to take the test twice (using different forms). On one test occasion, the traditional paper-and-pencil format was used. On the other testing occasion, the test was taken on a computer with an option for hearing the test items and directions spoken. Performance on some parts of the test, those with text passages longer than 100 words, were significantly better under the spoken aloud condition, with a slightly better performance overall using this format. Interestingly, for items related to shorter text passages, there was a slight, but not significant advantage for the traditional paper-and-pencil format. Surveys from the students indicated that they all preferred the computerized text-to-speech format and thought it was easiest. The authors suggest that a support option such as the technology available in this study is only helpful to students when it is used, and they may not have needed it for shorter passages. They also emphasize that the use of new technologies (and other elements of assessment designed to improve fair access) may be distracting or in some other way actually function as barriers to performance. That's why real-world research like this is necessary to determine if assessment design choices actually improve access and level the playing field.

WHAT ACCOMMODATIONS LOOK LIKE IN THE CLASSROOM

In the United States, each state has developed guidelines for the types of accommodations allowed and how they should be incorporated into testing

Text readers, which speak the words of a test, are most useful when written passages are long.

procedures. Each state's rules will be consistent with the federal policies described earlier in this chapter. The National Center on Educational Outcomes (Thurlow, 2007) collects and reports data on current state policies, and Table 10.1 lists some of the most common accommodations found across the country.

Table 10.1 Number of States Allowing Selected Test Accommodations

Accommodation	Allowed	Allowed With Some Restrictions
Oral Administration	8	37
Calculator	19	22
Proctor/Scribe	37	11
Extended Time	41	4
Sign Interpreter	8	25

Note: 2005 data from Thurlow (2007).

Example 1. Kansas

The Kansas state tests, the Kansas Computerized Assessments (KCA), provide an example of how these policies are operationalized. The policy starts with procedures for reading directions to students: "For students with disabilities, the directions may be clarified or paraphrased." Here is a sampling of other accommodation rules for the KCA tests. This is taken from several pages of detailed guidelines and policies. Portions in bold indicate policies that are particularly consistent with what we know about the universal design philosophy (in Chapter 9).

- IEP and 504 students may only use accommodations documented on IEP and 504 plans. (IEPs are Individualized Educational Plans for students who have an identified disability and require specialized instruction. 504 plans are for students with an identified disability who do not need specialized instruction, but may need accommodations.)
- General education students may only use accommodations permitted by KSDE. [Kansas State Department of Education].
- For the read-aloud and paper/pencil accommodations, EL students and general education students must have a student plan documenting the need.
- **Accommodations should not be used on the state assessments if they have not been a regular part of instruction.**
- In order to use the KCA audio voice, the read-aloud accommodation with individual students or the read-aloud accommodation with a group of two or three students, the proper test order type must be supplied in a TEST record submission at least two (2) weeks prior to administering the assessment.
- To use an accommodation other than one listed, contact your district test coordinator who will send the request to KSDE. **If the accommodation changes the construct being tested, the student will count as not tested.**

The policy is also specific as to which accommodations are not allowed:

- **Reading to students any text (including isolated words) in the reading passage on the reading test is prohibited.** Violations will result in the student being counted as "not tested."
- Use of a calculator or a fact table on the non-calculator portion of the mathematics assessment is prohibited. This prohibition applies to all students including 504 and IEP students. **If a student uses a calculator on the**

non-calculator portion of the assessment, the test will be invalid and the student will be counted as "not tested."

- Use of teacher-generated or student-generated journals, notes, logs, etc. is prohibited.
- Use of commercially-made, teacher-made, or teacher-generated graphic organizers (during testing) is prohibited.

There are accommodations designed especially for English Learner students:

- Directions may be read to the student in English or explained in the student's native language.
- **Reading passages, the test questions, answer choices, labels, graph titles, etc. may NOT be translated into the student's native language.**
- Electronic translators and bilingual dictionaries may be used to read directions, test questions and answer choices. **They cannot be used on the reading passage of the Kansas Reading Assessment.**
- The assessment may be given in small groups of not more than three students.
- The entire mathematics or science assessment, either English or Spanish version, may be read to students, but the reader is not allowed to translate.
- A Spanish version of the Mathematics Assessment and Science Assessment are available via the KCA.
- To request the Spanish version of the science assessment, submit a TEST record with a value of "7" as the student's science test order type.
- Students who need access to both Spanish and English version at the same time should take the Spanish version online and be provided with the English-language paper form (*pdf copy*).

There is a list of alternative forms available:

- Braille edition
- Large print edition
- KCA audio voice or individual received read-aloud accommodation
- Group read-aloud accommodation
- Paper/pencil accommodation
- Spanish math or Spanish science translation of the assessment

Here are some of the other specific accommodations allowed:

- Frequent breaks
- Visual magnification

- Scribe
- Communication device
- Directions signed
- Signed responses
- Braille writer/slate
- Student reads the test aloud
- Paper-and-pencil accommodations

The rules for allowing paper and pencil to be used (for what are normally computer-based assessments) are further specified:

1. All students will take the state assessment by computer except in very unusual circumstances.

2. The paper/pencil accommodation is an individual accommodation. It may NOT be requested for entire classes.

3. This accommodation must routinely be used in the classroom when other students are using the computer.

4. Questions to ask about the child when considering a paper/pencil accommodation:
   a. Has the student used the computer for the formative assessment(s)?
   b. Does the student have barriers to using the computer in individual or group instructional settings that require alternative assignments when the class is using the computer?

5. A student's need for the paper/pencil accommodation must be documented on one of the following plans:
   a. Pre-intervention plan (student improvement plan)
   b. EL (English Learners) plan
   c. 504 plan
   d. IEP

Example 2. Oklahoma

Another example of state policy on test accommodations is provided by Oklahoma. The state website at sde.state.ok.us lists accommodations allowed for students with IEPs (Individualized Educational Plans) or 504 Plan designations (for students with special needs who are in a regular education setting) on the state's core curriculum tests. This state's posted policies are specifically for students with disabilities (as officially recognized), while Kansas's policy explicitly allows for accommodations for all students when appropriate.

Oklahoma's accommodations include the following:

- Setting
  - o Test administration:
    - o Individually
    - o In small group (no more than 5)
    - o In testing carrel
    - o In separate location (such as a special resource classroom) that will minimize student distractions
    - o Provide special lighting
    - o Provide adaptive or special furniture
- Timing/Scheduling
  - o Time of day when student is most responsive
  - o Flexible schedule
  - o Administer subject area test over several sessions
  - o Allow frequent breaks during testing
- Presentation
  - o Large print or Braille (contracted) (Test Administrator must transcribe answers verbatim into a standard student Answer Document)
  - o Use of assistive devices/supports
  - o Magnifier
  - o Auditory amplification devices, such as hearing aids or noise buffers
  - o Read or sign test items if test is not a reading test (teacher reading items must read over the student's shoulder, not from a separate test booklet, except when "signing") (Groups of 5 or less)
  - o Color overlays to reduce glare
  - o Simplification/repetition/signage of directions (not test questions or answer choices)
  - o Student may ask for clarification of directions (not test questions or answer choices)
  - o Students utilizing Braille may be provided an abacus
  - o Calculator (3rd–8th Math, 5th and 8th Science—can use four-function calculator only; Algebra I and Biology—can use scientific calculator only)
  - o Provide cues (arrows, stop signs) on answer form
  - o Use templates to reduce the amount of visible print
  - o Secure paper to work area with tape or magnets

- o Reread directions for each page of questions
- o Masks or uses markers to maintain place
- o Test Administrators assist the student in tracking and/or monitor the placement of student responses on the answer document
- Response
  - o Mark answers in test booklet and not on answer sheet, for later transfer by Test Administrator to Answer Document
  - o Slant board or wedge for positioning
  - o Utilize assistive technology communication device(s)
  - o Brailler
  - o Pencil grip
  - o Colored overlays
  - o Abacus (for students using Braille)
  - o Give oral or signed responses to be marked on multiple-choice Answer Document by Test Administrator
  - o Dictate words to scribe (English II and writing test only) (Test Administrator must transcribe words verbatim into the standard student Answer Document)
  - o Utilize typewriter, word processor, or computer without the use of "help" features, such as spell check, and so on. (English II and writing test only)
  - o Student tapes response for verbatim transcription at a later time (English II and writing test only) (Tapes need to be destroyed by the District Coordinator)

Mr. West Wants to Help (Part II)

"Here's an update," Mr. West said to Ms. Bartels. "I spoke with Grace's parents to explain about the tests I use in my class and the accommodations I felt would be useful. They seemed to understand, but were worried about any accommodation that would make their daughter stand out and seem different than the other students. They also didn't want the test made easier just for their daughter. I told them I understood their concern and this would just make it fairer, not easier."

Ms. Bartels said, "That doesn't surprise me. Her parents are very involved and want what's best for Grace. What accommodations are you recommending?"

"I'm considering a Vietnamese/English dictionary for the Math portion. Although the vocabulary is important in my class, I want to make sure that the results reflect what she really knows without interference based on the level of the language used.

"I have one in my room that we have used in years past; you can borrow it now so she can have experience with it," said Ms. Bartels.

"Well, she already has one she brings to class. Also, I have spoken with a couple of students and their parents about a time accommodation, and I included Grace in that conversation. When I asked her if extending the time limits would help her she expressed concern about being the last one done and holding up the class from moving on to something different. She did admit that she felt rushed and didn't take her time on questions at the end of the test when she saw everyone else was already done. I told her that she would be in a different classroom with other students who have additional time, and she felt more comfortable about that situation," said Mr. West. "She understands that it is just extended time and not unlimited time."

Mr. West continued: "I allow this extended time during the classroom tests to make sure the students make the most of that time. I have planned to send them to the resource room where they should have the space and time to complete the test."

"Have you checked your decision against the state and federal rules and guidelines, just so you know what you can do?" Ms. Bartels was always concerned about the rules.

"Well, of course, before I brought in the parents I made sure I was giving them accurate information about the accommodations we could use. I think that as long as I document the accommodation I use in the classroom she will likely be allowed the same supports for the state test," said Mr. West.

Both teachers felt good about the decisions that were made for Grace. Ms. Bartels was happy that the rules allowed for this sort of accommodation on both classroom assessments and state tests. And Mr. West was happy because he always liked to help.

THINGS TO THINK ABOUT

1. Will computer-based testing and the many accommodations it provides increase or decrease the validity of assessment?

2. Thinking about the long list of accommodations for assessment allowed or recommended by states and at the locations shown in the list of web resources at the end of this chapter, do any of them go too far?

3. Should some students be exempt from statewide standardized testing?

4. Accommodations can positively influence test scores. Does this indicate that tests are often biased against students with disabilities?

Looking Back in This Chapter

- Federal policy mandates the full inclusion of all students as part of state testing programs, and it is reasonable to extend that philosophy to classroom assessment.
- Accommodations allow for changes or additions to the testing environments that promote the validity of scores for all students.
- Research shows that accommodations can work and can increase scores of students with disabilities.
- Different states vary regarding what accommodations are allowed and how and when they can be used.

ON THE WEB

An example of one state's guide to accommodations (New York)
http://www.p12.nysed.gov/specialed/publications/policy/testaccess/policyguide.htm

An almost exhaustive list of possible test accommodations
http://iris.peabody.vanderbilt.edu/agc/assess_accom_chklist.pdf

An almost exhaustive list of possible instructional accommodations
http://www.cpt.fsu.edu/ese/pdf/t3_list.pdf

Accommodations commonly found on Individualized Educational Plans (IEPs)
http://www.teachervision.fen.com/tv/printables/AccomCheck.pdf

STUDENT STUDY SITE

Visit www.sagepub.com/frey to access additional study tools including eFlashcards, web quizzes, web resources, additional rubrics, and links to SAGE journal articles.

REFERENCES

Conderman, G., & Pedersen, T. (2010). Preparing students with mild disabilities for taking state and district tests. *Intervention in School and Clinic, 45*(4), 232–241.

Cortiella, C. (2005). *No child left behind: Determining appropriate assessment accommodations for students with disabilities.* A parent advocacy brief from the National Center for Learning Disabilities.

Dolan, R. P., & Hall, T. E. (2001). Universal design for learning: Implications for large-scale assessment. *IDA Perspectives*, 27(4), 22–25.

Dolan, R., Hall, T. E., Banerjee, M., Chun, E., & Strangman, N. (2005). Applying principles of universal design to test delivery: The effect of computer-based read-aloud on test performance of high school students with learning disabilities. *Journal of Technology, Learning and Assessment*, 3, 7. Retrieved from http://ejournals.bc.edu/ojs/index.php/jtla/article/viewFile/1660/1496

Fuchs, L. S., & Fuchs, D. (2001). Helping teachers formulate sound test accommodation decisions for students with learning disabilities. *Learning Disabilities Research & Practice*, 16(3), 174–181.

IDEA Partnerships and CEC. (2000). *Making assessment accommodations: A toolkit for educators*. Reston, VA: The Council for Exceptional Children.

Salend, S. J. (2008). Determining appropriate testing accommodations complying with NCLB and IDEA. *Teaching Exceptional Children*, 40(4), 14–22.

Thompson, S., Johnstone, C., & Morse, A. B. (2002). *Accommodations research & universally designed assessments: Where we've been & where we're going.* Presented at the National Research Council, Best Practices for State, College of Education & Human Development, University of Minnesota.

Thurlow, M. L. (2007). *Research impact on state accommodation policies for students with disabilities.* Paper presented at the annual conference of the American Educational Research Association, Chicago, IL.

CHAPTER 11

UNDERSTANDING SCORES FROM CLASSROOM ASSESSMENTS

Looking Ahead in This Chapter

There are many ways to create scores, and different types of scores have different meaning. Groups of scores can be summarized and described with descriptive statistics. This chapter presents a variety of methods for understanding and producing assessment scores.

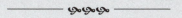

Objectives

After studying this chapter, you should be able to

- Produce and interpret a variety of types of scores including item scores and subscale scores
- Identify the characteristics of objective scores and subjective scores
- Compute and interpret descriptive statistics
- Apply an understanding of the normal curve
- Work with real-world classroom data to produce and interpret scores

"How full of error is the judgment of mankind! They wonder at results when they are ignorant of the reasons."

Metastasio (1698–1782), Italian Poet

"WITH GREAT POWER THERE MUST ALSO COME—GREAT RESPONSIBILITY!"

Stan Lee, *Amazing Fantasy, 15,* 1962 (1st Appearance of Spider-man)

The score a student gets on a teacher-made test, this modest, small piece of data, contains a power potentially far beyond its legitimate worth. As the opening quotations suggest, a test score is treated with great reverence. Interpreted correctly, it provides feedback to students, teachers, and others about how a student is doing regarding meeting objectives, or regarding learning and achievement. Used incorrectly, it becomes a symbol of self-worth and a measure of student character. A score is a simple thing, really, but it is important to know and reflect on what a score is and how it is made.

CREATING SCORES

This chapter describes traditional raw scores, how they are calculated, and when and why different score types might be used. Chapter 13 discusses standardized scores from large-scale district or state mandated tests and what they mean.

Raw Scores

Raw scores are the actual scores that a student receives on a test, the number that's often in red ink at the top of the first page when it is handed back. Raw scores can be calculated by simply summing the total number of items answered correctly or as a percentage of points possible. A raw score has not been converted or standardized in any way. Raw scores provide *criterion-referenced* information about student performance.

Number Correct

The simplest way to report scores from an assessment is by adding up the number of items a student answered correctly. For example, if a student answers 90 questions correctly, under a scoring system that awards 1 point for each correct answer, the number correct for this student would be a raw score of 90. Pretty straightforward.

By reporting the number of items a student has answered correctly we have some idea about how much a student understands. Using our raw score of 90 example, if each item on the assessment represented an objective, the teacher could interpret that the student has met 90 instructional objectives. By using the number correct a student receives, we might also infer, with at least moderate validity, how much overall knowledge that student has on the subject. Notice that the score does not tell us anything about how many items were on the exam. A score of 90 does not mean the student received an A grade or a 90%. Reporting the number correct only tells us how many items were answered correctly.

Computing a raw score by assigning one point for each correct answer has become so common that it may seem to be the obvious way of doing things. However, there are at least three assessment decisions that you have already made when you choose to report the number correct as the score for a test:

1. It's been decided that all items should be worth the same amount of points, so all items are equally weighted and equally important to the total score. This suggests that the classroom teacher, the test's author, has decided that the objectives or specific skills or knowledge domains are all equally important.

2. It's been decided that one should score each item so that partial credit is not possible. The answer is either correct or it is not correct; students get 1 point or 0 points.

3. Points will not be awarded for missing an item or failing a task. Students receive points for getting an item correct or accomplishing a task successfully.

Point 3 may seem too silly to even list; obviously we get points for being right, not wrong. Right? There is nothing about the rules of measurement, though, that mandates that points have to be assigned in a particular "direction"; a high score can be a bad thing; it doesn't have to be a good thing. For tests of depression, high scores indicate reason for concern. Golfers want low scores, not high scores. So assigning points for correct answers or good performance is arbitrary, though it is certainly a long-held tradition and a perfectly reasonable way of doing things.

Percent Correct

Consider the example of the number correct score of 90. If we know that there were 200 items on the exam, we could then convert that score into the percent correct. (Sheesh, this is an awfully long test! Good thing, because it makes the math easier.) We calculate the percent correct by simply dividing the number correct by the total number of items on the exam (90/200 = .45) and then multiplying by 100 to get a percentage (.45 = 45% correct). If a student had a number correct of 21 out of the 30 questions on an assessment, the percent correct would be 70%. And so on.

There is more information in a score that is reported as the percent correct because we now know the *proportion* of items that were answered correctly. The percent correct approach is still criterion-referenced scoring; the criterion is the number of items on the test.

Imagine that Mr. Duguid has developed an exam to measure his students' knowledge of insects. The classroom assessment is meant to be *summative*, as it comes at the end of the unit, after instruction has ended, and will affect his students' grades (in fact, it will substantially determine the grade). His test has 60 questions—50 multiple-choice, 8 matching, and 2 short-answer, with all items being worth one point. Mr. Duguid will combine the scores of several summative assessments together for a quarterly grade.

Table 11.1 shows assessment results for three students. Mr. Duguid has calculated both a *number correct* score and a *percent correct* score and might write both values at the top of each student's test. He might write neither of those scores and, instead, put a letter grade on the paper. For quarterly grades, Mr. Duguid will average the percent correct scores across all the summative assessments he has given during the quarter. Therefore, all of the summative tests will have equal weight for the quarterly grade, regardless of how many items were on each test.

Table 11.1   Raw Scores and Percent Correct Scores

Student	Number Correct	Percent Correct
Mark	42	42/60 = 70%
Emily	48	48/60 = 80%
Jared	60	60/60 = 100%

Table 11.2 Grading Scale Based on Percent Correct

Percent Correct	Letter Grade
90–100%	A
80–89%	B
70–79%	C
60–69%	D
59% and below	F

When using percent scores to convert to a letter grade for a student, one commonly used interpretation, the traditional approach, is shown in Table 11.2. As we discussed in Chapter 3, however, this "traditional" approach is not based on any statistical criteria, but is just something that has become a cultural custom utilized by teachers, parents, and students. (Classroom teachers often must use a district or schoolwide grading scale, but if they are allowed to choose their own, they should decide on one that makes sense to them.)

Subscale Scores

There are a number of ways that scores can represent a student's performance. The most common is for an individual to only receive a single score for an entire test. In classroom assessment, it is typical that separate assessments are designed to measure specific areas covered in the preceding unit. Even if the assessment is summative and treated as a final exam, the whole period of time is usually treated as if it represents a single topic or skill (i.e., geography, reading, or history). With standardized tests, however, designed to identify performance across a variety of domains or skill areas, single total scores are usually not the most informative. For these standardized tests, looking at a profile of subscale scores can be interesting. Likewise, classroom teachers use subscale scores, as well, to develop a profile of performance on a single exam or across multiple assessments.

Subscales are individual groups of items within a larger assessment or assessment system that are focused on a single domain, skill, or trait. Reporting subscale scores can increase the validity of score interpretation. Imagine a student who completed and received a raw score of 165 on a series of assessments or assignments that, when combined, represented 200 different questions or tasks. (There's that ridiculously long test again, but, at least, it's a nice, round number.) If the test covered math, science, reading, *and* history, that single score of 165 would provide limited information about the student's level of knowledge in any of these areas. So reporting a single score by itself does not always make sense. By reporting a raw score for each of the four content areas, math, science, reading, and history, more diagnostic information and a more complete picture of the student's ability in each of the four areas is reported.

Reporting subscale scores as a strategy for better understanding students' levels of performance is a practice that goes back to elementary school, one teacher for the whole day, and report cards. On a report card there is often a broad grade or score, with a listing of the items that determine the grade. These lists of items are subscales. Often the scores on these subscales are shown, suggesting that the subscale scores are combined in some way to produce the letter grade.

When subscales are thought to measure independent areas that are still somewhat related, the subscale scores will often be reported *and* combined into a single score. Standardized test reports do this all the time by showing subscale scores *and* a total score. A battery of subtests can produce a profile for students, which indicates a student's strengths and what areas offer opportunities for growth.

Using Subscale Scores

Let's return to the intrepid Mr. Duguid. (He was my 6th grade teacher, and his name really *was* pronounced "do good," but his tests were not really 200 questions long.) Imagine he taught for a month on the topic of terrain and biospheres. He spent a week on tundra, desert, plains, and rainforest. During instruction for these short units he administered many formative assessments to provide feedback to students and some guidance for himself about the pace of student learning, but these scores did not affect the students' grades. He decided to give a single summative exam to measure students learning at the end of the month to determine their grade. The exam was composed of four subscales, one covering each of the four topics. Three subscales had 8 questions, and the rainforest quiz had only 6 questions, for a total of 30 points possible. Table 11.3 gives the results of this exam for three students.

By comparing subscale scores to each other, Mr. Duguid can see a profile of highs and lows for each student. He can also use the subscale totals to assess his own teaching. By his own interpretation of the data, Mr. Duguid seemed to

Table 11.3   Using Subscale Scores

| Student | Subscale Scores Number Correct (Percent Correct) | | | | Total Score | | |
	Tundra	Desert	Plains	Rainforest	Number Correct	Percent Correct	Mean Percent Correct
Lydia	8 (100%)	6 (75%)	7 (87.5%)	6 (100%)	27	90%	90.6%
Tom	7 (87.5%)	8 (100%)	8 (100%)	6 (100%)	29	96.7%	96.9%
Karin	5 (62.5%)	7 (87.5%)	7 (87.5%)	5 (83.3%)	24	80%	80.2%
Total	83.3%	87.5%	91.7%	94.4%			

provide the best instruction for the plains and rainforest terrains, but was not as effective for the tundra and desert units. For determining the total score on the exam, he chose to treat all four subscales as equally important. To do this, he chose the Mean Percent Correct, which averaged the percent corrects across all four areas, as the best total score. This controls for the fact that the different assessments had differing amounts of points possible.

Item Scores

Just as there are test scores, responses to individual test items or tasks can be assigned scores, as well. In this book, we have described two basic item types that pretty much cover all possible formats. Items are either *selection* items or *supply* items. Either item format, of course, can be scored. Selection item scores are ones in which students select an answer from a list of possibilities, by marking, circling, writing, or otherwise indicating their response. With selection items there is usually only one correct answer. The typical scoring system for these items is to assign a 1 for a correct answer and a 0 for an incorrect answer. (These 1s and 0s provide the data for the item analyses described in some for the features in Chapter 5.) Supply items do not offer possible answers from which to choose but require the student to supply the answer (e.g., essay questions, short answer, fill-in-the-blank, and, essentially, all performance tasks). Supply items allow for many possible correct answers. The scoring for these items often ranges from 0 to some number greater than 1.

Objective Scores

Items with only one possible correct answer are scorable objectively. A computer could do the scoring, as could anyone with an answer key or a list of correct answers. Once the answer key is produced, it does not take any special knowledge or skill to score objectively scorable items. Selection items are almost always objectively scored. Of course, the term *objective* doesn't mean that students might not reasonably argue with a teacher about whether a given answer is correct; it only means that a scoring key indicates a concrete specific answer or answers that should be considered correct. No judgment is required for scoring.

The simplest approach to scoring objective items is to assign 1 point for a correct response and 0 for an incorrect response. Measurement people call this *either/or* type of scoring dichotomous (pronounced die-CAW-tum-us), which means there are only two values possible. Dichotomous scoring makes sense for scoring any learning objective that must be completely mastered or completely learned for a teacher to consider that the objective has been met. So this would likely be true for learning objectives that are at lower levels of understanding. More advanced objectives or skill development often require a range of scores to validly represent where the student is really "at." With multi-point scoring, a teacher may grant partial credit if only a part of the objective has been met or if students could have varying "amounts" of understanding.

Subjective Scores

If an item has a range of points possible, it is probable that there is some subjective judgment required for scoring. Items that are constructed response, essays or short answer, are generally scored with multi-point or partial credit to allow for the varying levels of knowledge or mastery among students.

Subjective scoring could help with the validity of an assessment if the scoring can truly differentiate the varying levels of performance among students. However, subjective scoring usually lowers reliability because of random, unpredictable, or unsystematic application of scoring rules or interpretations of the degree to which item responses match scoring criteria. These sorts of random errors in scoring are far less likely to occur with objectively scored items. The secret to the effective use of subjectively scored assessments is to work on maintaining high standards of reliability, while benefitting from the likely stronger validity of the approach.

DESCRIPTIVE STATISTICS

Educational measurement folks refer to a group of scores on an assessment as a **distribution**. It is convenient to summarize all the scores in a distribution rather than having to list each one of them every time we want to think about them. We can summarize a distribution in a number of ways. We could make a table or a graph or we can use a few values, *statistics*, to summarize all the values in a distribution.

Tables

A simple way of taking into account all the scores in a distribution is to produce a frequency table that lists all the scores received (or all the possible scores) and the number of students who received that score. Table 11.4 shows how this might look for a group of 50 scores.

In this table, possible scores are in the first column on the left, followed by the number of students who received each score, the percentage of students who received each score, and a final column that shows the accumulating percentage of students as one moves down the possible scores.

Table 11.4 A Frequency Table of Test Scores

Score	Frequency	%	Cumulative %
0	1	2%	2%
1	4	8%	10%
2	8	16%	26%
3	19	38%	64%
4	11	22%	86%
5	7	14%	100%
Total	50		

Figure 11.1 Graph of a Frequency Distribution

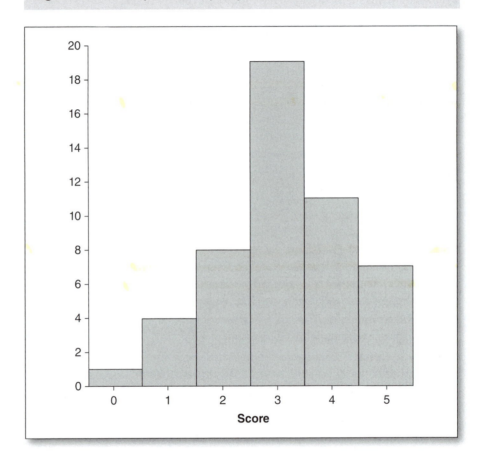

Graphs

For the visually minded, the same information shown in Table 11.4 can be displayed with vertical (or horizontal) bars representing the frequencies associated with each score. Figure 11.1 is an example of a graph or chart showing these scores. The highest bar is above the most frequently occurring score (a score of 3, in our example), allowing for a quick interpretation of how a group of students did as a whole.

Good Question!

Bar Graphs and Histograms

Q: That graph in Figure 11.1 is a bar graph, right? I've seen similar graphs called histograms. What's the difference?

A: Any graph that uses bars (and their relative length) to represent quantities is a bar chart or bar graph. One type of bar chart is called a histogram. If the bars do not touch each other, then the X-axis (the horizontal line along the bottom) represents a categorical (nominal or ordinal level; see the levels-of-measurement *Closer Look* in this chapter) variable and we just generically call it a bar chart. If the X-axis represents a continuous (interval or ratio level) variable, then the bars touch each other to indicate that the scores are on some continuum from low to high or high to low. We call those kinds of charts histograms. (*Histo* means *web* in Greek, so histograms are so named because they look like a web. I guess I can see that.)

Statistics

The numbers used to describe samples of scores are called *statistics*. Two types of descriptive statistics, *measures of central tendency* and *measures of variability*, provide almost all the information a teacher needs to understand the performance of a group of students. Measures of central tendency are different ways of reporting the average of a group of scores. Measures of variability describe how far apart or close together the scores are to each other. Because these numbers describe a group, they provide *norm-referenced* information.

Measures of Central Tendency

Three different numbers can be considered the average. The **mode** is the most commonly occurring, most popular score. (*Mode* is a French word meaning "in fashion" or trendy; the option of serving ice cream on top of pie is called *pie à la mode* because it was considered very chic and fashionable back in the day.) Whichever score most students got on a test is the mode. It's a handy way of summarizing your class performance. For the distribution below, the mode is 8.

0 5 6 6 7 7 7 <u>8</u> 8 8 8 9 9 10

The **median** is the score right in the middle of a distribution. If you put the scores in order from lowest to highest (or highest to lowest), the point at which 50% of the scores are above and 50% of the scores are below is the median score. Sometimes there is an actual score at that point (when there are an odd number of scores). Sometimes there is a point between two actual scores that is the middle (when there is an even number of scores). If an actual score is in the median position, it is reported; if there is no actual score at that point, the mean of the two scores on either side of that point is the median. For the distribution below, the median is 7.5, the imaginary score between 7 and 8.

0 5 6 6 7 7 7 | 8 8 8 8 9 9 10

The most useful measure of central tendency, the most informative average because it takes into account all the scores, is the **mean**. The mean is calculated by adding all the scores together and dividing by the number of scores in the distribution. This magic number is a very fair representation of all the scores because it is a value that is as close as possible to all the scores (technically it is the point that "minimizes the squared distances of each score"). The mean for the distribution of scores below is 7. (0 + 5 + 6 + 6 + 7 + 7 +7 + 8 + 8 + 8 + 8 + 9 + 9 +10 = 98. 98 ÷ 14 = 7).

0 5 6 6 7 7 7 8 8 8 8 9 9 10

Averages and Means

Good Question!

Q: So, in real life, when people say "average," they mean one of several different possible types of measures of central tendency?

A: No, they almost always mean *mean*. Technically, though, they are not using the word average correctly because, as you point out, mode, median, and mean are all "averages."

For the distribution we have been working with in our examples, we have three different measures of central tendency—a mode of 8, a median of 7.5, and a mean of 7. So which is right? Though there are mathematical rules that determine which measure of central tendency is best, basically, either the median or the mean works well for most classroom assessment score distributions. The difference tends to be whether the scores are fairly uniformly distributed. With our sample, the scores tend to be bunched near the top. Only 4 out of 14 scores are below the mean with this distribution, so it doesn't work well as a single representative value of all the scores. The median works better for our scores. The large sets of scores that are produced by assessments such as standardized tests, however, tend to be distributed more symmetrically, and the mean is the average that is reported for those large-scale tests.

A Closer Look

Levels of Measurement and Measures of Central Tendency

The "correct' measure of central tendency to use depends to a large extent on the **level of measurement** that is represented by a group of scores. Quantitatively minded folks have established that there are four levels of measurement; moving up the levels means more information is provided in the scores and allows for more powerful statistical analyses.

1. **Nominal Level**—At this lowest possible level, numbers are used only as labels for categories. They have no quantitative meaning. Analysis consists of counting the number of students in any given category. The mode is the proper average to report.
2. **Ordinal Level**—Numbers are used to show some order such as highest in the class, 2nd highest in the class, or like in a race with 1st, 2nd, and 3rd place finishes. One knows which score was higher or lower than another, but not how much higher or lower. The median is the proper average to report.
3. **Interval Level**—The distance between scores is equal in meaning. The temperature scale on a thermometer (almost any scale, e.g., Fahrenheit, Celsius) is at the interval level; the difference between 75 and 70 is equal to the difference between 50 and 45 regarding degrees of heat. The mean is usually best to report here as the average, especially if scores are normally distributed.
4. **Ratio Level**—This is similar to interval level, but is a higher level because it adds the extra requirement that there be a "true zero." This means that a student could literally have "none" of a trait and there are no negative numbers. This level is where you are if you are counting how much "stuff" someone has (e.g., number of dogs on a porch, years of teaching experience). There are actually academic debates over whether any interesting educational variables are at the ratio level (can a student have zero spelling ability or no intelligence?). The mean is usually the average reported for this level of measurement.

(Continued)

(Continued)

For most analyses, as long as the scoring level is at least interval level, all the useful analyses one would wish to perform can be done. Table 11.5 summarizes the characteristics of the four levels of measurement

Table 11.5 Levels of Measurement

Level of Measurement	Distinguishing Characteristic	Variable Examples	Average
Nominal	Categorical	Gender, classroom	Mode
Ordinal	In order	Grade level, Response to Intervention (RTI) tier	Median
Interval	Equal intervals between scores	Test scores, IQ	Mean
Ratio	True 0, no negative numbers	Days absent, number of objectives met	Mean

Measures of Variability

The mean is not enough by itself to tell us all we need to know about a group of scores in a sample. That's because very different distributions can have the same mean. Examine the distributions below:

A B

99, 100, 100, 100, 101 25, 50, 75, 100, 250

The mean of both distributions is 100, but it would not make sense to say that both groups of students performed the same way. There is a great deal of variability in B, the distribution on the right, and very little difference among the scores for A, on the left. Information on the variability, combined with knowledge of the mean, gives a fuller picture of how a group of students performed on an assessment.

A simple measure of variability is the **range**, which is the distance between the lowest and the highest score. The range for Distribution A is 2; the range for Distribution B is 225. That's quite a difference for two distributions with the same mean.

A more useful measure of variability, because of the variety of analyses and score transformations it makes possible, is the standard deviation. The standard deviation is the average distance of each score from the mean. The actual formula is a bit more complicated than that simple sentence suggests, however, because of some computational weirdness (summing distances of scores from the mean will always add to zero). Here it is in words:

Square root of ((Sum of (square of (each score subtracted from the mean))) ÷ Number of Scores)

Though resulting from a complex formula, the value gives a good indication of how much scores differ from each other and how well they hover around the mean. The standard deviations for the two sample distributions we have been playing with are A = .71, and B = 39.52. Quite a difference.

THE NORMAL CURVE

With the mean of a distribution and the standard deviation of the distribution firmly in hand, teachers not only can get a sense of how their class has done as a group, but can interpret performance of individuals. These two values are useful for interpreting student performance if one is interested in a norm-referenced interpretation because the mean and standard deviation define the normal curve. The **normal curve** is a well-known pattern of scores that is so commonly found with groups of test scores that it is assumed to be universal, regardless of what is being measured and what population is being tested. It is sometimes referred to as the normal distribution or bell-shaped curve.

Normal Distributions

Q: So, almost every variable in the universe is normally distributed?

A: No. But, if you measure the variable at the interval level of measurement or above AND the scoring scale you use includes a wide range of possible scores, then yes, almost every variable in the world is normally distributed. Spooky, huh?

The exact shape of the normal curve (at least as theoretically described if one had an infinite number of scores) is precisely defined and you can find a table in the back of many introductory statistics books that indicates the proportion

Good Question!

of scores you'll find above and below any given point under the normal curve. For example, scores tend to be close to the mean, and very few people score very far from the mean. Under the normal curve, scores tend to be within one standard deviation of the mean (being greater than *or* less than the mean is equally likely because the normal curve is symmetrical), fewer scores are one standard deviation away from the mean, and very few scores are two standard deviations away from the mean. For example, under the normal curve, about 68% of people score within one standard deviation of the mean. Another 28% or so will score between one and two standard deviations away from the mean. This leaves only about 4% to score at the extreme ends of the curve, more than two standard deviations away from the mean. These rounded-off values add up to 100% just for ease of discussion, but there is room in large distributions for students to score more than three standard deviations away from the mean. Very large groups of scores, such as those produced from standardized test administrations, have a small percentage of students who score very high or very low, very far from the mean regarding standard deviations. Figure 11.2 displays a simplified representation of the normal curve.

The normal curve has only a moderate influence on classroom assessment score interpretation. A quick and easy interpretation of any student's score is whether it is "about average" (within a standard deviation of the mean) or "above" or "below average" (more than a standard deviation away from the

Figure 11.2   Basics of the Normal Curve

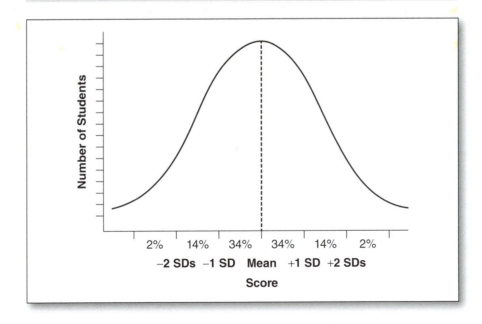

mean). Smaller groups of people (such as classroom sizes) will have scores that look less like a normal curve than the scores for massive groups, such as the thousands who take state tests or the hundreds of thousands who take college admission tests such as the SAT or ACT. Also, most teachers would expect that their own test scores would not distribute themselves in the symmetrical pattern of the normal curve with an equal number of students scoring "low" and "high." Consistent with an "all children can learn" philosophy and with a mastery (criterion-referenced) approach to scoring, effective classroom instruction tends to create curves where more people are near the top of possible points and fewer are at the extreme left, or low end of the scoring range.

WORKING WITH REAL DATA IN THE CLASSROOM

By using a sample of data from Mr. Duguid's class, we can work through the various organizational requirements and computations needed to summarize a classroom full of scores. Teachers usually use an Excel-type spreadsheet to keep track of (and calculate) the data they need for descriptive statistics of assessment results, but in this example we will work through the various steps in calculation that would be done automatically once a spreadsheet was set up. Imagine that the scores for 10 students (which represents a smaller sample than his actual 29 students) on a 25-question geography test were as shown in Table 11.6. Recalling that there were 25 points possible, a column has been added that divides the points received by that 25 (and then multiplied by 100, to show whole percentage points). So, for each student, we know their score in terms of percentage of points received.

> There are really no right or wrong ways to score performance, but there are certainly long-held customs and traditions.

Table 11.6   Scores From Ten Students

Student	Geography Test (25 points)	%
Chloe	22	88
Corey	19	76
David	24	96
Dimitry	13	52
Donovan	15	60
Jorge	18	72
Karla	19	76
Keisha	25	100
Michael	22	88
Teruna	25	100

The spreadsheet can easily compute the mean and standard deviation for us. For this distribution of scores, the mean is 80.8% and the standard deviation is 15.68%. The actual computational steps performed by a spreadsheet are as follows:

Sum all ten scores (use the percentages, not the raw scores).

808

Divide the sum by the number of scores (10 in our example).

808/10 = 80.8

For the standard deviation, the computations require these steps:

Subtract the mean from each score and produce "deviation" scores.

Square each deviation score. This turns all values into positive values.

Sum the squared deviation scores.

2458

Divide the sum by the number of scores (10 in our example). This computes the mean of the squared deviation scores.

2458/10 = 245.8

Table 11.7 Calculations Toward a Standard Deviation

Student	Geography Test (25)	Percent Correct Score	Percent-Mean	(Percent-Mean) Squared
Chloe	22	88	7.20	51.84
Corey	19	76	−4.80	23.04
David	24	96	15.20	231.04
Dimitry	13	52	−28.80	829.44
Donovan	15	60	−20.80	432.64
Jorge	18	72	−8.80	77.44
Karla	19	76	−4.80	23.04
Keisha	25	100	19.20	368.64
Michael	22	88	7.20	51.84
Teruna	25	100	19.20	368.64
	Sum:	808		2458
	Mean:	80.80		245.80

Take the square root of this mean. This is the standard deviation.

The square root of 245.8 is 15.68
Standard deviation = 15.68

Table 11.7 shows the various deviation scores and squared deviation scores for these calculations.

NORM-REFERENCED AND CRITERION-REFERENCED INTERPRETATIONS

Recall from Chapter 2 that scores, or any data, can be *norm-referenced* or *criterion-referenced*. A norm-referenced score has meaning when it is compared with other scores in the same distribution. A criterion-referenced score has meaning when it is compared with some standard of performance. Here are some common ways of understanding a norm-referenced piece of data:

- Bonnie did the best in the class.
- Bonnie did well; she was above average.
- Compared with other students, Bonnie had a lot of absences.

The following are some common ways of understanding a criterion-referenced piece of data:

- Bonnie met all instructional objectives.
- Bonnie received 86% of points possible; she demonstrated a high level of skill.
- Considering how much was covered this month, Bonnie had a lot of absences.

Let's return to Mr. Duguid and the data he had concerning three students that you can see in Table 11.3. For total scores, Tom received 96.9%, Lydia had 90.6%, and Karin got 80.2%. If he applied a criterion-referenced interpretation, he might be satisfied with the performance of all three students. Even the lowest score, Karin's 80.2%, Mr. Duguid might see as indicating pretty good success regarding meeting most instructional objectives. While he might prefer all students to reach mastery level, it is not unreasonable for him to treat all three scores as "good." If Mr. Duguid is applying a norm-referenced philosophy, though, he might automatically treat the lowest score in a distribution as "bad" and only the highest score(s) as "good."

Different teachers have different philosophies. Different tests have different philosophies, too, as is discussed in Chapter 13. Scores can be interpreted in a norm- or criterion-referenced fashion. As to which interpretation is the most *valid*, it depends on the test's purpose. Most classroom assessments are meant to assess the amount or quality of learning, understanding, or ability. The content of most assessments is driven by a well-defined domain, content, or set of criteria. Consequently, the most appropriate approach to score interpretation for classroom assessment would seem to be the criterion-referenced approach.

THINGS TO THINK ABOUT

1. How do the various types of scores differ regarding the information they provide?

2. Which types of graphs make it easier to understand test performance?

3. When might a classroom teacher be interested in the median or mode of test scores instead of the mean?

4. When might it be best to interpret data as norm-referenced instead of criterion-referenced? How about the other way around?

5. What are some of the advantages and disadvantages of using the normal curve to interpret a student's performance?

Looking Back in This Chapter

There are raw scores, number correct scores, percent correct scores, item scores, and subscale scores, just to name a few. They all have different purposes and provide different information. Scoring can be done objectively and subjectively. Objective scores are almost always more reliable, but in a classroom situation, they sometimes have weaker validity than subjective scores. The mean and standard deviation of a distribution of scores provides an effective summary for that group of scores. When scores have a wide range of possibilities, their shape when graphed tends to be bell-shaped.

ON THE WEB

Massive list with definitions of basic descriptive statistics
http://www.statsoft.com/textbook/basic-statistics/?button=1

A free statistics software program very similar to the commercial program SPSS
http://www.gnu.org/software/pspp/

Using Excel for data analysis
http://people.umass.edu/evagold/excel.html

Online doodads for a variety of simple statistical analyses
http://statpages.org/javasta2.html#Freebies

STUDENT STUDY SITE

Visit www.sagepub.com/frey to access additional study tools including eFlashcards, web quizzes, web resources, additional rubrics, and links to SAGE journal articles.

CHAPTER 12

MAKING THE GRADE

Looking Ahead in This Chapter

Just like with classroom assessment, there are different philosophies and approaches to assigning grades. Teachers make their decisions about the best grading approach based on concerns about validity, reliability, and their professional values.

Objectives

After studying this chapter, you should be able to

- Identify and distinguish different grading philosophies
- Identify the characteristics of the five different assessment approaches that relate to grading choices
- Develop a grading plan that is valid and reliable

Stories From the Classroom

Mr. Delatorre and Mrs. McGuiness Get Philosophical

Mr. Delatorre walked into the teachers' lounge during lunch break and heard Mrs. McGuiness asking about last night's parent-teacher conferences. Mrs. McGuiness said, "Some of my parents last night wanted different things from my grading system. One parent actually suggested that I shouldn't use effort as part of the grade, even though it's only a tiny percentage."

Mr. Delatorre asked, "What did you tell them?"

"That the school district says I can and that grades should be used to help motivate students. It is also not fair to students who work really hard to get C's and those students who do not even try get A's," said Mrs. McGuiness.

Mr. Delatorre said, "I have often wondered how to answer those questions to parents because my grading system is based on what the district tells me to do, but when parents come in it is almost like I don't know what my grades mean."

"I have questions like that. What does an A or B even mean! The art teacher takes away points for behavior, but then how does the grade reflect art ability or whatever?" said Mrs. McGuiness.

"Right! Like in high school, I had a teacher grade on the curve. I could miss the majority of questions on a test and still "pass" or I could get most of the questions right and still fail. One teacher weighted the final exam so heavily that all I needed to do was pass the test at the end and it didn't matter if I didn't do any homework," continued Mr. Delatorre.

"Now that I think about it," Mrs. McGuiness said, "I have made all of these decisions without really thinking about my overall approach or philosophy or whether I even *have* a philosophy. I just do things as I go. I should sit down sometime and plan how my grading should work to be fair and precise and consistent. That might really help the parent conversations go smoother."

"That is a great idea. I am going to do that, too; you know, describe my own philosophy of grading. It would be fun to see how ours compare when we are finished, if you don't mind?"

"Just let me know when you have yours done!" said Mrs. McGuiness.

(To Be Continued)

"[In the early 1900s], it was common practice to grade in terms of a percentage score based on an absolute score of 100, [but a groundbreaking study showed that any two teachers were likely to

disagree strongly on the correct grade for an assignment]. . . . The question was raised loud and clear: if grades were going to play such an important role in determining a student's academic career, shouldn't teachers ensure that these wide varieties in their grading practices be eliminated? So, educators began moving away from the 100-point scale to those scales which had fewer and larger categories. One was a three-point scale, which employed Excellent, Average or Poor as the grading criteria. Another was the (now) familiar five-point scale—Excellent, Good, Average, Poor, Failing (or A, B, C, D, F). . . . One popular new method was 'grading on a curve'. . . . One advocate suggested that 2% of the students should qualify for an A grade, 23% for a B, 50% for a C, 23% for a D, and 2% should fail."

Wad-ja-get? The Grading Game in American Education
Kirshcenbaum, Simon, and Napier (1971, pp. 55, 57)

As can be seen in the brief history of grading quoted as the opening passage in this chapter, most classroom grading systems have developed for somewhat arbitrary reasons of convenience and custom, and, occasionally, reasonable concerns about reliability. Most have not been developed based on validity concerns. It should come as no surprise, though, that in the modern classroom, the same big picture approach taken in designing and administering assessments so that they are valid and reliable is taken when designing a grading system or plan. A good grading plan is valid (it fairly reflects performance in terms of the knowledge and ability goals chosen by the teacher), and it is reliable (the grade is objectively determined and summarizes multiple components and observations).

First, an issue of definition: A grade is different from a score. Grades are categories of quality or performance placed in some meaningful order. They can be letters, descriptive words or phrases, or (rarely) numbers. Scores also express accomplishment, but are always numbers and typically represent a summing of points from a test or assessment. So if you got a B+ on a test, that is the *grade* you got, not the *score*. In school, scores are magically transformed into grades. Grades are sometimes placed on an individual assignment, but they are more commonly used at the end of a unit, course, quarter, term, semester, or year and represent a broad composite of many assignments and many assessments.

PHILOSOPHIES OF GRADING

The grading procedures a teacher uses, especially regarding the labels one uses (e.g., A, B, C, D, F), is likely mandated by a school or district or by tradition. When choosing a broad general philosophy about what grades are, how they should be determined, and what they should mean, however, teachers report four common sources of inspiration:

1. The policies and practices they experienced as students

2. Their personal philosophies of teaching and learning

3. District-, building-, department-, or grade-level policies on grading and reporting

4. What they learned about grading and reporting in their undergraduate teacher preparation programs (Guskey & Bailey, 2001, 2009)

Among these reasons, listed in order of popularity, reasons 1, 3, and, maybe, 4, do not involve professional teachers making a decision based on their own perspectives and expertise. Reassuringly though, the second most common reason given for choosing a grading approach is teachers' personal philosophies.

Norm-Referenced and Criterion-Referenced Grading

Grading philosophies tend to center on applications of four of the "important words" present in Chapter 2: *norm-referenced*, *criterion-referenced*, *validity*, and *reliability*. Here's how those terms are reflected in the various grading approaches found in the modern classroom. Performance on a test or an assignment can be interpreted by comparison with other students, the norm-referenced approach, or by comparison with some benchmark, standard, objective, or expectation, the criterion-referenced approach. Because modern classroom assessment involves alignment between instructional objectives, classroom activities and assignments, and assessment, almost every contemporary educational researcher, philosopher, trainer, and essayist advocates for adoption of a criterion-referenced approach toward classroom assessment. This just seems to make the most sense for real-world classrooms. Standardized statewide testing programs have some rational reasons for designing norm-referenced assessments (maybe), but that doesn't

Table 12.1 Comparing Criterion-Referenced and Norm-Referenced Approaches to Grading and Assessment

Criterion-Referenced	Norm-Referenced
All students can get an *A*.	Only some students can get an *A*.
All students can succeed.	Some students must "fail."
A student's performance is "good" or "bad" depending on how that student did.	A student's performance is "good" or "bad" depending on how other students did.
Assessments are designed to assess learning.	Assessments are designed to differentiate students from each other.
Formative assessment can allow students to know how well they are doing in comparison with classroom objectives.	Students do not know how well they are doing until they know how other students are doing.
Teachers know whether an assessment is fair before the assessment is given by basing its content on instructional objectives.	Teachers know whether an assessment is fair only after the assessment is given by seeing how difficult it was.
Grades are usually based on a range of teacher-chosen cut scores that determine which grade a student receives.	Grades are usually based on the proportion of students who happen to perform above or below particular scores.
The standards of quality performance are chosen before the assessment is administered by an expert (the teacher) after careful consideration of the important classroom objectives.	The standards of quality performance are chosen by chance.

mean that classroom assessment should be norm-referenced. Table 12.1 provides a quick "objective" comparison of norm-referenced and criterion-referenced grading.

A criterion-referenced style to grading is conveniently consistent with a *mastery* approach to learning, as well. Teachers with mastery goals believe that with enough time and effective instruction students can master any subject or skill. While sometimes very complex tasks may need to be broken down into smaller, more manageable steps, mastery teachers set achievable goals and expect all students to reach those goals. Their grades are based on their level of mastery set against predetermined standards. Grading based on a mastery approach, and, for that matter, any criterion-referenced approach, will ideally have clearly and concretely defined competency levels. Additionally, the assessment environment should allow for multiple opportunities to achieve and demonstrate mastery.

Validity and Reliability of Grading

Aspects of validity and reliability also play a role in the choices teachers make when embracing a grading philosophy. For grading, *validity* refers to the value and appropriateness of how grades are interpreted. Issues to consider in determining the validity of a grading system are whether the grade truly reflects the construct of interest (construct validity) and does so in a fairly representative way (content validity). For example, if grades are meant to represent learning in a subject (e.g., history, English, math), are the components that determine a grade representative of the important aspects of the subject? Are they given the correct weighting to accurately represent the relative importance of the universe of assignments and assessments that could have been used to evaluate learning in the subject?

The primary reliability issues for grading concern *internal consistency* reliability and *inter-rater* reliability. If a grade is produced to represent a group of assessments, this is parallel to a single test score produced to represent a group of items. Consistency in performance across the different pieces (assessments, assignments) that are combined into the single grade reassures classroom teachers that they are using a reliable grading plan. If a teacher notices that there is a wide variety of performance across the different components within a student and this is true for many students, the teacher might consider whether all the components should reasonably be counted toward a single broad indicator of performance. *Inter-rater reliability* refers, in this case, to the subjective nature of the grading. Conveniently, subjectivity in grading is not a big concern if a teacher is using a predetermined grading scheme. In those cases, the issue of subjectivity moves to individual assessments and assignments. Inter-rater reliability for individual assessments and assignments will usually be high for traditional paper-and-pencil assessments and somewhat lower for performance-based assessments. Solutions for dealing with the subjective nature of scoring performance-based assessments tend to be based on the use of rubrics and other predefined, well-organized sets of concrete scoring rules. These approaches are explored in Chapters 5, 6, and 8.

Using grades as motivation can lead to grade inflation, where everyone gets A's.

There are several potential purposes of grading (McMillan, 2011). The most obvious purpose and the most traditional is that grades provide feedback. They let students, parents, and others know how students are "doing." Grades are usually understood to reflect levels of achievement, and they are usually assumed to be an indicator of learning. So the primary use of grades traditionally has been as summative assessment, an indicator of learning after instruction has ended. A second possible use of grades is as feedback *during* instruction as formative assessment. Providing grades to students while they are still engaged in classroom activities, or better yet, teaching students to grade themselves, can have a powerful effect on learning. A third purpose of grades has traditionally been as a motivator. Research suggests that students can increase self-efficacy (self-confidence that they can learn and improve) when teachers demonstrate the link between efforts, performance, and the grades they receive.

Adopting a norm-referenced vs. criterion-referenced approach and identifying the intended purpose of grading are two factors that define a teacher's grading philosophy. A third piece of the puzzle is whether to include student characteristics other than achievement or learning as customarily defined. Teachers sometimes choose to include other aspects of student performance:

- **Effort.** Grades can be used to reward students who try hard. The idea is that by reinforcing good school behaviors, students will become better students and be more successful both in and out of the classroom. There are some validity concerns with this approach. First, measuring "effort" is notoriously difficult because it is hard to define and hard to see. Second, grades are almost always expected to mostly represent learning, so they may be misunderstood if effort is part of the calculation.
- **Ability.** Students differ in their ability levels and some teachers choose to assign grades based on what the students are capable of and how well they met their individual potential. The disadvantage of this approach is, again, an issue of validity. Potential is just about the hardest construct to measure in all of educational and psychological measurement.
- **Improvement.** Students who improve the most have, almost by definition, learned the most. So it is reasonable that those who improve the

Should grades be used to reward hard work?

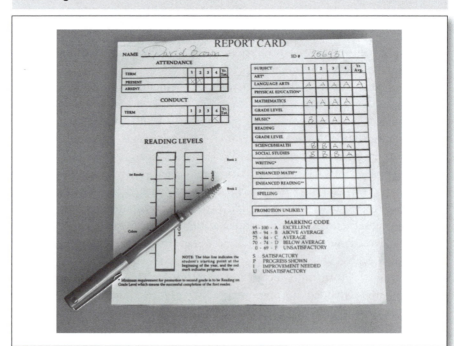

most should get the highest grades. This isn't a crazy idea on its face, but operationalizing this idea in practice is tricky. Students who are high achievers from the very beginning cannot "improve" much, for example.

- **Attendance.** Some teachers include attendance as part of the grading scheme. Indeed, some school districts have grade-related penalties tied to absences. While attendance is not an indication of whether instructional objectives are being met or learning is occurring, some feel that it is important to foster work-related and real-world skills while children are young, and the real world values "showing up."

Standards-Based Grading

Some teachers, schools, and districts are choosing a new approach to the traditional A, B, C, D, and F letter grades, especially in elementary school. This method, *standards-based grading*, differs in two important ways from the letter grades approach (Marzano & Heflebower, 2010; Scriffiny, 2008). First, descriptive phrases replace the letters, and there are usually fewer levels of performance. For example, a third-grade student might be *Advanced* in Reading, *Proficient* in Math, and *Partially Proficient* in Writing. The second difference is that those traditional content areas, such as *Reading, Math,* and *Writing,* are typically broken down into specific skill areas identified by a standard set of instructional objectives. So, within Reading for example, a student could get "grades" of *Proficient* in "Can write an alternative ending to a story," an *Advanced* in "Can identify elements of a story," and an *Advanced* in "Can compare and contrast two stories" (Tomlinson & McTighe, 2006).

Advantages of standards-based grading are that it provides a great deal more meaning to grades than the old way, it makes clear to parents and administrators what the objectives are, and it ties the assessment system directly to performance that theoretically substantially strengthens the validity of grades. When it is implemented, though, it is often controversial and meets resistance. Parents, and sometimes teachers, too, often prefer the traditional letter grade system. They are used to that system, it was what they got in school, it has some shared meaning, and high school and college are likely to use the letter grade system, so students can get used

(Continued)

(Continued)

to that system early. There are other concerns with standards-based grading, as well. Often, not all students are expected to meet the same objectives. Additionally, some of the same validity problems with the old system (e.g., What does a "C" mean?) remain in a standards-based system (e.g., What does "Partially Proficient" mean?).

Form a validity and reliability perspective, standards-based grading fits in well with modern approaches to classroom assessment. Teachers, students, and parents should develop a shared understanding of the criteria for the various levels of achievement, which should help validity. Grades now describe specific, individual, well-defined objectives and are no longer a broad summary of possibly unrelated items. This should increase the reliability of report cards.

GRADING AND THE DIFFERENT APPROACHES TO ASSESSMENT

Modern classroom assessment applies the methods of five different approaches to classroom assessment. They each have earned a separate chapter in this book. The different assessment approaches suggested are consistent with certain grading approaches.

Traditional Paper-and-Pencil Assessment

The traditional grading systems have long assumed that grades should be based on "percent of points possible," and traditional paper-and-pencil tests are also typically scored and "graded" using the same system. Consequently, the validity of a grading system, whether for a course, an assignment, or an assessment, depends to the validity of the grade assignment rules. Does 90% = A and 80% = B, and so on, for example, because that is the way the teacher has always seen it done? Or has the teacher considered the knowledge-based objectives covered by a test or in a unit and made a professional decision that answering 90% of the questions on a multiple-choice test represents excellent "A-level" achievement?

Performance-Based Assessment

One unique issue regarding assigning letter grades related to performance-based assessment is whether grades should be determined by improvement or development. Though any assessment system can contribute scores used to evaluate improvement or change over time, it is portfolio assessment that is often designed to specifically illustrate change across time. So should improvement or development affect student grades?

Teachers, as professionals, make philosophical choices about their teaching approach. Teachers' approaches to classroom assessment, for example, are clearly driven by their values and how they see the role of assessment in the modern classroom. Grades are the same; how a teacher defines the meaning of a letter grade depends on the teacher's values. Grading based on the kind of improvement that can be seen with portfolio assessment makes sense if grades are meant

- to reflect growth (obviously, perhaps),
- to reflect effort (students who try harder across time might "deserve" a high grade), or
- to be used as motivation.

Those who advocate for grades to be used to reflect improvement believe that it will increase student motivation or can "jump-start" improved performance among students who have a history of low grades. If you adopt this grading approach, be sure that students have the ability to improve. Although it is likely that all students can learn and have the general ability to improve, if improvement is tied to a baseline standard that the student has not, or cannot, reach, grades based on improvement cannot act as effective motivation.

Formative Assessment

The grading guidelines for formative assessment discussed in Chapter 4 apply here. Formative assessment is designed to give feedback during instruction, while learning is happening, so performance on formative assessment rarely should affect grades.

Table 12.2 Whether to Assign Grades to Authentic Assessment

Assessment Purpose	Examples	Reporting Methods
Instruction and assessment are embedded in a process approach	• Collaborative projects • Research reports • Debates • Interviews • Journals	• Not graded • Student-led conference • Detailed written summaries
To motivate and inform students	• Student-led portfolios • Frequent writing • Pair-and-share	• Not graded • Self-scored
To inform students and parents	• Total score from scoring rubric	• Grade based on cumulative points

Authentic Assessment

Special grading issues related to authentic assessment depend on the extent to which the assessment includes portfolios and the extent to which the assessment includes formative assessment. Chapter 7 explores the irony inherent in summarizing portfolios with a letter grade. The collection of student work and evidence of growth and development was meant to replace single scores or grades as indicators of student accomplishment and learning. Fischer and King (1995) point out that whether to grade authentic assessment such as portfolios depends on their purpose. Table 12.2 reflects their decision-making process as to whether to assign grades for authentic assessment.

Universal Test Design

The underlying philosophy of universal design, regarding classroom assessment, is "one test for all." If we extend this goal to grading systems, then the same grading rules, and the definition of those grades, should be used for all students. It is common, and not unreasonable, though, that teachers have different expectations for different students or different student populations (e.g., students with disabilities, students whose first language is not English). Applying different grading standards to different students in this context might be justified, but it is inconsistent with the universal test design way of thinking.

A Closer Look

The Game of Grades

Game Theory is a way of thinking about human behavior that assumes people adapt their behavior so as to maximize "wins" and minimize "losses." Classrooms can be thought of that way with high grades as a *win* and low grades as a *loss* (Newfields, 2007).

One way to categorize games is whether they are *zero-sum* games or *non-zero-sum* games. In zero-sum games, there must be some winners and some losers. In non-zero-sum games, all players can win (or lose). The differences between norm-referenced and criterion-referenced grading parallel the differences in these two game types. Another way to describe games is in terms of how much information is known about what one has to do to "win." *Perfect information* games have crystal clear rules and scoring systems known and fully understood to all players. *Bayesian* games provide only incomplete information to players, and the possible outcomes are not known. A classroom assessment system that emphasizes the performance criteria that matter most, and may even have determined the scoring rules collaboratively with students, represents the perfect information game. Based on what we know about different grading philosophies and the power of modern classroom assessment approaches such as formative and authentic assessment, the fairest and most instructionally effective grading game would seem to be a *non-zero-sum, perfect information* game.

TALKING WITH PARENTS ABOUT GRADES

The number one question that parents have when talking with teachers about assessment information is probably "What does this say about my child's learning?" While parents tend to favor standardized testing as one assessment tool, they overwhelmingly prefer talking with teachers about student grades as the best way to really understand their children's learning. Even better is when a teacher shows parents an actual example of student work and the grade the work earned (Shepard & Bliem, 1995).

A parent can understand what a grade means, what it tells us about learning, and what should happen next when a teacher shares the process that led to the grade. The same transparency that exists in modern classrooms between teachers and students regarding the objectives of assessments and assignments and the rules used for both scoring and the subsequent assignment of letter grades should be applied to parents. These guidelines may be helpful when talking to parents about student grades:

- Provide examples of actual student work. If you already use a portfolio assessment system where you have collected examples of student work, this is all part of the conferencing with parents and students that comes along with that approach.
- Share the scoring rubric (if there is one) that you used for the relevant assignments. If parents can see the concrete criteria for what indicates high quality work, they are more likely to conclude that the assignment of a score and subsequent grade was fair and sensible. Explain how those criteria were chosen.
- Share the grading rules you used for choosing between different levels of letter grades. If these standards are tougher (or easier) than what parents experienced when they were in school, you might explain your philosophy (or, perhaps, your school's philosophy or guidelines) for setting those "cut scores." It is likely that your grading system is criterion-referenced, not norm-referenced, so make it clear that this grade doesn't categorize their student as below (or above) average.
- Talk about your expectation for what happens next. Will you be changing your instructional strategy? Do you expect your students to change their classroom behaviors? How do you think this grade relates to student learning and student effort? What do you expect from the parents?
- Listen. The most important thing a teacher can do in a parent-teacher conference is to listen to parents without anticipating their concerns. What do they want to know? What do they expect of you and their child? Parents, of course, are not the enemy. They may be anxious, though, especially if they anticipate "bad news" about their child's performance. Solid, specific, and accurate information in response to their heard concerns helps.

GRADING PLANS

Grading plans are made up of two components: the "*recipe*" (the ingredients, which are the assessments and their scores that are combined to produce a grade and the relative weight given to each score), and a **grading scale**, which determines which scores become which grades. The recipe is usually determined by the classroom teacher, whereas the grading scale is often mandated by a school or district. Here are real-world examples of each.

Recipes

Example 1: Secondary Level

Grades are based on four homework assignments and five exams. A total of 200 points is possible.

Homework = 60 points.

Homeworks 1–3 are worth 10 points each; Homework 4 is worth 30 points.

Exams are worth 140 points.

Exams 1–4 are worth 25 points each; The final is worth 40 points.

In Example 1, grades are based on many different assessments, five exams and four homework assignments. This is likely more reliable than assigning grades based on just one or two tests or assignments.

Example 2: Secondary Level

"Course grades are based on 10 quizzes (50%) and a written report (50%). A total of 100 points is possible. The quizzes consist of 10 multiple-choice questions based on the previous week's lesson. You write your report as part of a group of about four people. Your group will turn in a single report."

Different ways of demonstrating learning are combined in Example 2. Traditional paper-and-pencil tests are combined with a group, written project, with both parts of equal weight.

Example 3: Elementary Level (from an elementary school in Chesterfield, Virginia)

"All children receive grades in PE, Art and Music classes. This grade is based on a student's performance of skills that are taught in the nine-week grading period. Keep in mind that resource classes meet once a week for 45 minutes of instruction.

PLEASE BE AWARE THAT YOUR CHILD'S GRADE REFLECTS A SPECIFIC PIECE OF THE SYLLABUS, NOT AN OVERALL MEASURE OF YOUR CHILD'S ATHLETIC, MUSICAL, AND/OR ARTISTIC ABILITY."

The information to parents shown in Example 3 indicates that grades are not meant to be treated as indicators of student ability.

Example 4: Elementary Level—Math (from an elementary classroom in Walkersville, Maryland)

Assessments—30% of final grade

     Teacher-created quizzes and tests

     District- or textbook -developed end-of-unit assessments

Guided/Independent Practice—65% of final grade

     Activity and textbook pages

     Daily practice

Participation/Homework/Effort—5% of final grade

     Discussion

     Journals

     Exit cards

     Participation

     Homework

The following rubric will be used for both math and science to evaluate participation, homework, and effort.

Participation, Effort, and Homework Rubric

5 Student consistently demonstrates excellent performance in participation, effort, and homework.

4 Student consistently demonstrates satisfactory performance in participation, effort, and homework.

3 Student demonstrates inconsistent participation, effort, and homework completion, but student performance is generally satisfactory.

2 Student demonstrates inconsistent participation, effort, and homework completion, but student performance is generally unsatisfactory.

1 Student consistently demonstrates poor performance in participation, effort, and homework.

In Example 4, the actual rubric for assigning grades is shared with parents and students.

Grading Scales

Just as there are a variety of different components that can be combined to produce a letter grade, there are a variety of grading scales that are used. A grading scale consists of the numerical rules for what percentage of points results in each letter grade. Sometimes a qualitative, verbal description is used instead of percentage of points, but a simple table with Column A being full of different percentages and Column B made up of descending letter grades is traditional and almost always used. In these real-world examples, notice that while specifics vary, a 93% cutoff score, is now the norm for what constitutes an "A." This is likely different from what your parents experienced, when 90% usually meant "A" work. Theoretically, at least, A's are tougher to get now than in the old days.

Example 1: Secondary Level (from a private, Catholic Missouri high school)

Reports for the first and third quarters are distributed to all parents at parent-teacher conferences. Reports for first and second semester are mailed home. This school uses a software program as a means to communicate up-to-date grades for each student electronically with the student and his or her parents. Exams are given at the end of each semester. The exam grade will count for 20% of the semester grade. Semester grades are calculated by averaging the two quarters in the semester along with the semester exam. Each quarter receives 40% weight while the exam is weighted 20% of the semester grade. Grades are interpreted as follows:

A   =   93–100 Superior Work

B   =   86–92 Above Average Work

C   =   77–85 Average Work

D   =   70–76 Below Average Work

F   =   0–69 Failing Work

I   =   Incomplete Work

CONDUCT: Satisfactory Conduct

Conduct Needs Improvement

Unsatisfactory Conduct

Example 2: Secondary Level (from a middle school in Manassas, Virginia)

Achievement is based on actual academic assignments directly related to the Curriculum Action Plan, whereas effort and conduct are based on the observed behaviors of the student.

A = Excellent 93–100%   4.0

Demonstrates outstanding scholarship and achievement:
Achieves maximum growth in relation to the established objectives. Is self-directed in his/her attainment. Evidences understanding and appreciation of the fundamental concepts of the subject area. Exercises superior ability in problem solving and in arriving at logical conclusions. Shows originality in preparation of assignments. Is responsible and participates positively in class activities. Expresses ideas clearly both orally and in writing. Submits all work on or before due date. Displays neatness, legibility, and accuracy in work.

B+ = Very Good   90–92%   3.4

Displays all of the characteristics of the "B" student and some of the characteristics of the "A" student. Modulates between the characteristics of the "B" and "A" student.

B = Good   84–89%   3.0

Displays many of the same characteristics of the "A" student. Demonstrates above average scholarship and achievement. Does his/her assignments thoroughly and accurately and makes creative contributions. Is responsible and participates in class activities.

C+ = High Average   81–83%   2.4

Displays all the characteristics of the "C" student and some of the characteristics of the "B" student. Modulates between the characteristics of the "C" student and the "B" student.

C = Average   74–80%   2.0

Achieves many of the objectives developed for the class. Is responsible and participates in class activities. Frequently requires individual direction. Demonstrates average scholarship and achievement. Finishes most projects or assignments within the time allotted.

D+ = Fair   71–73%   1.4

Displays all the characteristics of the "D" student and some of the characteristics of the "C" student. Modulates between the characteristics of the "D" student and the "C" student.

D = Below Average   65–70%   1.0

Frequently falls below the level of achievement of which he/she is capable. Seldom completes an undertaking without teacher directions and encouragement. Demonstrates little understanding of instructional objectives. May be irregular in attendance and generally fails to make up missed work. Although efforts may have been made to improve, submitted work is still of poor quality. Shows little interest in the class and rarely contributes.

F = Failing   64% and below 0.0

Infrequently completes assignments. Demonstrates no effort though he/she has ability. Receives an "incomplete" and does nothing to warrant its change in the time allotted. Has excessive unexcused absences. Fails to meet the minimum requirements of the course. Fails to complete course work due to excessive absences. Fails to complete 65% of the assigned evaluated work

Example 3: Secondary Level (from a middle school classroom in Ann Arbor, Michigan)

A+   Exceptional mastery of standards—100%

A   Exceptional mastery of standards—93–99%

A–   Exceptional mastery of standards—90–92%

B+   Above Average mastery of standards—87–89%

B   Above Average mastery of standards—83–86%

B–   Above Average mastery of standards—80–82%

C+   Average mastery of standards—77–79%

C   Average mastery of standards—73–76%

C–   Average mastery of standards—70–72%

D+   Needs improvement—67–69%

D   Needs improvement—63–66%

D–   Needs improvement—60–62%

E   Failing—59% and below

S+   Satisfactory—available option for 6th grade exploratory, special ed, hospitalizations, temporary students, extraordinary circumstances use only

S   Satisfactory—available option for 6th grade exploratory, special ed, hospitalizations, temporary students, extraordinary circumstances use only

S–   Satisfactory—available option for 6th grade exploratory, special ed, hospitalizations, temporary students, extraordinary circumstances use only

U   Unsatisfactory—available option for 6th grade exploratory, special ed, hospitalizations, temporary students, extraordinary circumstances use only

I   Incomplete—extenuating circumstances, opportunity to make up work

NM   not enough information—too short a time to give a grade also used for advisory

Example 4: Elementary and Secondary Level (from a district in Tennessee)

GRADING SYSTEM

The Board believes that the issuance of grades serves to promote continuous evaluation of student performance, to inform the student and his or her parents of the student's performance, and to provide a basis for bringing about change, when necessary, in student performance.

GRADES K–2

The basic grading system for Grades K–2 shall be:

S........Satisfactory Performance

N.......Performance in Need of Improvement

A percentage grading system shall not be used in Grades K–2.

GRADE 3:

The basic grading system for Grade 3 in Science, Social Studies, Health and Safety, Handwriting, Music, Art, and Physical Education shall be the same as the basic grading system for Grades 4–12.

The basic grading system for Grade 3 in Reading, English, Spelling, and Math shall be the same as the basic grading system for Grades 4–12.

GRADES 4–12:

The basic grading system for Grades 4–12 shall be:

A.............100–93

B............. 92–85

C............. 84–75

D............. 74–70

F............. Below 70

CITIZENSHIP:

Citizenship grades are based on behavior and should not be deducted from scholastic grades. Citizenship shall be marked as follows:

Good   Fair   Poor

INCOMPLETED ASSIGNMENTS:

The student is responsible for completing all work missed during absences. (EXCEPTIONS: In case of modified day and/or suspension, see Board Policies "Code of Behavior and Discipline" and "Student Suspensions.") It is the responsibility of the student to contact the teacher(s) in order to obtain required assignment(s) missed during absences.

The work of a student whose grades are satisfactory, but are withheld because of failure to complete the required work shall be reported as incomplete "I." If the incomplete is not removed within the following nine weeks period, it will then become an "F." Also, if the incomplete is not removed between the time school is out in the spring and the time school begins in the fall, the incomplete "I" will become an "F."

Example 5: Elementary Level (from a Walkersville, Maryland school)

I hope that the following information will help you understand the grades your 3rd grader earns this year. Please feel free to call with any questions. Term or quarterly grades will be noted on the report card following the following guidelines from Reg. No. 500-06:

A—Exemplary Performance

Consistently meets and/or exceeds curriculum standards and class requirements.

B—Skilled Performance

Frequently meets and/or exceeds curriculum standards and class requirements

C—Satisfactory Performance

Generally meets curriculum standards and class requirements, though some curriculum standards and class requirements may remain as yet unmet

D—Minimally Acceptable

Meets some curriculum standards and class performance requirements, though many curriculum standards and class requirements remain as yet unmet

F—Unacceptable Performance

Meets few, if any, curriculum standards and class requirements

Letter grades are based on the following percentages.

A   90–100

B   80–89

C   70–79

D   60–69

F   59 or below

In grades K–5, teachers also record an instructional level on the report card each term for language arts and mathematics using symbols as follows:

+ Receives Essential Curriculum with Enrichment

√ Receives Essential Curriculum

/ Receives Essential Curriculum with Intensive Intervention

* Receives Alternative Curriculum Based on IEP

In grades 1–5, the following evaluation code is used to indicate progress in student learning skills in the areas of effort and behavior:

X Consistently

\ Sometimes

Rarely

Example 6: Elementary Level (from an elementary school in Manassas, Virginia)

Figure 12.3

Grading Scales

Kindergarten		1st–2nd Grades	
S	Satisfactory	S+	Consistently meets or exceeds objectives
N	Needs Improvement	S	Satisfactorily meets objectives
P	Progressing	S–	Inconsistently meets objectives
U	Unsatisfactory	N	Needs Improvement
		U	Unsatisfactory Progress

3rd–5th Grades					
Grading Scale		Handwriting, Art, Music, P.E.		Work Habits	
100–93	A	4	Outstanding	O	Outstanding
92–84	B	3	Satisfactory Progress	S	Satisfactory Progress
83–74	C	2	Needs Improvement	N	Needs Improvement
73–65	D	1	Unsatisfactory	U	Unsatisfactory
64–0	F			NA	Not Applicable

Mr. Delatorre and Mrs. McGuiness Get Philosophical (Part II)

Mr. Delatorre and Mrs. McGuiness got back together a few days later to discuss their personal grading philosophies. Mr. Delatorre confessed first.

"I really found that my grading system needed better alignment with my teaching philosophy. An overwhelming amount of my assignments are individual, because I feel like it is hard to gauge a student's understanding when part of a group product. And when students work on their individual assignments, the more effort they put into it, the higher the level of quality will be. So it seems like effort is already built into that performance. So I award points based on effort. I want my students to know that, yes, mastering the skills is the only important thing. Also, knowing where they stand relative to their peers is very important, so I expect to give as many D's as A's," explained Mr. Delatorre.

Mrs. McGuiness was surprised that they had such different teaching philosophies. They had worked together for a few years, and they had never had this talk before. "Mr. Delatorre, we are on two different pages there. I believe that every student should have the opportunity to get an A if they have done everything I have asked them to. I want my students to reach a goal not through competition with each other, but against themselves. My A's mean that a student has mastered everything I have taught. What do your grades mean?"

"Well, they mean that on any particular assignment, some students did well above average and others did average and some did below average. After all, that's what I think letter grades should mean; who's average, who's above average, who's below, and so on. Most of my students will fall around the average. I will also have control over the cut scores to determine where the grades are so there might not be an equal number of A's and F's and maybe none of either. If I wanted my grades to say that a student has mastered an objective but there are only 10 questions and most of them miss two, then nobody has mastered that objective. I might make my test a little easier to ensure A's are obtained. Could an 80 percent actually mean proficient or maybe only a 100 percent means proficient," said Mr. Delatorre.

"But you are not taking into consideration how well the child has done according to the objectives. I know that my grading system is based on what 'normal' students should be able to do. And in terms of weighting your grades . . . ?"

Mr. Delatorre said, "I still have more weight placed on tests and less placed on homework and then combine them at the end for their final quarter grade just like the district asks me to do. I still choose not to include attendance or effort, but I have even eliminated taking off points for being late because that would throw off my distribution and not really show a student's achievement relative to their classmates."

"I think that attendance and effort play a role in grades anyway, so why not separate it out to demonstrate to parents that attendance is important and to help motivate students to be there and put forth effort?" Mrs. McGuiness asked. "This might not work for all students, but it targets those who might not have the motivation to begin with," she explained.

"It makes sense that our grading philosophies would align with our teaching philosophies, I guess," said Mr. Delatorre. "Even though we don't agree on the right way to do it. A B in your class does not mean the same thing as a B in my class."

"True, but we both have a sense of what our grades do mean. That may put us ahead of our nonphilosopher colleagues, at least!" Mrs. McGuiness joked. "I know there was a reason for why I grade the way I do." She smiled. "At least now I know I have a philosophy about grading and can answer questions about it!"

On that, they could both agree.

THINGS TO THINK ABOUT

1. What do you think of the massively popular grading scale of A, B, C, D, and F?

2. Should grades be assigned based on anything other than performance?

3. What does the future hold for **standards-based grading** where you will be teaching?

4. What are the important differences among the five real-world examples of grading plans shown in this chapter?

5. What are the consequences of giving a student an F? What should the consequences be?

Looking Back in This Chapter

Grading systems can be norm-referenced or criterion-referenced and can be used for a variety of purposes. Grades can be designed to motivate, inform, or encourage development and learning. The different approaches to modern classroom assessment (traditional, performance-based, formative, authentic, and universal design) have different implications for how grades are determined and their purpose in the classroom. There is a variety of different real-world grading plans that serve different purposes.

ON THE WEB

Information on a grade tracking tool to share with students
http://udi.uconn.edu/index.php?q=node/464

A handy chart to convert grades to points and vice versa
http://inquiry.princetonreview.com/leadgentemplate/GPA_popup.asp

Modern grading approaches
http://www.education.com/magazine/article/traditional-grades/

An almost exhaustive list of different grading approaches
http://taskmasters.pbworks.com/w/page/19500480/Grading%20Methods

STUDENT STUDY SITE

Visit **www.sagepub.com/frey** to access additional study tools including eFlashcards, web quizzes, web resources, additional rubrics, and links to SAGE journal articles.

REFERENCES

Fischer, C., & King, R. M. (1995). *Authentic assessment: A guide to implementation*. Thousand Oaks, CA: Corwin.

Guskey, T. R., & Bailey, J. M. (2001). *Developing grading and reporting systems for student learning*. Thousand Oaks, CA: Corwin.

Guskey, T. R., & Bailey, J. M. (Eds.). (2009). *Developing standards-based report cards*. Thousand Oaks, CA: Corwin.

Kirshcenbaum, H., Simon, S. B., & Napier, R. W. (1971). *Wad-ja-get? The grading game in American education*. New York, NY: Hart.

Marzano, R. J., & Heflebower, T. (2010). *Formative assessment & standards-based grading*. Bloomington, IN: Solution Tree.

McMillan, J. H. (2011). *Classroom assessment: Principles and practice for effective standards-based instruction* (5th ed.). Boston, MA: Pearson.

Newfields, T. (2007). Game theory approaches to grading: An experiment with two incentive point systems. *Tokyo University Keizai Ronshu, 32*(2), 33–43.

Scriffiny, P. L. (2008). Standards-based grading. *Educational Leadership, 66*(2), 70–74.

Shepard, L. A., & Bliem, C. L. (1995). Parents' thinking about standardized tests and performance assessments. *Educational Researcher, 24*(8), 25–32.

Tomlinson, C., & McTighe, J. (2006). *Integrating differentiated instruction and understanding by design: Connecting content and kids*. Alexandria, VA: Association for Supervision and Curriculum Development.

CHAPTER 13

STANDARDIZED TESTS

Looking Ahead in This Chapter

Standardized tests are meant for large-scale assessment and are norm-referenced. They are produced following structured procedures and often use specialized, "standardized" scores. In addition to common standardized tests, examples of statewide "*No Child Left Behind*" tests are discussed. The ethics involved when preparing students to do well on standardized tests are presented.

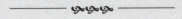

Objectives

After studying this chapter, you should be able to

- Define standardized tests
- Describe the steps involved in creating standardized tests
- List the validity and reliability issues for standardized tests
- Interpret Z scores, T scores, percentile ranks, stanines, and other common standardized scores
- Provide examples of real-life statewide standardized tests
- Evaluate the ethics of "teaching to the test" and other test preparation issues

From about 100 years ago:

> *The importance of these new standards of measurement for our educational service is indeed large. Their use means nothing less than the ultimate transformation of school work from guesswork to scientific accuracy; the elimination of favoritism and politics from the work; the ending forever of the day when a personal or political enemy of a superintendent can secure his removal, without regard to the efficiency of the school system he has built up; the substitution of well-trained experts as superintendents of schools for the old successful practitioners; and the changing of school supervision from a temporary or political job, for which little or no preparation need be made, to that of a highly skilled piece of social engineering. . . . To the teacher it cannot help but eventually mean not only concise and definite statements as to what she is expected to do in the different subjects of the course of study, but the reduction of instruction to those items which can be proved to be of importance in preparation for intelligent living and future usefulness in life.*

Ellwood P. Cubberly (1868–1941), Professor of Education,
Stanford University (Cubberly, 1924, pp. xii–xiii)

An assumption that is common when people, or the media, or students think about assessment in the schools is that *assessment* means standardized tests and standardized tests only. Of course, at this point in this book, it is clear that most of the assessment that goes on in classrooms is teacher-developed, not those made (and mandated) by others. It is standardized tests, though, that are the focus of most of the political, administrative, and social discussions about testing in the schools. As the opening quotation from almost 100 years ago makes clear, standardized tests have long been given a great amount of reverence and power. These assessments are the focus of the *No Child Left Behind* policy discussions or anxieties about performance on college admissions tests. Though teachers do not develop these assessments and the data they produce are likely not precisely relevant to teachers' classroom instructional objectives, they are a part of the classroom teachers' world, and it is important to know what they are, how they come to be, and what their scores mean.

WHAT IS A STANDARDIZED TEST?

A **standardized test** has two characteristics that make it "standardized." A test is considered standardized when it is administered in a *standard* way and when the scores it produces are *standardized*.

By definition, an assessment is standardized when a standard, unvarying set of instructions are followed in its administration. For example, the SAT college admission test, produced by the College Board, includes a detailed set of directions for how it is to be administered—time limits, layout of the testing room, type of computers to use (if it is online), type of pencil to be used (if it is a paper form), and so on. The SAT test is clearly a standardized test. By this definition, though, almost all assessments given in any context are technically *standardized*. A teacher-made quiz is likely administered in such a way that all students must follow the same rules and, thus, is standardized. Even if the teacher hastily threw the quiz together on a smart phone while driving late to school, the quiz is still a standardized test. The term is typically used in a way, though, that goes beyond its dictionary meaning. To call a test *standardized* usually implies that it is meant for large-scale use; was developed in a carefully organized manner; has very reliable, usually objective, scoring methods; and produces scores that are interpreted in a norm-referenced way.

Standardized tests usually produce scores that are transformed in some way onto a simple scale that allows for easy interpretation. These transformed scores are called standardized scores because a known, standard set of guidelines is used to understand their meaning. Some standardized scores you may be familiar with are IQ scores, ACT and SAT scores, and percentile ranks. Later in this chapter, these scores are dissected and ways of interpreting these mysterious and powerful numbers are presented.

Generally speaking, standardized tests are designed to measure either learned knowledge and mastered skills or less concretely defined constructs such as traits and "potential." These types of tests are called achievement tests and aptitude tests. Commercially produced standardized tests for educational settings, as well as the many state tests produced under the requirements of U.S. *No Child Left Behind* legislative requirements, are all meant either to predict the future (aptitude tests, such as college admissions tests) or to assess learning that has already occurred (achievement tests, such as your state's statewide math test).

A Closer Look

College Admissions Tests: Measuring Achievement or Aptitude?

Achievement tests are supposed to measure what has already happened, learning that has occurred. Aptitude tests are, by definition, supposed to predict future performance and only measure the *potential* of today. So is the SAT test, the most widely used

(Continued)

(Continued)

college admissions test, an achievement test or an aptitude test? This is not a simple question. Surely we can just find out what the "A" stands for, right? Is it the Scholastic Achievement Test or the Scholastic Aptitude Test or something else, like the Scholastic Assessment Test, or maybe Admissions Test? Interestingly, the "A," according to the organization that produces the test, the College Board, no longer stands for anything. Nothing in their official materials ever spells out the S, A, and T these days.

Historically, and officially, the test was never called an "Achievement" test, despite the fact that most of the items clearly represent categories of knowledge or skills that students are meant to have learned or *achieved* by the time they finish high school if they hope to do well in college.

The letters did stand, initially, for *Scholastic Aptitude Test*. This makes sense because the test is meant to predict the future. This changed about 10 years ago. It turns out that the word *aptitude* had become something of a political hot potato. For many, it has a genetic connotation, meaning that students might not be able to control or change their *aptitude* for success in college. Because there have long been patterns of disparity in SAT scores between males and females and between White and non-White students, if one claims that the test measures aptitude, then that can be seen as a racist or sexist belief.

Of course, another reason to stop calling the SAT and other college admissions tests "aptitude" tests is that they don't do a particularly good job of predicting college success. By traditional educational measurement standards for strength of statistical relationships, the correlation between SAT or ACT scores with undergraduate college performance (e.g., grade point average) has always been relatively weak. Requiring test scores remains popular as a college admissions strategy, however, because even a small relationship provides some information on which to make decisions. Another wrinkle in figuring out what is measured by the SAT is that many researchers have pointed out the very high correlation of SAT scores with intelligence tests. They suggest that regardless of what name the test is given, it functions primarily as a measure of general intelligence.

HOW STANDARDIZED TESTS ARE BUILT

Standardized tests are developed by teams of psychometricians (scientists who are experts at measuring the mind) and other research and content professionals. In designing a test, the same procedures teachers use to ensure validity and reliability for their classroom assessments are used by the test development team, so these processes will sound familiar. There are several steps involved in producing a standardized test:

1. **Identify the purpose of the assessment.** Will it be used as a criterion-referenced instrument to assess a current level of student mastery, for example, or is it meant to measure a student trait, like intelligence? What is the target population; who will take the test?

2. **Define the domain or content area that the items on the test should represent.** A theoretical universe of content (and associated potential items or tasks) to be measured is identified, such as U.S. history before the Civil War, or analytic writing skills that predict college success. For state mandated tests, the areas to be assessed often are chosen to match state standards, goals, and objectives.

3. **Specify the structural and technical aspects of the test.** What format for items or components will be used? Will it be administered on computer (either local or online) or through paper and pencil? Will the scoring be subjective or objective; must humans score it (e.g., most intelligence tests, most writing tests) or can a computer do it (e.g., anything using those bubble sheets)? A crucial element of this step is the creation of a *table of specifications*. (See Chapter 2 for how teachers do this.) This table specifies the exact topics, categories, domains, and subdomains that the items will represent and the relative proportion (or weighting) of those topics. The degree to which the final instrument contains items that match the table becomes *content validity* evidence.

4. **Write items.** A large pool of potential items is created. If the test is an achievement test, experts in the content areas are trained and provided with the guidelines for item writing. During this stage, the wording of items is often examined by panels of experts to identify questions that, on their face, might be culturally biased, insensitive, or otherwise unfair based on gender, race, or ethnicity (and sometimes other characteristics). There are statistical analyses that come in the next step that also seek to identify biased items.

5. **Field test and analyze the items.** A series of both small- and large-scale "pilot" studies are typically conducted. This provides information on how these items "work" with real students (e.g., discrimination and difficulty indices such as those described in Chapter 2, typical patterns for answers or performance). Because of the large sample sizes often used in these studies, very sophisticated statistical analyses can be performed.

With large-scale test development, a powerful set of analytic tools collectively referred to as *Item Response Theory* is usually applied. Item Response Theory, essentially, allows for more precise estimates of reliability, by taking into account the ability level of the student. These techniques are also used to identify, using a statistical criterion, items that might be biased based on race, gender, whether English is a student's first language, and so on.

6. **Construct a test (or multiple forms of the "same" test).** Following the table of specifications, the advice from expert panels, and the statistical analyses, the "final" test is constructed. The items that work best, in terms of reliability (do the items work well together to produce a precise score?) and validity (content validity and construct validity, and, sometimes, criterion validity), are selected from the larger pool, and put together to form a test.

These steps take time, money, and careful attention, but, as you might imagine, they can produce very high quality (and *standardized*) tests. There is much criticism these days of standardized tests, but these criticisms are seldom of the technical quality of most of these tests. Attacks on *testing* as a concept are usually based on concerns about the social and instructional consequences of a system that places so much weight on these tests, and not about whether the tests are "any good."

There's a Stat for That!

Differential Item Functioning (DIF)

Item Response Theory provides a variety of statistical methods for test development and item analysis. One analytic method possible under this measurement approach allows for a statistical identification of item *bias*. The word *bias* has different meanings in different contexts, and determining that any educational assessment is biased toward a particular group of students is possible through a variety of lines of evidence. The psychometrician's definition of bias is as follows:

An item is biased if the *relationship* between student ability and the probability *of* getting an item correct is different for different groups of students.

For example, if White students with average overall ability have a 70% chance of getting Question 14 correct and Hispanic students with the same average overall ability have only a 40% chance of getting Question 14 correct, then Question 14 might be biased against Hispanic students.

Using large samples of student response data, test developers can investigate whether items function differently for students with different sets of characteristics. Graphs of curves are produced that show the relationship between the chance of getting an item correct and the range of student abilities. Psychometricians call these graphs *DIF curves*. If items work the same way for all groups, the curves should be roughly the same for each group of students (e.g., males and females). If they are not the same, then that indicates differential item functioning: items measure something differently for different groups. Notice that an item is not considered biased simply because it is more difficult for one group of students. Items are considered as possibly biased when they are more difficult for one group of students even after controlling for ability level.

VALIDITY AND RELIABILITY OF STANDARDIZED TESTS

Depending on the purpose of a standardized test, there are three approaches for determining its validity. If the test is an achievement test, then the extent to which there is a close match between the items on a test and a reasonable table of specifications supports claims for content validity. Standardized tests often do a good job of ensuring *content* validity. If the test is meant to measure an abstract construct or student trait, such as an intelligence test or a psychological assessment, it is the *construct* validity of the instrument that is the center of discussion. Validity for these tests is a matter of whether one agrees with the test developers' definition of the construct and interpretation of research studies that examine the underlying measurement effectiveness of these tests. For aptitude tests meant to predict future performance, the relevant validity argument is clear. It is the category of *criterion* validity evidence known as predictive validity that is most compelling.

Reliability as an indicator of technical quality for standardized tests is seldom a problem. These tests are usually very long, and long tests with many items are almost always very reliable regarding *internal* reliability; the amount of random error is due to there being too few opportunities to respond. Scoring also tends to be objective (indeed, most are computer scored), which results in high *inter-rater* reliability, which, theoretically, should be perfect (in the absence of a technical or computer error). Some standardized tests, though, are designed for human scoring. One-on-one intelligence tests, for example, require the examiner to do the scoring. It is somewhat subjective, and judgment is required. Some portions of state tests and other tests that assess writing ability are also subjectively scored and require trained experts to assign scores. Inter-rater reliability is the concern here, and much effort is placed on the training of those who score and, in the case of intelligence tests, those who administer the tests. High levels of inter-rater reliability must be demonstrated before the scores produced by these "raters" are trusted.

Another reliability concern can arise when some *part* of a test is scored and interpreted. The high internal reliability estimates almost always found for state tests, for example, do not apply to the shorter subtests that are often reported. Test reports often include a profile that might provide scores for specific math sections or specific reading skills. These scores might be produced from just a few items. Though they are pulled out from a longer test with a large number of items, they themselves are really shorter tests created from that long test. So the reliability estimates for the long test do not transfer to the shorter test, and research shows that these shorter tests (or "testlets" as they are sometimes called) often do not have the excellent levels of internal reliability required for reporting a total score in other contexts.

INTERPRETING STANDARDIZED TEST SCORES

Some standardized tests are designed to be criterion-referenced. For example, most state-level tests developed to meet the reporting requirements of *No Child Left Behind* produce scores that are interpreted against a chosen set of standards with *cut scores*. Cut scores are particular scores that one must reach to be placed in some category of quality (state testing programs often institute *proficiency* categories). The common "90%, 80%, 70%" letter grade scale uses cut scores and is an obvious example of criterion-referenced scoring. Most standardized tests, however, are norm-referenced and use information about how large groups of students have performed to create scores that are interpreted against a backdrop of what is "normal."

Norm-referenced standardized scores all use the same strategy in their calculation. They start with a raw score and change it following some mathematical rules so that it reflects whether the individual student performance is above or below the mean and how far above or below the mean it is. This allows teachers, school psychologists, counselors, parents, and administrators to understand a score without having to know how many points were possible, how difficult the test was, and so on.

To change raw scores to standardized scores, one needs to know the *mean* and *standard deviation* of the distribution of scores (all the scores of all students who took a test). To get a sense of how common or rare a particular standardized score is, one needs to be familiar with the *normal curve*. We introduced these statistics and concepts in Chapter 12. Here's a reminder:

- The *mean* is the arithmetic average of all scores.
  - Sum all the scores and divide by the number of scores.
- The *standard deviation* is the mean distance of each score from the mean.
  - Square each distance, average those values, and take the square root.
- The *normal curve* is the common, nearly universal shape of a distribution of scores.

Most scores are near the mean with fewer scores far away from the mean. If scores are normally distributed, then about 68% of all scores are within one standard deviation of the mean. Only 2% or so of scores are more than two standard deviations above or below the mean.

Figure 13.1 The Normal Curve

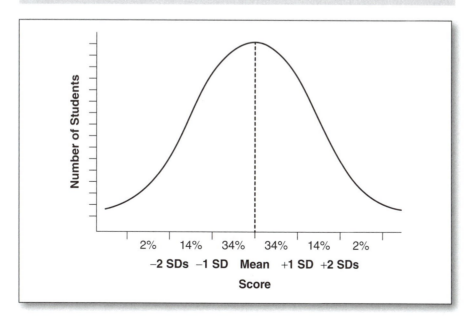

Z Scores

The simplest standardized score, and the one that is used as the basis of almost all the others, is a Z score. Z scores are raw scores that have been transformed so that the distribution is such that the mean score is 0 and the standard deviation is 1. Because a normal distribution has room for about 3 standard deviations above and below the mean, Z scores tend to range from –3 to +3, though with large samples, Z scores can be –4 and +4 or even more extreme. Here's the formula for Z scores:

$$Z = \frac{\text{raw score} - \text{mean score}}{\text{standard deviation}}$$

So to transform a raw score into a Z score just subtract the mean of the distribution from the raw score and divide by the standard deviation. The resulting Z score is either positive or negative. If it is positive, you know the raw score is above average; if it is negative, then the raw score is below average. The number itself tells you how far above or below average the score is. For example, if a student receives a Z score of 1.26, she performed about $1\frac{1}{4}$ standard deviations above the mean. We know from the normal curve that this means she likely performed better than more than 84% of all students, because 34% of students score between the mean and 1 standard deviation above the mean on the normal curve. Add the 50% who, by definition, likely fall below the mean, and we are above 84%.

A Z score provides much more information than a raw score. If I receive a raw score of 78 on some test, I have no idea if that is good or bad, high or low. If I see it as a Z score, though, I know, at least, if I am above or below the mean and how far above or below the mean I am. Table 13.1 gives examples of some

Table 13.1 Examples of Z Score Transformations

Test	Raw Score	Mean	Standard Deviation	Z Score	Interpretation
1	9	8	2	.50	A little bit above average
2	87	96	7	–1.29	About $1\frac{1}{3}$ standard deviations below the mean
3	45	45	10	0.0	Average

raw scores, the required statistics, transformations into Z scores, and interpretations of those scores. Notice that the score interpretations are impossible until they are standardized.

Z scores have many advantages over raw scores and are useful anytime one wishes to compare the score of one student on a test with the scores of other students on the same test. It is also useful for comparing the performance of one student across many different tests. For any given student, a profile of scores for a range of measures can be produced with Z scores to identify strengths and areas of concern. By placing scores on a standard scale (Z's always have a mean of 0 and a standard deviation of 1), fair comparisons can be made.

T Scores

Z scores are used in real life all the time, but they are usually calculated as a step along the way to producing some other standardized scores and are rarely reported. That's because the common scores produced by the Z transformation are unpleasant and troublesome. A score of 0 is perfectly fine (because it is average) and students can score negative numbers (half of all Z scores are below 0). The highest scoring students get scores like 1 and 2. Parents, students, and most teachers aren't used to such odd scores. Consequently, other scales are commonly used to report standardized scores. A popular standardized score format that teachers often see on test reports is the T score distribution. T scores have a mean of 50 and a standard deviation of 10, so scores tend to range from 20 to 80 (remember, there is usually room under the normal curve for about three standard deviations on either side of the mean). The scores produced under this system are much more palatable than with Z scores. T scores begin as Z scores but are changed using this formula:

$$T = 50 + Z (10)$$

Applying this equation, a Z score of 0 become a T score of 50. That sounds more like average performance than a score of 0 does. Positive Z scores will produce T scores greater than 50 and negative Z scores produce scores less than 50. The range of T scores is more palatable than the range of Z scores, but one disadvantage still remains. Students will probably never receive a T score as high as 100 no matter how well they do (unless they outperform many tens of millions who took the same very difficult test).

Percentile Ranks

The most commonly reported standardized scores and the ones most people are familiar with are percentile ranks. By taking a Z score and placing it against the normal curve, the percentage of students who are at or below a given score can be determined. So a Z score of 1 becomes a percentile rank of 84 because 84% of scores are at or below 1 standard deviation above the mean. Likewise, a student scoring a Z of 0 is at the 50th percentile. Teachers, parents, and students have become very used to percentiles, and most interpret them correctly, though some confuse a percentile with a "percent correct," thinking that if a student scored at the 63rd percentile, then she got 63% of the questions correct. Notice that a percentile rank answers the same question as a Z score or T score or any standardized score; is the score above or below

Figure 13.2 Standardized Scores

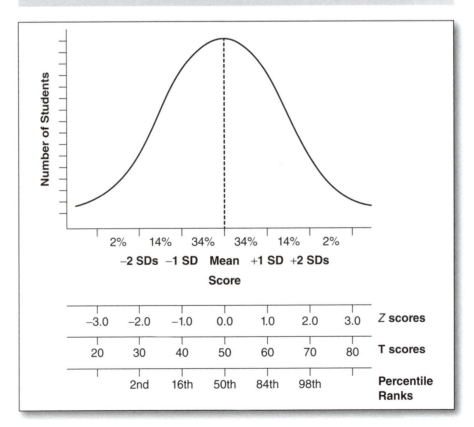

average and how far above or below is it? Because of this consistency, any standardized score can easily be transformed into any other standardized score. Take a look at the normal curve we first used in Chapter 11 (Figure 13.2) and see how these three common standardized scores line up below it.

Stanines

An even simpler way of reporting scores is the stanine system. Stanines (a shortened form of the name *standard nines*) have a range of 1 to 9 and only the whole number is used. The area under the normal curve has been sliced eight times, creating nine different levels of performance. With 5 in the middle, each stanine represents half of a standard deviation. The lowest is 1, and 9 is the highest. The normal curve is such that fewer and fewer scores are found as you go farther away from the middle, so most scores will be close to 5 with fewer scores in the intervals near 1 and 9. Table 13.2 shows the distribution of stanines. One advantage of stanines is that they remind us that there is not much meaningful difference for students who are close to the mean but just happen to be above or below it, or for students who score near each other anywhere on the distribution. A disadvantage of stanines is that much precise information is lost when one stops using digits past the decimal. Advocates for the use of stanines would argue, however, that that extra information isn't very meaningful, so nothing is lost.

Table 13.2 Stanines

Stanine	Z Score Range	Percentage of Students in Interval
1	Below −1.75	Lowest 4%
2	−1.75 to −1.25	7%
3	−1.25 to −.75	12%
4	−.75 to −.25	17%
5	−.25 to .25	20%
6	.25 to .75	17%
7	.75 to 1.25	12%
8	1.25 to 1.75	7%
9	Above 1.75	Highest 4%

Table 13.3 Well-Known Standardized Scores

Score	Mean	Standard Deviation
Z	0	1
T	50	10
American College Test (ACT)	18	6
SAT	500	100
Graduate Record Exam (GRE)	500	100
Law School Admission Test (LSAT)	150	10
Medical College Admission Test (MCAT)	8	2.5
Wechsler Intelligence Scales (IQ)	100	15
Stanford-Binet Intelligence Test (IQ)	100	16

Note: Some tests report the "official" mean and standard deviation but allow these values to vary each year so they can show increases or decreases over time. For example, the ACT national standardized mean is calculated by comparing it with an original norming group's mean and standard deviation; lately this has been around 21 for each test, not 18.

Other Standardized Scores

Just about every standardized test you can think of—college admissions tests, personality tests, intelligence tests has its own standardized scoring system. All of these customized and, sometimes, trademarked scores began as Z scores, and then they were changed into whatever scale the test developer wished to use. The transformation process for changing a Z into a different standardized score with its own predetermined mean and standard deviation follows the same steps as is used by the T score. Start with whatever value you wish to have as the mean in your new scoring system or distribution. Add to that value the product of the Z score multiplied by whatever value you wish to have as the standard deviation in your new distribution. Some common standardized tests' scoring rules are shown in Table 13.3.

TALKING TO PARENTS ABOUT STANDARDIZED TEST SCORES

When talking with parents about their student's standardized test performance, there are two concerns most teachers have. They want the information to be useful, and they want the information to be accurate and interpreted and explained correctly. Research suggests that most parents do not find information from standardized tests by itself to be useful in understanding their children's learning. Talking one-on-one with a teacher, however, is much more helpful. One classic study found that almost all parents (94%) found talking with teachers about student progress to be useful, compared with only about 37% who found information from standardized tests to be useful (Shepard & Bliem, 1995). So it is very valuable to sit with parents and conference with them to ensure that they benefit from receiving the data of test scores.

The other goal for most teachers, the accuracy goal, requires a good understanding of the nature of the standardized scores presented. Here are some suggestions for talking with parents about their child's test results:

- Explain the purpose of the test. What is supposed to be measured by the test? Does it provide an indicator of learning? Is it meant to be formative and provide feedback helpful to teachers and students? Is it meant to reflect progress over time? Is it a requirement from the state or district? How are results meant to be used?

- Explain how the test was made. Were topics and items driven by state goals and objectives? Were teachers involved in test development (this is often the case for state tests)? Is the test "new and improved"?

- Explain what the score means regarding whether it is norm-referenced or criterion-referenced. No need to use the jargon of "norm-referenced" or "criterion-referenced," of course, but you should explain whether to interpret the score as a comparison with other students or as an indicator of whether certain objectives are being met. If the score is standardized based on a normal distribution (with known means and standard deviations), interpret performance based on your understanding of what that score means statistically. For example, if the score is a percentile rank, explain that this is the percentage of all students who scored at or below their student, not the percentage of questions a student got right. Unless a student's norm-referenced score is far away from the mean (i.e., more than a standard deviation), it is probably best (and more meaningful) to describe it as in the average range. When tests are criterion-referenced, share with parents what those standards are and how they were chosen.

- Be precise if being critical of the test. It is unlikely that a test is literally "no good" or "of no value" or "doesn't tell us anything." It is very unlikely that the test is "not reliable" as we use the term. It is possible, though, that a test is not useful for a particular purpose. It is also possible that a test does not cover your specific classroom objectives and that you assess learning in ways that are more meaningful or authentic. As professionals, teachers should feel free to criticize the inappropriate use or interpretation of any test, but it is important, of course, to be clear about what the criticism is. Parents expect teachers to be honest with them about the strengths and limitations of assessment.

- Listen and answer parents' questions. Parents want to be heard. The most powerful communication strategy is not to talk, but to listen. Most parents will have some questions and may hesitate to ask them. So it is important to listen carefully to identify parents' concerns. It is likely that the most useful conversation about test scores will focus on what the score means in terms of student learning and what guidance it provides for parents, teachers, and the student.

STATEWIDE STANDARDIZED TESTS

The *No Child Left Behind Act of 2001* is U.S. federal legislation that, among other things, requires states to develop assessments in basic skills to be given to all students. (States are not actually required to do this, but they will lose federal funds if they do not. Consequently, all states have chosen to follow the act's provisions.) The standards for proficiency or success, what a "good" score is, are set by each individual state. Passage of this legislation has, obviously, resulted in a huge increase in the emphasis placed on standardized test scores by administrators and the development of dozens of new standardized tests that are meant to align with each state's curricular standards. This chapter presents information about three of these statewide tests to illustrate what these measures are like.

Kansas State Assessment (KSA)

Kansas administers tests for five different content areas. The grades and tests involved are shown in Table 13.4. The standard format for testing is on a computer, with pencil-and-paper forms allowed as an accommodation. All questions, with the exception of the writing assessment, are multiple-choice. The test developers report that they follow universal test design guidelines (see Chapter 10).

Scores are meant to be interpreted as *percent correct*, which defines five different categories or "performance levels." The particular cut scores vary a bit

Table 13.4 Kansas State Testing Schedule by Grade Level

Test	3rd	4th	5th	6th	7th	8th	9th	10th	11th
Reading	x	x	x	x	x	x			
Mathematics	x	x	x	x	x	x			
Science		x			x				x
Writing			x			x			x
History/Government				x		x			x

from test to test and grade level to grade level. For example, the 6th-grade reading test breaks down performance in this way:

- 0–51% Academic Warning
- 52–63% Approaches Standard
- 64–78% Meets Standard
- 79–88% Exceeds Standard
- 89–100% Exemplary

Adequate yearly progress is defined as a specific percentage of all students in a school receiving scores in the *Meets Standard* range or higher. Schools not making Adequate Yearly Progress are listed at an annual State Board of Education meeting.

New York State Testing Program (NYSTP)

The New York State Testing Program was meant to complement existing *Regents Examinations*, which already assessed students statewide in high school (over college preparation–type subjects). The newer tests assess English language arts and mathematics each year for Grades 3 through 8. The language arts test includes a writing assessment. There are statewide science tests, given to 4th and 8th graders, and social studies tests, given to 5th and 8th graders, as well.

All state testing programs begin with a precise table of specifications based on state standards, which define what students are expected to learn each year. These tables also often define the formats for test items and their relative frequency. From the New York 4th grade math test, the tables of specifications are shown in Table 13.5. Items are a mix of multiple-choice, short answer, and essay. Here is a sample 4th grade item the testing developers provide:

Table 13.5 New York State Test Tables of Specifications for 4th Grade Math

	Multiple-Choice Questions	Short-Response Questions	Extended-Response Questions	Total Number of Questions	Testing Time
Section 1	45	0	0	45	70 minutes
Section 2	0	8	4	12	70 minutes
Total	45	8	4	57	140 minutes

Topic	Percentage of Items
Number Sense and Operations	45%
Algebra	14%
Geometry	12%
Measurement	17%
Probability and Statistics	12%

Which sentence best combines the two sentences?
The train sped through the tunnel. The train sped across the bridge.

    A. The train sped through the tunnel and across the bridge.
    B. The train sped through and across the tunnel and the bridge.
    C. The train that sped through the tunnel sped across the bridge.
    D. The train sped through the tunnel and it sped across the bridge.

The correct answer is A.

California Standards Test (CST)

In California, *No Child Left Behind* tests are part of the *Standardized Testing and Reporting Program.* They were developed to align with California's standards in English–language arts, mathematics, science, and history–social science. The schedule for test administration is shown in Table 13.6.

An example of a table of specifications used for the CSTs comes from the reading standards. A simplified version of this table is shown in Table 13.7.

Tests are mostly multiple-choice items. A sample item from the 4th grade math test looks like this:

Table 13.6 California State Testing Schedule by Grade Level

Test	2nd	3rd	4th	5th	6th	7th	8th	9th	10th	11th
English/Language Arts	x	x	x	x	x	x	x	x	x	x
Mathematics	x	x	x	x	x	x		x	x	x
History/Social Science							x		x	x
Science				x			x	x	x	x

Note: The specific math and science test administered in high school depends on the courses in which students are enrolled.

There were sixty-two thousand, seven hundred twenty-one seagulls nesting on an island. What is this number in standard form?

   A. 62,721
   B. 627,021
   C. 62,000,721
   D. 62,700,021

The correct answer is A.

ETHICS OF PREPARING STUDENTS FOR STANDARDIZED TESTS

Fellow teachers are explaining things to Mr. Prez, a first-year middle school math teacher at a struggling inner-city school.

Mrs. Scott:	The test in April is the difference between the state taking over the school or not.
Mrs. Shapiro:	Look, you don't teach math (for the next six weeks), you teach the test. North Avenue is all about the *Leave No Child Behind* stuff getting spoon-fed.
Mr. Prez:	And what do they learn?
Ms. Sampson:	Find some middle ground. Every day, try to do a little for the statewide . . . for (the principal), you know, if she comes to visit, she thinks you're on point. The rest of the time, do what you feel like you need to do.
Mrs. Scott:	But be careful. You're still on the far side of your evaluation.

From *The Wire*, HBO Television Series, 2002–2008

Table 13.7   Portion of Table of Specifications for Grades 4–11 (Based on a 75-item Reading Exam)

WORD ANALYSIS, FLUENCY, AND SYSTEMATIC VOCABULARY DEVELOPMENT: Students understand the basic features of reading. They select letter patterns and know how to translate them into spoken language by using phonics, syllabication, and word parts. They apply this knowledge to achieve fluent oral and silent reading.	18 items
Vocabulary and Concept Development: apply knowledge of word origins, derivations, synonyms, antonyms, and idioms to determine the meaning of words and phrases	8
Vocabulary and Concept Development: use knowledge of root words to determine the meaning of unknown words within a passage	3
Vocabulary and Concept Development: know common roots and affixes derived from Greek and Latin and use this knowledge to analyze the meaning of complex words (e.g., international)	1
Vocabulary and Concept Development: use a thesaurus to determine related words and concepts	1
Vocabulary and Concept Development: distinguish and interpret multiple meaning words	5
Literary Response and Analysis	9
READING COMPREHENSION: Students read and understand grade-level-appropriate material. They draw on a variety of comprehension strategies as needed (e.g., generating and responding to essential questions, making predictions, comparing information from several sources). The selections in *Recommended Readings in Literature, Kindergarten Through Grade Eight* illustrate the quality and complexity of the materials to be read by students. In addition to their regular school reading, students read one-half million words annually, including a good representation of grade-level-appropriate narrative and expository text (e.g., classic and contemporary literature, magazines, newspapers, online information).	15 items
Structural Features of Informational Materials: identify structural patterns found in informational text (e.g., compare and contrast, cause and effect, sequential or chronological order, proposition and support) to strengthen comprehension	1
Comprehension and Analysis of Grade-Level-Appropriate Text: make and confirm predictions about text by using prior knowledge and ideas presented in the text itself, including illustrations, titles, topic sentences, important words, and foreshadowing clues	2
Comprehension and Analysis of Grade-Level-Appropriate Text: evaluate new information and hypotheses by testing them against known information and ideas	3
Comprehension and Analysis of Grade-Level-Appropriate Text: compare and contrast information on the same topic after reading several passages or articles	3
Comprehension and Analysis of Grade-Level-Appropriate Text: distinguish between cause and effect and between fact and opinion in expository text	3
Comprehension and Analysis of Grade-Level-Appropriate Text: follow multiple-step instructions in a basic technical manual (e.g., how to use computer commands or video games)	3

Because of the growing trust and reliance on statewide standardized tests for making a variety of decisions about students, teachers, administrators, and schools, there is growing pressure by administrators, teachers, and parents to increase test scores. As with the new teacher in the scenario presented at the start of this section, real-world teachers try to find some middle ground where they can prepare students to do their best on statewide tests, cover the objectives that the tests are designed to assess, but avoid "teaching to the test." What does it mean, though, to teach to the test, and is it right or wrong? Chapter 2 presents some of the ethical guidelines and issues related to classroom assessment in general, and it should come as no surprise that preparing students for standardized, statewide, high-stakes tests has its own set of ethical questions.

Teaching to the test seems to have a variety of possible definitions, depending on the context, the speaker, and the attitude toward statewide testing that one holds. Teaching to the test can mean any of the following:

- **Providing practice and specific answers to actual test questions that will be on the test**

   Because statewide test items are meant to be secure (unavailable until the test is actually administered), even if a teacher or administrator wished to do this, it would be difficult to do in any sort of comprehensive way. Of course, if tests do not change from administration to administration (and for comparison across time purposes they usually need to stay substantially the same), teachers and students can recall items they have seen and share this information. With their own classroom tests, on the other hand, teachers can and sometimes do teach to specific items they know will be on a test. This is one way that state test scores lose value and leads to what educational researchers call "test score pollution" (Haladyna, Bobbit, Nolen, & Haas, 1991). Because this clearly lessens or completely eliminates any validity eventual test scores would have, engaging in this practice, most would agree, is unethical. Obviously, knowing that the answer to question 1 is "C" does not mean that a student has learned the underlying knowledge or skill.

- **Providing practice and specific answers to questions that are similar in format and content to actual test questions**

   This way of teaching to the test is probably what is described in the television excerpt that opens this section. It is often public knowledge, using information purposefully shared with teachers and parents, as to the format and what sample questions (or questions used on earlier forms of a test) look like. This sort of practice, regardless of whether it is a reasonable use of instructional time, may or may not be ethical regarding measurement ethics. The key is whether, knowing which particular content or specific objectives are covered on the test, a teacher focuses on that important subset. Leaving out important objectives because a teacher knows it won't be covered on the state test sounds unethical. Even using similar items is considered unethical by some (Haladyna et al., 1991). Of course, a quality state test covers all objectives, not just some. Even then, if the context of specific items is known (e.g., items ask about measuring the height of trees), a teacher could use class examples that focus on the same context.

- **Providing training in general strategies for doing well on standardized tests**
  Teaching students how to think and behave while being tested is an important school skill that should be included among instructional objectives from the moment that assessment begins in students' lives. Classrooms that are formative assessment environments include discussions about how to demonstrate knowledge regularly. Even for these classrooms, though, the objectively scorable multiple-choice format of many standardized tests seems artificial or strange, and certainly is only seen for the most part in the classroom (and on a few select television game shows). Making sure that students are "testwise," that they understand and know how to take tests, is reasonable and should be taught as part of all assessment activities, not just in the days before a statewide test.
- **Teaching to meet the instructional objectives that are assessed on the test**
  If a test covers what a teacher should be teaching, then teaching that content is not teaching to the test. In a perfect system, both the classroom teacher and the state test developers work from the same set of standards. Under this reality, it's not that teachers teach what they do because test developers put it on the test; test developers put it on the test because it is what teachers teach.

THINGS TO THINK ABOUT

1. Which form of assessment provides more information about students, standardized tests or teacher-made classroom assessment?

2. How do the various types of standardized scores differ from each other regarding the information they provide?

3. Most states are moving toward sharing "common core" standards and objectives. Should there be common educational standards nationwide?

4. More and more often, teachers' jobs can depend on their students' scores from standardized tests. Should this be the case?

Looking Back in This Chapter

The majority of classroom assessments in the modern classroom are teacher-designed. It is the standardized test, however, that gets all the attention. Standardized tests usually provide norm-referenced scores. These standardized scores transform raw scores into a score with a known mean and standard deviation. This way, one can easily tell whether the performance of a student is above or below the mean and how far away from the mean it is. This chapter presented Z scores, T scores, percentile ranks, stanines, and a variety of other commonly seen standardized scores. While most standardized tests produce scores that are norm-referenced, many state tests produced criterion-referenced scores. These statewide tests are typically used under the requirements of the 2001 *No Child Left Behind* federal legislation to place students into categories of proficiency. There are ethical ways to prepare students for success on these tests.

ON THE WEB

Newspaper article about the myths of standardized tests
http://www.washingtonpost.com/blogs/answer-sheet/post/the-myths-of-standardized-testing/2011/04/14/AFNxTggD_blog.html

One state's (California) test reporting cite
http://star.cde.ca.gov/

Information on a variety of standardized tests
http://www.educationbug.org/a/standardized-testing-statistics.html

How ETS (makers of the SAT and GRE tests) computes and interprets test scores
http://www.ets.org/understanding_testing/scoring/

STUDENT STUDY SITE

Visit **www.sagepub.com/frey** to access additional study tools including eFlashcards, web quizzes, web resources, additional rubrics, and links to SAGE journal articles.

REFERENCES

Cubberly, E. O. (1924). Editor's introduction. In W. S. Monroe, J. C. DeVoss, & F. J. Kelly (Eds.), *Educational tests and measurements*. Cambridge, MA: Riverside Press.

Haladyna, T. M., Bobbit Nolen, S., & Haas, N. S. (1991). Raising standardized achievement test scores and the origins of test score pollution. *Educational Researcher*, *20*(5), 2–7.

Shepard, L. A., & Bliem, C. L. (1995). Parents' thinking about standardized tests and performance assessments. *Educational Researcher*, *24*(8), 25–32.

GLOSSARY

Accommodations: Physical and procedural changes in testing conditions, such as a separate room, lighting changes, more time, and so on.

Analytic Approach: A scoring method that evaluates each of the pieces or steps of a product or performance.

Authentic Assessment: Assessment that includes tasks, content, expectations, and evaluation methods similar to those that are valued outside of the classroom.

Classroom Assessment: The systematic collection of information about students designed, administered, and scored by teachers or students.

Coefficient Alpha: A number generally ranging from 0 to 1 indicating the level of internal reliability for a group of test items. The closer to 1, the higher the reliability.

Construct: The invisible trait that one wishes to assess. Pronounced CON-struct. In the classroom, constructs are typically knowledge, understanding, skills, attitudes, traits, and so on. In the broader world of educational and psychological measurement, constructs include things like intelligence, depression, learning disabilities, aptitude, and personality.

Construct Validity: The broadest category of validity. A construct validity argument is that performance on the assessment reflects the underlying knowledge, skill, or trait that one intends to measure.

Constructed-Response Items: Assessment tasks that ask students to create a complex written answer or a complex, frequently creative, product.

Content Validity: A content validity argument is that the items on a test are a fair and representative sample of the items that could or should be on the test. For example, teachers may have a well-defined set of instructional objectives that an assessment should cover.

Content Validity Ratio: A number ranging from 0 to 1 that indicates the extent to which an item is essential when covering a particular topic.

Criterion-Based Validity: A criterion validity argument is that performance on an assessment is related to scores on another assessment in a way that makes sense.

Criterion-Referenced: An approach to score interpretation that judges performance against some criterion (such as instructional objectives, percentage of points possible, and so on).

Criterion Validity: A type of validity argument that provides evidence that the scores on one test correlate with the scores on some other measure.

Cut Scores: Specific scores that define categories of performance.

Dichotomous Scoring: A scoring system with only two possible scores.

Difficulty Index: The proportion of students who answered a question correctly.

Distribution: A set of scores and their associated frequencies.

Effect Sizes: Numbers that represent the strength of relationships between variables. Effect sizes are used in educational research to judge, for example, the effectiveness of an instructional approach.

Feedback Intervention Theory: A theory suggesting that formative assessment feedback is most effective when it is narrowly focused on specific tasks and behaviors related to success and least effective when it is broad (such as "Good work!").

Formative Assessment: Feedback produced while learning is occurring and concepts and knowledge bases are still being developed. It allows students and teachers to modify their behaviors and understanding before instruction has ended.

Grade: Categories of quality or performance placed in some meaningful order.

Grading Scale: A set of rules for assigning letter grades based on points or performance.

Internal Reliability: Consistency in scores within the various items on a test.

Inter-rater Reliability: Consistency in scores between two different scorers or raters.

Interval Level: A level of measurement with equal intervals in meaning between any two adjacent scores.

Item Difficulty Index: The proportion of students getting a question right. Technically, it's the average score from a single item. Calculated by dividing the number of students who got an item correct by the total number of student who took an assessment.

Item Discrimination Index: A number indicating how well a single item discriminates between high scorers on a test and low scorers.

Item Score: The number of points a student received for a single question or assessment task.

Level of Measurement: The amount of information provided by a given scoring format. There are four levels, with *nominal*, where numbers are used only as names for categories, as the least informative and *ratio*, where scores represent equally spaced quantities and there are no possible scores below 0, as the most informative.

Mean: The arithmetic average. Calculated by adding all the scores together and dividing by the number of scores in the distribution.

Median: The score right in the middle of a distribution. 50% of scores are greater; 50% are lesser.

Mode: The most commonly occurring score in a distribution.

Modifications: Changes made for an individual student in a test in order to increase validity for that student. For example, a different version might be used, or there may be different directions.

Nominal Level: A level of measurement with numbers being used only as names or labels, not as quantities.

Norm-Referenced: An approach to understanding scores by comparing scores with each other. The information in a score comes from referencing what is normal.

Normal Curve: A very common shape of the distribution of scores. If one graphs a moderate number of scores from almost any assessment with the scores in order along the X axis and the frequency of the scores placed along the Y axis, then the distribution tends to be symmetrical around the mean with most scores close to the mean and very few scores far from the mean.

Number Correct: A common scoring system where students get a point for each correct answer.

Objective Scoring: A scoring system where no judgment is involved in assigning a score. If a computer can do the scoring, it is an objective scoring system (e.g., multiple-choice tests).

Ordinal Level: A level of measurement where numbers are used to show some ranking (such as listing students in order of their performance) but there is not an expectation that the intervals between ranks are equal.

Percent Correct: A common scoring system that indicates the percentage of points possible that a student received. Most commonly it is the percentage of questions answered correctly.

Percentile Rank: The percentage of students scoring at or below a given score.

Performance-Based Assessment: An approach to assessment that requires students to perform or produce something for evaluation. It is most commonly used to assess a skill or ability.

Primary Trait Approach: A common approach to scoring performance-based assessment that involves the identification

of a few major constructs or traits and then judging the level of each.

Range: In a distribution, the distance between the highest score and the lowest score.

Ratio Level : A level of measurement that includes the characteristics of interval level measurement, with the extra requirement that there is a "true zero"; one can literally have none of the trait of interest. No negative numbers are used in ratio scoring.

Raw Scores: The actual scores that students receive on a test. They have not been altered or standardized.

Reliability: Consistency and precision in scores. Scores that are very close to what a student would typically receive on a given test are reliable.

Scoring Rubrics: A written set of scoring rules, often in the form of a table. They provide guidance for the assignment of scores.

Selection Item: An item format where the answer is provided to students and they must select it or indicate it (such as multiple-choice or matching items).

Self-Directed Learners: Students who are self-managing, self-monitoring, and self-modifying.

Standardized Score: A score that had been modified from a raw score using known, standardized rules. Usually, standardized scores provide information on where a student performed in terms of standard deviations above or below the mean.

Standardized Test: A test that is administered in a standard way. Sometimes the term is reserved only for large-scale "official" high-stakes tests that produce standardized scores.

Stanines: Areas under a normal curve that has been sliced into nine convenient roughly equal levels of performance. The term is short for *standard nines*.

Subjective Scoring: Scoring systems that require some human judgment.

Subscale Scores: Scores of groups of items within a larger assessment that are focused on a single domain, skill, or trait.

Summative Assessment: An assessment approach with the goal of summarizing student performance at the end of a period of instruction. Grades are usually assigned based on summative assessments.

Supply Item: An item format where the correct answer is not provided; students must supply it.

T Score: A standardized score with a mean of 50 and a standard deviation of 10.

Table of Specifications: Typically, a matrix with columns and rows that provides guidance as to the nature of the items which should appear on a test in terms of content, for example, or level of Bloom's Taxonomy. These tables form the blueprint for an assessment.

Test-Retest Reliability: A type of consistency in scores that are stable across time.

Traditional Paper-and-Pencil Assessment: Very popular, efficient, objectively scored approach to assessment (such as multiple-choice questions, matching, true-false, fill-in-the-blank, and some short answer formats).

Universal Design : The design of products and environments to be usable in a meaningful and similar way by all people.

Universal Test design : An approach to test design that emphasizes accessibility and fairness for all children, regardless of gender, first language, ethnicity, or disability.

Validity: The characteristic of an assessment that measures what it is supposed to measure. *Supposed* means that the assessment measures what you assume it does, and it also means that the assessment measures what it is intended to measure.

Z Score: A standardized score that transforms a raw score by subtracting the mean from it and then dividing by the standard deviation of the score's distribution. Z scores have a mean of 0 and a standard deviation of 1.

INDEX

⑤SAGE research**methods**

The essential online tool for researchers from the world's leading methods publisher

Find exactly what you are looking for, from basic explanations to advanced discussion

More content and new features added this year!

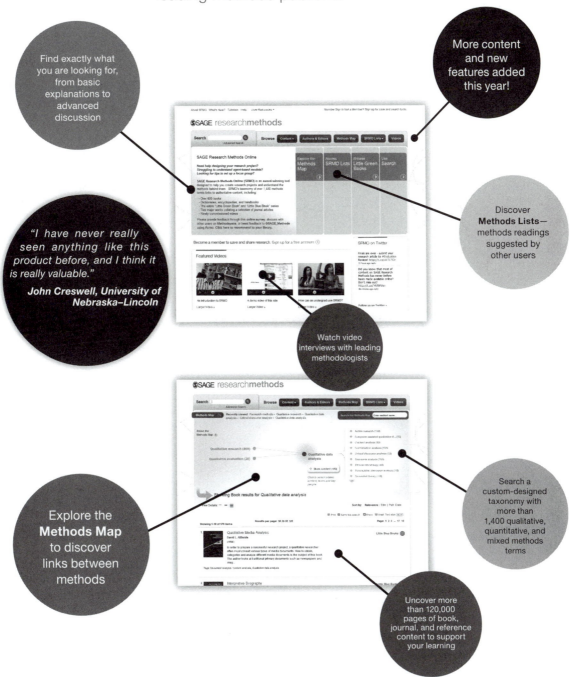

"I have never really seen anything like this product before, and I think it is really valuable."

John Creswell, University of Nebraska–Lincoln

Discover **Methods Lists**— methods readings suggested by other users

Watch video interviews with leading methodologists

Explore the **Methods Map** to discover links between methods

Search a custom-designed taxonomy with more than 1,400 qualitative, quantitative, and mixed methods terms

Uncover more than 120,000 pages of book, journal, and reference content to support your learning

Find out more at
www.sageresearchmethods.com